Aspects of Violence

Cultural Criminology

Series editor: **Mike Presdee**, Sometime Senior Lecturer in Criminology,
University of Kent, UK

Titles include:

Ruth Penfold-Mounce
CELEBRITY CULTURE AND CRIME
The Joy of Trangression

Willem Schinkel
ASPECTS OF VIOLENCE
A Critical Theory

Cultural Criminology
Series Standing Order ISBN 978–0–230–53558–9
(*outside North America only*)

You can receive future titles in this series as they are published by placing a standing
order. Please contact your bookseller or, in case of difficulty, write to us at the address
below with your name and address, the title of the series and the ISBN quoted above.

Customer Services Department, Macmillan Distribution Ltd, Houndmills,
Basingstoke, Hampshire RG21 6XS, England

Aspects of Violence

A Critical Theory

Willem Schinkel
Erasmus University of Rotterdam, The Netherlands

palgrave
macmillan

First published 2010 by
PALGRAVE MACMILLAN

Palgrave Macmillan in the UK is an imprint of Macmillan Publishers Limited, registered in England, company number 785998, of Houndmills, Basingstoke, Hampshire RG21 6XS.

Palgrave Macmillan in the US is a division of St Martin's Press LLC, 175 Fifth Avenue, New York, NY 10010.

Palgrave Macmillan is the global academic imprint of the above companies and has companies and representatives throughout the world.

Palgrave® and Macmillan® are registered trademarks in the United States, the United Kingdom, Europe and other countries.

ISBN 978–0–230–57719–0   hardback

This book is printed on paper suitable for recycling and made from fully managed and sustained forest sources. Logging, pulping and manufacturing processes are expected to conform to the environmental regulations of the country of origin.

A catalogue record for this book is available from the British Library.

A catalog record for this book is available from the Library of Congress.

Printed and bound in Great Britain by
CPI Antony Rowe, Chippenham and Eastbourne

Contents

List of Illustrations

Acknowledgements

I would like to thank the following people for their advice/help/support in writing this book.

Zygmunt Bauman, Marguerite van den Berg, Godfried Engbersen, the guys from F and C-block, Philippa Grand, Mart-Jan de Jong, Rudi Laermans, Olivia Middleton, Liesbeth Noordegraaf-Eelens, Mirko Noordegraaf, Rutger Noordegraaf, Thomas Noordegraaf, Casper Noordegraaf, Jeroen Noordegraaf, Oma Geerse, Oma Schinkel, Mike Presdee, Sonja Pruimers, Anders Schinkel, Eva Schinkel, Els Schinkel, Kees Schinkel, Jeroen van Tilborg, Charlotte van Tilborg, Debby Vermeulen, Raymond Visser, Annemieke Vreugdenhil and Loïc Wacquant.

Part I The Concept and Observation of Violence

1
Introduction: Aspects of Violence

Introduction: Writing about violence

There are two ways of expressing the difficulties inherent in writing about violence. These two perspectives come together in the statement that *violence has a tendency of being misrecognized*. On the one hand, this is taken to mean that violence hides itself from any interpretative act towards it, that it is an essential feature of violence to be ill-recognizable. On the other hand, it is said that there is a tendency to misrecognize violence as such, because there exists an *illusio* that functions as a cover-up for violence. These positions are widely different, and yet they have in common the idea – the intuition if such is allowed – that violence is a slippery object, covering a plethora of things, actions mostly, being ill-definable (cf. Stanko, 2003). It is an object which escapes objectification. As Bauman (1995: 139) has said: 'There must be something about violence that makes it elude all conceptual nets.' If one finds paradigm-centred nomenclature enlightening, one might be satisfied here with an opposition along the lines of phenomenology versus structuralism. Thus, in sociology, debate may centre on the proper recognition of violence, on its 'immediate understanding' versus its structural antecedents and mythological or ideological masks. In philosophy, another issue appears to be at stake. The problem of the definition of violence can here, equally roughly, be divided into an essentialist and an anti-essentialist stance, or a conceptual nominalist and a realist stance. Is violence to be regarded as a Wittgensteinian family concept or as an Aristotelian form? These two debates – the one in sociology, the other in philosophy – are of course contaminated with each other. No understanding of violence will be propagated without a philosophical stance concerning the question what violence is. And no ideological masks are uncovered without debunking both commonsensical and philosophical essentialist notions of violence. Yet the reality of violence shows no respect for academic wobbling; it disregards the analytic dissection of its conceptual use and the causal dissection of its perpetrators. If a further claim is to be made, it is that *no one perspective*

3

'captures' violence. No academic discipline has it on a leash in a proper view that is all encompassing. Next to the sociological and the philosophical fields of enquiry are those of psychology, anthropology, biology and neuro-biology, all facing the same difficulty: how to handle violence without being contaminated with it? How to re-present it without doubling its presence? How to choose between reduction and abstraction, depth and surface, gram-mar and history, between motivation and causation? Are these even proper oppositions? How to avoid 'epistemological violence' (Shiva, 1988)? It is no coincidence that the supposed 'crisis of (re)presentation' in Western thought is said to have been brought about by two *violent events*: the Holocaust and the Gulag. It seems that the difficulty violence poses to the subject undergo-ing it is mirrored in the difficulty of the representation of violence.

Such speech, involving issues such as 'the violence of writing' or 'the violence of the social science of violence', involves a choice that is both consequential and controversial. It opts to utilize a notion of 'violence' as something other than physical, intentional violence between individuals. Rather, it aims to encompass something that has been called 'structural vio-lence' or 'symbolic violence'. In the discussion between a 'limited' and an 'expanded' concept of violence, this book is intended as one forceful albeit qualified argument in favour of the latter.

Liquidation as method

In order to develop this argument, it is important to start by outlining the method used to search for a definition of violence that intends to transcend existing worn out debates on the definition of violence. To use a violent metaphor, I opt for a perspective best called 'liquidation'. The liquidation of violence quite simply entails the critique of absolute definitions and theo-ries of violence, of theories that claim to capture violence as a whole. It is an attempt to liquify, or make fluid, what theories of violence all too often solidify, and to thereby harvest and preserve the *aspects of violence* that many theories do correctly but incorporate in a one-sided manner. Straight up, a sociological theory of violence has to reckon with certain strongly felt intui-tive understandings of what violence is. Such intuitions are always also of a moral nature. There is, for example, no doubt that if I were to randomly pick a stranger and hit that person in the face, he or she would feel violated. There is also no doubt that anyone reading this will agree with the adequacy of that feeling in that situation, or that early Pleistocene australopithecines would probably have experienced this as a violation in at least a comparable sense.

So there is, in such a case, a kind of immediate apprehension of the presence of violence. Surely not in the form of a theoretical-thematic knowledge, but certainly on the level of emotional response and practical knowledge in re-acting to violence. Any study of violence, any questioning of the nature of violence, cannot avoid the claim that there exists, in some cases, a *pre-reflexive apprehension* of violence. But 'some cases' are only some cases. Objections against this notion of a pre-reflexive understanding will be made saying that, in many cases, people tend to differ in their interpretations of what constitutes violence and what doesn't. And empirical research illustrates that people's intuitive sense of violence covers a wide array of acts and situations (Waddington et al., 2005). In other words, people's intuitions of what violence is vary significantly. Furthermore, what is recognized as violence and what isn't is a matter of violence itself, since it is a power to be able to use force without it being recognized as such.

These objections are, each in their own domain, justified. Just as the notion of a pre-reflexive understanding of violence is justified in its own sphere of recognition. Therefore, when I state that violence is an object that is difficult to objectify, I do not mean to claim that no substantial claims concerning its nature and presence can be made. What I do mean to do thereby is to *liquidate* any *theory* of violence, and to similarly *liquidate* any *empirical definition* of violence. To liquidate, that is, to tear down, to counter claims of absoluteness, and at the same time to liquify, to make fluid. A conceptual liquidation is a way of not accepting any claim of wholly describing or explaining a phenomenon in a stipulated definition or a determining cause, while preserving that which is at the core of such a claim and which may be of fundamental relevance. To liquidate a theory is to strip it bare to its most fundamental insights, and to then preserve those insights by storing them in a horizon of aspects that each shed their own distinctive light on a certain phenomenon. Each theory of violence and each empirical definition of it will possibly have at its core a relevant aspect, a relevant searchlight that sheds light on one side of the phenomenon of violence, but since each theory and each empirical definition tends to overstate its case, these turn into abstractions that freeze the flowing reality of violence. To liquidate is to recognize that with each objectification something is lost, since the processual character of reality does not allow freeze-framing without the loss of relevant aspects. Therefore, to keep those aspects from totalizing, like, for instance, a pre-reflexive understanding of violence has the tendency to become a naive realistic view on what violence 'is', is to keep open the possibility of, as Wittgenstein has said, 'changing the aspect'.

Observing aspects

Even assuming a universal pre-reflexive apprehension of violence exists, it is characterized by what Saint Augustine has said of time: so long as I don't think about it, I know what it is. In his *Réflections sur la violence* (1919), Sorel similarly wrote that the problems of violence remained 'obscure'. That does not mean there has not been significant work on violence, but it does mean that such work had not always fully recognized the complexities involved.

In his recent and rich book on violence, for instance, Randall Collins (2008) adopts a micro-sociological perspective and analyses violence in what he calls violent situations. He thereby assumes we know what a 'violent situation' is. But what is it that makes a situation 'violent'? Is it the raising of the arm or the blow on the head? Is it the 'face-work' of the individual actors involved or the collective definition of the situation of those standing by? Is the situation violent before a blow has been struck or a gun fired? And for how long after that has happened does it remain violent? Collins' book offers many rich empirical insights into the nature of violent situations, but he in the end evades the theoretical question of the definition of violence. He is unable to precisely demarcate the boundaries between 'violence' and 'non-violence' in situations. I am not pretending that such a demarcation is feasible. My point is, rather, that if such boundaries are fuzzy, an analysis like Collins' operates on the basis of some decision of what violence 'is'. A decision that is not made wholly explicit and that hence may not be the *only* way to speak meaningfully of violence.

There are many places where the study of violence can be liquidated. That means that there are many viewpoints that are easily made absolute, seen from which violence takes different shapes. It takes a focus on a particular aspect to see violence the way it appears to the victim of a physical assault, and it takes a change of aspect to see it from the perpetrator's perspective. With so many aspects to violence, a choice has to be made explicit concerning the aspects that are selected for closer study. Where such reflexivity is absent, the social scientific study of violence runs the risk of falling under the description Hannah Arendt gave it:

> [T]hat strictly scientific research in the humanities, the so-called Geisteswissenschaften that deal with the products of the human spirit, must come to an end by definition is obvious. The ceaseless, senseless demand for original scholarship in a number of fields, where only erudition is now possible, has led either to sheer irrelevance, the famous knowing of more and more about less and less, or to the development of a pseudo-scholarship which actually destroys its object.
>
> (Arendt, 1970: 29)

In order to avoid this, I choose to be very explicit about those aspects of violence I will study and those I will not. First, I wish to explicate what it is I mean by the fact that different 'aspects' may be discerned in violence.

Seeing aspects and changing the aspect

Wittgenstein's remarks on aspect-seeing are centred round the idea of 'seeing as', of seeing something as that which it is, when it is seen as such. Although Wittgenstein was, in the end, more concerned with a grammar of seeing, perhaps with certain language games of seeing and knowing, and not with perception in a realist sense, I shall largely ignore Wittgenstein's own emphasis, and put his remarks to use for my own purposes in illustrating the different possible ways of seeing a phenomenon such as violence, and the connections between those ways of seeing. Wittgenstein uses many examples to explain what he means by aspect-seeing. He for instance discusses seeing a face, recognizing that it has not changed yet somehow seeing it differently. That is what he calls 'seeing an aspect' (Wittgenstein, 1984: 518). The point is here that suddenly, one sees in the same image something else. This is Wittgenstein's way of saying that there always exists a certain articulation in conscious perception. Another example Wittgenstein gives concerns the illustration of a triangle. The triangle has, he says, many aspects, for it can be seen as a hole with three corners, a body of some sort or as a geometrical drawing. But it can also be seen as standing on its baseline or hanging from its top. Or it can be seen as a mountain, an arrow, or as one half of a parallelogram and so on. These are all possible aspects of the same illustration. And that same illustration may justify one person in seeing a mountain, while it may facilitate the perception of a geometrical drawing in another. So the same 'raw material' can become articulated in perception as entirely different things (Wittgenstein, 1989: 39). These different 'things' can then be called 'aspects' of that 'raw material', which may be an illustration or a face, or, as I want to demonstrate, a phenomenon such as violence.

There is an important distinction to be made when seeing something *as* something. On the one hand, there is a continuous seeing of an aspect. From this, the highlighting of an aspect (Wittgenstein, 1984: 520), which I will henceforth also call the *actualization* of an aspect, has to be distinguished. Wittgenstein illustrates his ideas on aspect-seeing using the famous figure, commonly called the 'duck-rabbit' figure (although it is Jastrow's picture of a hare). In this figure the fact that one can see at least two different aspects becomes easily visible. One can either see this as a drawing of a duck, or one can see it as a drawing of a hare (or a rabbit). What is important is that seeing the one excludes the perception of the other. I cannot see both hare and duck at the same time. So at times there may be a change of aspect in my perception. These are moments at which I suddenly see a hare instead of a duck, or at which I all of a sudden see a similarity between two faces. Something changes, but the perceptions before and after that change cannot be attributed solely to the subject, because the aspects of an object are, so to speak, in between subject and object. A change of aspect is described *as if* the object changes before one's eyes, because it is really seen 'in a different light', and thereby it looks like another object altogether. That has to do with the fact that after a change of aspect, parts of the object are seen as joining, as related, in a way they weren't before (Wittgenstein, 1984: 543). Other connections are being seen. When we see something as something, we have a certain relation to it. And also, when the aspect changes, our relation to the object changes.

In this book, I discuss certain aspects of violence. I will try to change the aspect several times. My use of Wittgenstein is indicative of a *method* of approaching violence. I don't mean to set a certain methodology loose on 'violence' in order to explain 'it'. My attitude is that of what one might call a *fractured realism*, in which I use a method of highlighting aspects of violence, and of changing between them. In doing so, any unified and all-embracing approach is liquidated. The ways in which such an approach highlights certain aspects of violence will be incorporated in a less rigid, more *fluid* account of aspects. This amounts to a 'fractured realism' in the sense that these aspects cannot then be combined *a posteriori* into a realist representation of violence in all its aspects. There will be fractures between aspects. Gluing them together will leave a distorted picture.

This fractured realist perspective takes in some highly relevant remarks by Edmund Husserl. Starting from phenomenology's basic tenet, the idea that consciousness is intentional, Husserl describes, by way of transcendental reduction, the perception of spatial objects in the natural attitude. Noesis, the intentional act(s), gives a noematic structure of an object that is never a unity in itself, but which consists of parts, of aspects in different experiences. Husserl (1976a: 73–4) gives the example of a table. The perception of a table continuously changes, and yet the table is perceived as a continuity itself. Although repeated perception gives me the assurance that the table is what it is and will be when I close my eyes, my perceptions are part of a flow of consciousness in which temporal perceptions are interconnected. In order to experience the table as what it is, consciousness has to transcend itself. Each experience of the table in fact consists of more than one perception; other perceptions are always already included in a single act of consciousness. For the perception of the table 'now' immediately flows into a 'just-now' perception, a perception of the past, while a new 'now' becomes actual (Husserl, 1976a: 74, 164–5). These different perceptions are, by means of retention and, concerning expectations towards the future, protention, included in any intentional act of consciousness, which is therefore transcendent.

Husserl makes a distinction between aspects of objects and profiles of these aspects (see Sokolowski, 2000: 19). An aspect is a continuous characteristic of the object. Such an aspect is experienced by means of a perceptual adumbration: successive perceptions that are part of the system of profiles (*Abschattungssystem*) of an aspect. Take, for example, the colour of an object. The same colour appears, according to Husserl, in a multifariousness of profiles. Each time I perceive the colour of an object, I perceive a profile of the aspect 'colour' of the object. Continuous perception gives me many profiles of such continuously present aspects. Husserl (1976: 202–3) gives the example of the colour of a tree. While the position of the eyes continuously changes and the gaze moves from trunk to twig, while we take a closer look or step back, we bring different perceptions into flow. Yet each profile points at the same aspect – in this case, the colour of the tree – and out of a multifariousness, unity is experienced. I can perceive an object because it adumbrates or variegates itself according to its aspects (Husserl, 1976a: 77). Not only does consciousness transcend the immediate perception of the object because of past or possible future perceptions, it also extrapolates on aspects of the object I am not immediately able to experience, such as the fact that a table has a backside, or that it has several legs while I might not even see one. I also extrapolate when I assume that the earth is spatially extended in many directions beyond my room without being able to verify that perceptually. Any object can only be given in a one-sided fashion (Husserl, 1976a: 81). But with each one-sided givenness of the object, other possible sides or ways of perceiving it are included. Those remain at hand in what Husserl calls a *horizon* or *background* of an act of consciousness. At each moment a certain selection out of that horizon becomes actualized (Husserl, 1976a: 167n) – a notion incorporated into sociology for instance by Niklas Luhmann (1971). Because so much is at each moment, though at hand, not selected, there is always a certain vagueness that surrounds the actually experienced object (Husserl, 1976a: 81). This vagueness concerns all those profiles that aren't selected. Yet each of them may at any time become selected and lose its vagueness. Then, the profile that was selected before, now moves into the background as part of the horizon of all those possible profiles not selected. This background is, however, partly constitutive of the experience of an object. In their negation, those aspects that are not selected still 'work' upon what is selected. I will always keep in mind that a table has a backside, since if I wouldn't, it would not make sense to experience a table. Without this relative inadequacy of an absent presence of many aspects, the experience of the object would be inadequate (Husserl, 1976a: 80). An experience contains a 'sense' ('Sinn') because it consists of a perception accompanied by less clear alternative perceptions in a backgrounding horizon of the experience (Husserl, 1976a: 181).

Aspects of violence

My use of both Wittgenstein's way of seeing aspects and Husserlian phenomenology is, admittedly, rather parasitic. Its aim is not exegetic. It is rather to come to an epistemology that can be utilized in analysing violence in the social sciences. I believe a non-dogmatic combination of pure phenomenology with Wittgenstein's insights will offer a *method* (in the sense of a *way* of seeing) of observing violence from the point of view of the social sciences that departs from naïve realism while at the same time eluding the trap of epistemological relativism. In a similar vain, the opposites of one-sided absolutism and endless conceptual dissemination are avoided. Fractured realism departs, as any epistemology or ontology does, from a few basic intuitions regarding reality. In this case, two such intuitions are present, and 'making it explicit' is preferable to silently presume them but at the same time pretend no such ultimate 'intuitions' are the foundation of a social science. A first intuition of fractured realism is the *realist intuition*, which entails that the world is an overwhelming presence to which I am subjected; I am knowing-in-the-world. Complementing this is what can be called the *fractured intuition* that holds that the world is endlessly complex. In order to know and to act, selection or articulation is necessary; 'world' as such cannot be represented.

In order to come to such a fractured realism, a first step is to define aspects and profiles in a manner suitable for these purposes. I will regard as an *aspect* of a phenomenon the *selective highlighting of a certain relational identity*. That focus of attention differs according to the specific thought-style that forces a scientist immersed in a thought-collective to see things in what is, for him or her, the only possible way of seeing them. Yet a different thought style, either within the same thought-collective or within another, leads one to see things in light of another aspect. One may, for example, see a phenomenon from a functionalist point of view, that is, with regard to its actual or possible functions for the social whole or for social subsystems. It can then appear to be an identity with causal relations to other phenomena with which it stands in some teleological relation. Seen in light of this aspect – its function – certain relations, both internal and external to the phenomenon, are highlighted that lead to a 'seeing as ...' of the object *in light of* its functions. The functionalist perspective leads to one view of the object, emphasizes one aspect of it, and by doing so, it (re)arranges its internal relations and its relations to other objects in such a way that several other possible aspects are for the moment blotted out.

Any view of 'violence' as a phenomenon therefore always concerns an *aspect* of violence that entails the view of violence as .... This means 'violence' is narrowed down to one aspect in which it *becomes* what is seen: a certain identity, a phenomenon, having certain internal and external relations. An aspect is always seen with a focus that is, in the thought-style from which it emanates, presupposed. The functionalist thought-style thus presupposes a focus on the function of a phenomenon, and this leads to an aspect of that phenomenon that shows those functions. Seen in light of those functions, the phenomenon may become a different relational identity compared to what it would be when seen in light of its means–end relations. As such, the same aspect of a phenomenon may still, in two different situations, differ in detail, since what is shared is a relatively general focus. What the phenomenon observed in light of an aspect looks like in detail, depends on the profile in which the aspect is seen.

I will regard as a *profile* of an aspect any *theoretical* view of an aspect. I will, therefore, not regard every description of an aspect as a profile, but rather every theory to which such a description adheres, either explicitly or implicitly.

To describe the functional aspect of a phenomenon, one may adhere to different theoretical 'search-lights'. While the same aspect is described, this still occurs in a different manner, varying according to which *theory* is used to describe the aspect. There is, therefore, in each approach of a phenomenon, a dissemination of ways of seeing according to aspects and to profiles of these aspects. In the study of violence, there is always a selection of a certain aspect out of a horizon of aspects. This selection allows for certain relations, along with an identity of violence, to be seen, whereas others, constituting a different identity, are obscured. As Peter Winch (1958: 102) has said, 'science [...] is wrapped up in its own way of making things intelligible to the exclusion of all others'. The focus on one aspect means a negation of other possible aspects. And similarly, there is a horizon of profiles at hand for each alternative aspect. An aspect can be approached in many different theoretical ways that may only have the focus on a specific aspect in common. And each of these profiles offers a more or less different picture of the selected aspect. Like Goya's etches in the *Desastres de la guerra* are a series of sketches of the horror of the violence of war – which can be regarded as the selected aspect of, in this case, the phenomenon of war violence – each etch can be seen as a different profile, showing the same aspect from a slightly different angle.

In the social scientific study of violence, a selection of aspect may, for instance, be that of the 'means–end' relation in which violence exists. Several theoretical approaches have this in common, leading nonetheless to very distinct profiles. Rational choice theory and (feminist) theories of masculinity and violence may share a focus on the aspect that is seen from a means–end perspective, but their profiles differ radically, and therefore, though they both see violence in light of the same aspect, they still see the aspect itself in a different light. Moreover, with the selection of an aspect comes a blindness to several other aspects. Only in a change of aspect can these be actualized out of a backgrounding horizon of aspects. However, several aspects are often at the same time selected. Unlike in Wittgenstein's hare–duck figure, selection of an aspect need not exclude simultaneous selection of certain other aspects, though it will always exclude some; namely those that shed light on the opposite of the selected aspects. So violence may be seen in light of its means-end aspect, and at the same time in lights of its aspect of the destruction of order. These are compatible aspects, which may be incorporated in the same profile, that is, which are presuppositions of the same theoretical approach. Aspects that are automatically excluded in that selection are, to name two, the *intrinsic attraction of violence* as a goal in itself (discussed in Chapter 5) and the *productive* or *constitutive aspect of violence* in social life. In this case, these remain unactualized in a horizon of alternative aspects, since the focus on means and ends tends to obscure the view of means and ends coinciding in violence as a goal in itself, and since a focus on the violent destruction of order is blinding to the view of the constitution of order through violence. Or to take another example, in seeking to explain juvenile criminal violence, a Mertonian analysis would focus primarily on the materialistic aspect of violence (which relates deviance in general to the opposition employment/unemployment). Yet especially in the case of juvenile criminal violence, the materialistic aspect is often less relevant as a causal factor than other factors, such as those that become apparent in the aspect of juvenile criminal violence as a group-process conveying intra-group status to individual members of the group (cf. Hassemer, 1973: 137; Katz, 1988: 313–17). The focus on the materialistic aspect blots out the view of such an aspect that is probably more relevant to a causal theory.

It is my goal in this book to further a proliferation of aspects of violence. To shed light on the fact that there are always many aspects to violence and that the theoretical profiles that the social sciences deploy are necessarily one-sided due to an implicit reduction of violence to but one aspect of violence. A liquidation of the study of violence intends to break through such rigid schemes of capturing their object in pointing towards the fluidity of aspects of violence. For to regard certain aspects of violence as violence itself is to disregard other aspects, other forms, effects, victims and agents of violence. The definition of violence is a matter of *politics*, and it will be dealt with in the next two chapters.

A crucial question is what counts as an aspect of violence. It is fine to speak of a proliferation of aspects that, together, offer a fractured representation of violence as a phenomenon, but if anything will do for an aspect, not much will be gained in the sense of a fractured *realism*, nor will any warnings against ideologically constructed images of violence hit home. I will therefore regard as an aspect of violence one selective construction of the identity 'violence', with a relative degree of consistency and coherence. Such an identity can be regarded as a relatively autonomous field of relations, a 'social formation' (compare White, 2008). A 'field of relations' here means a certain identity of violence as ..., brought about by certain internal and external connections. These can be probed in their consistency and coherence, and only when these are established as existing to a certain intersubjectively verifiable degree do I speak of an aspect of violence that forges that field of relations out of a multiplicity of factors, such as events, causes, motives, actors. That always at the same time involves a certain aspect-blindness. In subsequent chapters, it will become clear that in the social scientific study of violence, aspect-blindness amounts to a very specific form of violence itself. To the fractured realism based on Husserl and Wittgenstein, a political dimension will thus be added: the question of the recognition of aspects of violence is a question of *politics*.

The structure of the argument

What this book proposes to do is to change the aspect of both violence and its scientific study several times. I will take a critically reflexive stance towards the social sciences in my discussions of studies of violence, and shed light on different though not unrelated aspects of violence. This means that I will shed light on certain aspects of the study of violence, as well as on violence itself. The first discussion, espoused in Part I and in the concluding chapter, focuses on the *aspect of the study of violence*, which entails the fact that only a limited number of *forms and aspects of violence* are recognized by it, which are thereby universalized. Throughout this book, a critique of the social sciences and of philosophy in their way of analysing violence is brought forward.

When, in the next chapters, a distinction is made between private violence, state violence and structural violence, these will be seen as ideal-typical forms of violence. The following chapters will discuss the criteria on the basis of which a phenomenon may be called 'violence'. Ideal-typical forms of violence are distinguished from aspects of violence. It makes as little sense to say that structural violence is an aspect of violence as it makes sense to say that a tiger is an aspect of the generic type 'animal'. Yet it is possible to see a certain case of structural violence in light of the aspect of its being 'structural violence', like it makes sense to consider a tiger in light of its being an animal. The fact that a certain violence can be called structural violence means that certain things can become visible when this violence is considered in relation to a certain differentiation of the social system, things that are otherwise unseen. Other aspects of violence are highlighted in various chapters. They include the intrinsic attractiveness of violence, the productivity of violence, the legitimacy of violence, the causes of violence, the autopoiesis or self-reproduction of violence, but also the fact that certain forms (types, kinds) of 'violence' lead to other forms of violence. For the relations between the three basic forms of violence are aspects of 'violence' in general.

In the next two chapters, the vital conceptual issue of the definition of violence will be elaborated upon. Chapters 1–4 make up the first part of this book, in which a metatheoretical foundation is laid for reflexive analysis of violence. Subsequent to a discussion of the problems in defining violence, Chapter 2 provides an analysis of the etymology and semantics of the concept of violence. This will include a historical analysis of the gradual formation of the modern concept of violence which arose as a consequence of the autonomization of the state. The consequences of the historical differentiation between the concepts of *potestas* and *violentia* will be the main focus here. On the basis of what is said in Chapter 2, an ontological definition of violence will then be put forward in Chapter 3, and why an apparently abstract and admittedly broad definition of violence is the only way of realistically defining it will be explained. In addition, it is argued that alternative ways of defining violence are always more *violent* than the definition proposed. Chapter 4 offers a critical reading of Walter Benjamin's *Zur Kritik der Gewalt*. From the discussion in this chapter, the concept of *autotelic violence* – a violence for the sake of itself – will be concluded as designating a self-referential aspect of violence. This is one significant change of aspect that is usually unrecognized in the social science of violence. Part II consists of Chapters 5–9. Chapter 5 tacks on to the concept of autotelic violence, as espoused in Chapter 4, and discusses the role of a 'will to violence'. Chapter 6 deals with the definition of terrorism and specifically highlights the political character of notions of violence. Chapter 7 offers a tentative analysis of 'high school violence', which is highlighted in light of often-neglected aspects. A perspective is sought that differs radically from the common sense understandings of phenomena such as 'high school violence'. Chapter 8 draws different aspects of violence together in an attempt to conceptually raise the understanding of three main ideal-typical forms of violence by integrating them into a perspective that will be termed the *trias violentiae*. Chapter 9 concludes the book with a discussion in which the contemporary semantics of violence, as discussed in Chapter 2, are connected to the social scientific discourse on violence. This continues on a thread that runs throughout the book: observing aspects of violence is paradoxical and neglecting aspects of violence is characterized by a certain violence itself. The need for reflexive social science of violence arises from the very definition of violence, as elaborated in Part I.

From the perspective of a fractured realism it will not be possible, as Wittgenstein tries to do in his *Vortrag über Ethik* (1989: 10), to reach an effect similar to that of Galton, taking photographs of different faces on one photographic plate, in order to gain a total picture of those aspects characteristic of a face. Rather, violence may, when seen in the light of one aspect, appear to be incompatible with the way it looks after a change of aspect. Therefore, what is said in one chapter simply may not be wholly interpretable from the perspective of another. There is a certain incommensurability that has to be acknowledged as present in the study of violence. One might, then, compare this book to those late Renaissance collections of curiosities, constructed by rich aristocrats (the *Wunderkammer*), in which works of art and other artefacts were supposed to represent *aspects* of the world and in which a collection of all these aspects would be possible as a representation of the world in all its varieties – an idea still present in Louis XIV's Versailles. Such a collection can, from the point of view of a fractured realism, never be unequivocal and all encompassing; it would be fractured, paradoxical. Chapters in this book may be at odds with one another.

The motto of this book might be said to be, in Spinoza's words, *omnis determinatio est negatio*. Paradoxes are continuously present in the social scientific observation of violence. To observe the paradoxes of that observation is a work of reflexivity that unfolds under way. It now remains to be seen where a fractured realism takes the social scientific observation of violence. However, in the end, my enterprise can be considered as failed not when it is oblivious to relevant aspects of violence, but rather when it delivers a consistent but entirely uniform view of violence.

The antinomies of violence

Therefore, several antinomies can be formulated which underscore much of the discussion throughout the following chapters. In order to make the tensions that define this perspective explicit, ten of the most pressing antinomies are formulated below:

1   Violence breaks down social order – violence is constitutive of social order.
2   Violence is a social problem – violence is a standardized solution to social problems.
3   Violence is a purely destructive form of sociality – violence is a positive form of sociality bringing people together.
4   Violence is a way of dealing with contingency – violence is a prominent form and source of contingency.
5   Violence is norm-breaking – violence is norm-strengthening.
6   Violence is a visible situation – violence is a hidden process.
7   The violence of the state is reactive towards illegitimate violence – the violence of the state is already active in the very distinction between legitimate and illegitimate violence.
8   Violence is a meaningful social process, which has a meaning in referring to an external referent – violence is a social process characterized exclusively by self-reference.
9   Violence is a repellent – violence is a magnet.
10 Violence is a means to an end – violence is an end in itself.

2
The Definition of Violence – Part I

The definition of violence in social science

Problems of defining violence usually begin with reflections on the many denotations of violence (cf. Michaud, 1986; Collins, 2008; Crettiez, 2008). In doing so, many approaches start and end with an enumeration of the various actions that fall under the general heading of 'violence'. The following is one example of such a list:

1   To violate (do violence to) a church, a country's borders, a confidence, a promise, a treaty, one's office.
2   Obscenity does violence to one's senses.
3   Do violence to the dignity of another.
4   Do violence to a scriptural text.
5   A threat of violence.
6   Acts of violence such as to murder, maim, injure bodily.
7   Crimes of violence.
8   Violence of a storm.
9   Violence of pain.
10 Violent (impassioned) words.
11 A violent death.
12 Violent (severe) punishment.

(Wade, 1971: 369)

Regarding such lists as appropriate definitions of violence raises questions. For example, is there or is there not already *violence* in what is usually called the *threat* of violence? And most importantly, if we do not speak about the *same* violence when comparing, for instance, the violence being done to a text and the violence of a violent crime, then are we speaking of the same 'thing' [violence] at all? Can we say that, in the end, there is an identity of violence, an *essence* that lies at the core of all the things we call violence? This is the basic question when it comes down to finding a

16

definition of violence. Why would one even bother finding such a thing? One obvious answer would be that because not defining the basic concept one researches would seem to inevitably reflect negatively on the validity and general relevance of that research. Yet very often, this does not seem to be the case. Social scientists seem to operate under a general consensus, silently agreed to, that one usually does not need to define violence. If no one starts to raise problems about it, all will be well, and the social scientific industry of violence-research can operate at full steam. When a student shoots a teacher in the head, who cares about a definition of violence? It is obvious to any observer (sociologist or not) that whatever the precise conceptualization is, this qualifies as violence. Zygmunt Bauman has therefore commented on the common social scientific practice to not define violence:

> Virtually all writers attempting to come to grips with the phenomenon of violence find the concept either under-, or over-defined, or both. They also report in other writers (if they not display it themselves) an amazing reluctance, or ineptitude, to resolve the confusion and put things straight. Above all, they find in the texts they read plenty of understatements and half-truths, a lot of embarrassed silence, and other signs of shamefacedness
>
> (Bauman, 1995: 139)

Luhmann (1991: 16) has suggested that questions of definition in social science serve less the accurate description of phenomena, than they do the distinguishment thereof. The result being that research fields are maintained that leave each other in peace. This chapter and the following are written in light of the premise that both defining and not defining violence will lead to blind spots, as a result of which certain forms of violence go unnoticed. That is why Mary Jackman has stated that 'we must analyze the ideology of violence, to try to assess how and why various acts of violence are repudiated, ignored, denied, praised, or glorified' (Jackman, 2002: 408). For not noticing violence when it nonetheless exists – albeit not in a way that conforms to the prevalent legalistic definition of violence – is to silently condone it, to ratify and legitimize it. The violence of not defining violence is a violence that is necessarily overlooked by the social scientific industry of violence-research.

Linguistic problems: Etymologies of violence

So is there an 'essence' of violence? And what does that even mean? The possibility of finding such an essence will be discussed below. First, it is enlightening to review the etymological roots of the Anglo-Saxon concept of 'violence', alongside those of the similar Germanic concept of *Gewalt*.

Dictionary definitions

It is, first of all, helpful to review some of the common definitions of violence given in dictionaries. *Webster's Third New International Dictionary of the English Language* gives the following meanings of 'violence':

> 1 a exertion of any physical force so as to injure or abuse (as in warfare or in effecting an entrance into a house) b: an instance of violent treatment or procedure 2: injury in the form of revoking, repudiation, distortion, infringement, or irreverence to a thing, notion, or quality fitly valued or observed 3 a: intense, turbulent, or furious action, force, or feeling often destructive b: vehement feeling or expression: fervor, passion, fury c: an instance or show of such action or feeling: a tendency to violent action d: clashing, jarring, discordant, or abrupt quality 4: undue alteration of wording or sense (as in editing or interpreting a text) syn see FORCE

The *Oxford English Dictionary* gives:

> 1. The exercise of physical force so as to inflict injury on, or cause damage to, persons or property; action or conduct characterized by this; treatment or usage tending to cause bodily injury or forcibly interfering with personal freedom. b. In the phr. *to do violence to, unto* (or with indirect object): To inflict harm or injury upon; to outrage or violate. c. In a weakened sense: Improper treatment or use of a word; wresting or perversion of meaning or application; unauthorized alteration of wording. d. Undue constraint applied to some natural process, habit, etc., so as to prevent its free development or exercise. e. *Law* (...) 2. An instance or case of violent, injurious, or severe treatment; a violent act or proceeding. 3. Force or strength of physical action in natural agents; forcible, powerful or violent action or motion (in early use freq. connoting destructive force or capacity). 4. Great force, severity, or vehemence; intensity of some condition or influence. 5. Vehemence of personal feeling or action; great, excessive, or extreme ardour or fervour; also, violent or passionate conduct in language; passion, fury. 6. Violation of some condition.

Common transitive meanings in this list are '1. To do violence to; to violate' and '2. To compel or constrain; to force (a person) to or from a place, etc, or to do something, by violence'. Before singling out what would appear to be the core elements in these dictionary definitions, it is relevant to consider a continental equivalent of the English word 'violence'. Since the French 'violence' can obviously be assumed to be of similar stem, the German 'Gewalt' (also in Dutch: 'geweld') will be better suited as a comparison. The *Duden* dictionary reads on *Gewalt*: 'Power, authority, right and means to exercise control over somebody or someone'.

Some striking differences appear when 'violence' and 'Gewalt' are compared in their dictionary definitions. Most obvious is the integral part played by power (*Macht*) in the German definition. In fact, *Gewalt* is often used as a synonym for *Macht*, as in the German translation of Montesquieu's famous formulation in *L'Esprit des Lois*: 'the division of powers' (*Gewalten* or quite simply *die Gewaltenteilung*). And the *Europäische Enzyklopädie zu Philosophie und Wissenschaften* lists *Gewalt* as 'Macht/Herrschaft/Gewalt' (Sandkühler et al., 1990: 114–21). The difference between *Macht* and *Gewalt* has been stressed by Kant, who states in his *Kritik der Urteilskraft* that 'violence' or 'force' (*Gewalt*) is a power that is able to overcome that which has power itself (Kant, 1957: 184). However, this would appear to mean nothing more than that *Gewalt* is simply the highest power: the ability to overcome the greatest obstacles, in Kant's definition. New in Kant's definition is the idea that *Macht* and *Gewalt* are what they are according to their degree of overcoming obstacles. In Kant's definition, they are, on the one hand, separated from each other, while on the other hand they are brought closer together. For power (*Macht*) does not 'need' violence (*Gewalt*) to assert itself, but violence rather resides at the top of a continuum of power. Hegel, on the other hand, defines *Gewalt* as 'appearance of power' (Hegel, 1969: 715). What remains obvious is an intricate relation between violence and power.

This connection between *Gewalt* and *Macht* is an old one that seems to reveal a fundamental, or a continuously culturally present, aspect of violence. The English 'violence' also has a connection, albeit less explicit, with power. To explore this, it is necessary to briefly delve into the etymology of the words 'violence' and 'Gewalt'.

Etymology: 'violence'

Violence has its roots in a concept of *force*, hence the primary dictionary definitions of violence: 'the exercise of (physical) force'. It is derived from the Latin noun *violentia* ('vehemence', 'impetuosity') and the adjective *violentus* ('vehement', 'forcible', 'impetuous', 'violent') and it appears to have become an independent word in Anglo-French and Old French somewhere around the fourteenth century. The verb to which both *violentia* and *violentus* relate is *violare*, meaning 'to outrage, to dishonour' or 'to treat with violence'. Furthermore, there is a relation between *violare* and *vis*, which translates as 'strength, force'. The Latin *vis* is related to the Greek *is*, which is itself related to *bia* (βια), meaning the vital (living) force, the force of the body and, consequently, the use of force and violence (Michaud, 1986: 4). There furthermore exists a relation between *vis* and *vir*, a concept which is found in the great humanist works of the Roman moralists such as Seneca and Cicero and which denotes 'man', in the sense of a 'real' or 'strong man', which then means a *virtuous* man, a man endowed with the virtues of which wisdom, justice, courage and temperance were the most important ones, taking his fate in his own hands, thus seducing the goddess of

Fortuna to favour him in his strife for glory and honour. Only the *vir*, the man in possession of *virtus* could do so. This classical theme, after being dismissed completely in scholastic thought, was then revitalized by Italian Renaissance writers, such as Pontano, Piccolomini and, most importantly, Machiavelli. Yet for the latter, *virtus*, or as he called it, *virtù*, did not consist of the humanist virtues that Cicero or Livy associated with it. Instead, Machiavelli turns this tradition upside down (cf. Wiener, 1973). Though he assumed the *virtuoso* to be able to seduce Fortuna, he saw the *virtù* of a princely ruler as the readiness to, at any time, do whatever is necessary (the concept of *necessità* occupies a central place in *The Prince*) for the maintenance of order. This would include actions many would think of as immoral or characteristics generally regarded as vices rather than virtues: the good prince does not 'swerve from the good if possible', but does also 'know how to resort to evil if necessity demands it' (Machiavelli, 1997: 68). In Machiavelli, therefore, a more explicit connection between power and the *vir* becomes apparent. Whereas the Roman moralists and historians tended to neglect the relationship between *vis* and *vir*, in Machiavelli this connection is (re)established. The existence of a strong connection between honour and violence has been argued also in social science, for instance by Anton Blok, who relates diverse violent practices – from the Spanish bull fight or the Sicilian mafia liquidations (*lupara*) to ritual sacrifice and banditry or terrorism – to each other on the basis of a ritualized threesome of honour, violence and power (Blok, 2001).

'gewalt ist aber sô manicfalt' – Etymology: 'Gewalt'

As the contemporary use of 'Gewalt' not merely echoes connotations with power, but explicitly conveys them, the etymology equally shows a certain duality in the concept. This duality is indicative of the close connections that would seem to exist between violence and power. 'Gewalt', as the Dutch 'geweld', stems from the old Germanic *waldan* (also *wouden*), which means 'to reign, to control'. Similar terms can be found in old Slavic-Germanic languages (such as the noun *vlada*, which similarly means 'reign'). These forms are comparable Latin *valēre*, which means 'to be strong'. Here, the etymology of 'violence' and the Germanic forms of 'Gewalt' and 'geweld' do not come together, since the Germanic forms existed before the Roman dominion, and since there is no evidence of a direct connection between *violare* and *valēre* anyway, although the latter word also bears much of the content of *vir* and *virtus* and is connected to these. An indirect connection between *violare* and *valere* might therefore be a common root in *vis*. As for 'Gewalt', then, a form derived from *waldan*, *wäl*, has furthermore been used to denote 'king'. Etymologically, *waldan* is related to the later Gothic *ulfilas*, of which one noun (*vulbus*) captures the meanings of 'honour', 'reputation' and 'splendour' that are also denotations of *vis*. The duality of the concept of 'Gewalt' is rooted in the fact that 'Gewalt' (also in older forms such as *giwald/giwalt*) did not serve as a juridical term in old Germanic law. With the Roman upsurge and the expansion and increased importance of Latin substantial differences between Germanic and Roman law led to the translation of a multitude of, more or less related, Latin concepts by 'Gewalt' (Grimm and Grimm, 1911: 4913; Ritter, 1974: 569). Out of these, *potestas* became the dominant translation of 'Gewalt', but this shifted when *potestas* came to be thought of as 'power' (*Macht*) during the Middle Ages, which can be seen to have influenced Hobbes' separation of *vis* ('force') and *potestas* ('power') (Hobbes, 1969). Then, 'Gewalt' gained a second meaning which was rooted in *violentia*.[1] The genesis of this semantic duality, which exists until today, must have been prompted by the fact that 'Gewalt' had always carried the ambiguity of this duality in itself, therefore needing a new form to be grounded in when *potestas* became used more and more as 'power'.

When I speak of a 'semantics of violence' I am concerned with a constellation of meanings that is historically contingent but intricately tied up with socio-structural developments pertaining to the nature of political organization and regimes of punishment. The following analysis of the historical development of the semantics of violence has one goal: it highlights the historical genesis of the conditions of possibility of the Western commonsensical notion of violence.

The semantics of violence

In delineating some of the historical semantic changes involving concepts of violence, contemporary historical research on violence is of little use, since it hardly ever focuses on historical views of violence, but presupposes views similar to contemporary ones, involving mostly the semantic construct of physical intentional hurt. What can instead be enlightening is a brief review of some of the ways in which the relationship between man, law and the state have been conceived over time. Surely the most significant process in this relationship has been the creation of sovereign states. It was this gradual autonomization of the state that necessitated first of all a view of the urgency of the problematic of physical violence and second of all an attempt to eradicate it from the newly born civil society. The taken-for-grantedness of violence as physical violence is no doubt connected to the taken-for-grantedness of the 'monopoly of legitimate violence' of the state, which is nothing other than a monopoly of *physical* violence. Physical violence has not always been the obsession of the predecessors of the state. In ancient Germanic law, 'Gewalt' did not serve as a juridical concept. In ancient Germanic tribes, crime in general was often punished not by corporal punishment of the perpetrator, but by retribution in terms of money or property and by reconciliation of victim and perpetrator. Only the severe cases of murder and treason were punished by exile, in which case the perpetrator was outlawed. 'Gewalt', however, was deemed part of the freedom the law did not pertain to (Ritter, 1974: 562). 'Gewalt' remains an ambiguous concept until today, since it became translated both as *potestas* and as *violentia* in the Middle Ages. This difference already marks the autonomization of the state and its appropriation of legitimate violence. While in scholastic thought, divine power was equally translated as *Gottesgewalt* and as *violentia spiritualis*, the connotation of 'power' was gradually transferred to *potestas* – *potesta* being, in medieval law from the twelfth century on, magistrates to whom conflicting parties turned for mediation (Sprandel, 1975: 112ff.). This difference exists equally in the semantic history of 'violence', and is pressed for instance by Hobbes, who equates *vis* or *violentia* to the violence of the state of nature and *potestas* to the (legitimate) violence of the sovereign state. A similar difference is denoted by the French *pouvoir* and *force (violence)*. By the eighteenth century, the opposition between legitimate and illegitimate force has driven a wedge between the concepts of 'power' and 'violence', two concepts originally hard to distinguish. We read for instance in Zedler's *Universallexikon*:

> Force [Gewalt] means the capacity to bring something about, either lawfully – and then it is a lawful force, potestas, pouvoir – or unlawfully and intentionally so – and then it is a punishable forcefulness, vis, violentia
>
> (Zedler, 1732ff.: 1377)

Similarly, it is not *violentia spiritualis*, but illegitimate *violentia*, that Milton refers to when he says: 'Looking down, he saw the whole earth filled with violence.' Luther translates *potestas* by 'Macht' and *violentia* by 'Gewalt' when he translates Luke 10, 49, 'potestam calcandi [...] supra omnem virtutem inimici', as 'Ich habe euch Macht gegeben [...] uber alle Gewalt des Feindes' ['I have given thee power [...] over all enemy violence'] (Grimm and Grimm, 1911: 4915). The structural context of these semantic changes is complex, since these changes allowed for a greater complexity to be dealt with by the social system at large. The differentiation into a legitimate and an illegitimate form enabled two positions to be taken instead of one. As a general course of history the autonomization of the state is highly relevant here, but this process did not take place independently of semantic changes in the conception of cosmic order and of the place of man therein, that is, of political theology. It is possible to roughly identify several stages of autonomization of the state that each have their own view of man. These stages are identifiable according to the nature of the political theology that serves as legitimation of the state. It is furthermore possible to relate conceptions of violence to the specific legitimation that is provided for the existence of the state. To deploy Carl Schmitt's classic thesis of political theology – which states that all political concepts are rooted in theological concepts (Schmitt, 1996) – is to see to what extent the state is thought of as man-made. This, in turn, reflects notions of legitimate and/or illegitimate violence. As precursors to the Western theory of the state, the Greek theory of the *polis* and the Roman concept of the *res publica* may be mentioned, although Voegelin (1951) rightly assumes that Plato's *Republic* is not so much a theory of the polis but rather of the demise of the polis and its ideal constitution. The *res publica*, on the other hand, is but a faint conception of the state, literally meaning the 'public cause', and perhaps best translated as 'society'. Modern states, on the other hand, are defined with the help of the opposition state/society.

The definition of violence and the autonomization of the state

It is relevant here to briefly discuss the development of a semantics of the state that separates it from 'society' in direct opposition, reserving legitimate violence (*potestas*) for the state and illegitimate violence (*vis, violentia*) for society. The first influential conceptualization of the state after the era of Roman hegemony is St Augustine's *City of God*. Augustine differentiates between a *civitas Dei* (City of God) and a *civitas terrena*, the worldly state. The *civitas terrena* is devoid of justice if it is not receptive to the *civitas Dei*. Without subordination to the *civitas Dei*, all legitimation that befalls a ruler is gone, and banditry would prevail. Augustine famously asks what differentiated Alexander from a common pirate. Any ruler not embracing the authority of God is without legitimation, since worldly power in the end derives from divine power. With this formulation, a statement of political theology is given that survives until well into the modern era, albeit then often in secularized form. From the early Middle Ages on, royal rule was theocratic (Southern, 1970). The hierarchical order inherent in this political theology is derived from Plato's analogy between the *polis* and the human body, with a head at the top (*logos*), the higher passions such as courage (*thymos*) in between as the guardians, and the people – the lower regions of the body and its lower passions (*eros*) – at the bottom (Schinkel, 2007). This analogy, which still finds expression in notions like the one, the view and the many, was given Christian theocratic content in the Middle Ages. The king mirrored himself through God on the one hand, above him, and through the people below him. However, the state was held in check by the church, which is the first ever supranational organization, and which also held great worldly power. For a long time, state and church, though rivals, kept each other in balance. Thomas Aquinas' views are an expression of this dual structure. Aquinas added to Aristotle's political theory a theological superstructure and connected the two (Copleston, 1972: 300). This 'theory of two powers' was significant in that it allowed for a legitimization of a feudal status quo. Regicide, even if it amounted to tyrannycide, was obviously a difficult issue but was mostly deemed illegitimate, while a feudal order was in place that was allotted a divine nature, since it was the divine rule of the universe that the status quo mirrored. In opinions on criminal law and punishment, the balance between state and church lead to a subtle change that eventually found its place at the heart of the modern theory of punishment. In the later days of the Roman Empire, private violence and crime in general were kept in check to the extent that threats to order were countered. There was, therefore, no real need to suit punishment to the conditions of the offender and the offence, as becomes apparent in Augustine saying:

> Surely, it is not without purpose that we have the institution of the power of kings, the death penalty of the judge, the barbed hooks of the executioner, the weapons of the soldier, the right of punishment of the ruler, even the severity of the good father [...]. While these things are feared, the wicked are kept within bounds and the good live more peacefully among the wicked
>
> (quoted in Kelly, 1992: 113)

The death penalty was, however, not as often executed as many moderns have thought, since the church, seeing the offender as a sinner in need of repentance and reclamation had a mitigating effect on criminal law (Kelly, 1992: 113). We then find Aquinas, centuries later, saying that

> there are others, of evil disposition and prone to vice, who are not easily moved by words. These it is necessary to restrain from wrongdoing by force and fear (*per vim et metum*) so that, they ceasing to do evil, a quiet life is assured to the rest of the community; and they are themselves drawn eventually, by force of habit, to do voluntarily what one stated only out of fear, and so to practise virtue. Such discipline which compels under fear of penalty is the discipline of law
>
> (quoted in Kelly, 1992: 155)

It is, however, significant that a modern monopoly of the use of legitimate violence did not exist, since the ruler was dependent upon a decentralized layer of feudal fiefs, down to a layer of knights. The king depended on these, and while they could not be counted as part of the state, they were in possession of a large extent of the potential of organized physical violence of medieval society. That means, however, that physical violence was not centralized, nor was it punishable if it struck people in the lower regions of society. In fact, the ruler often had difficulties controlling his knights in their violence. Elias (1980: 270) quotes Huizinga on the 'chronic form' of war in the Middle Ages, and reminds of the pleasure the knights derived from war. Not only was there a kind of autotelic violence in war, but a knight derived from combat his whole identity. His honour depended largely on his ability to fight (Elias, 1980). War means friendship for the knight; his social status was dependent on fighting. While knights were thus extremely useful in times of war, they were less useful when peace reigned. One reason for this is still prominent in Machiavelli's dissatisfaction with mercenary armies, which ravaged the country they were supposed to protect, especially in relatively peaceful times, when no one paid them (Machiavelli, 1997). Machiavelli's plea for a citizen army was in fact a move towards the monopoly of legitimate violence of the state. The knight's desire for physical violence, which was bound up with his entire social existence, also posed problems in the sense that a duelling culture existed, which led to excesses of violence that both harmed the ruler's base directly and, indirectly, provided cause for conflict that might disturb peace. There are indeed 'serious questions about the ability (and, indeed, willingness) of so-called higher authorities in later medieval France and the low countries to take effective action against private acts of aggression, committed by members of what was still, in so many respects, a warrior nobility' (Vale, 2000: 181). In order to come to grips with the problems for instance of aristocratic duels in at least a rudimentary sense, these were formalized. Impetus to formalization came from the king, but also from the church, which did not approve of the violence of the duel. Whenever two noblemen were engaged in conflict, a *gage de bataille* ('pledge of battle') was a formal trial by combat that was thus relatively well regulated. It was wholly banned at the end of the 1560s. Yet while the last public trial by battle in England was held in 1571, a private duelling culture survived until well into the nineteenth century as a sign of the risen yet still in certain respects limited autonomy of the state. The tournaments among knights were one of the greatest causes of concern to medieval rulers. Such tournaments existed especially during relatively peaceful times and were thus a proxy for war, even to the extent that knights of different kingdoms participated. These tournaments posed a threat to sovereignty to the extent that they were sometimes so bloody that a king could lose too many knights and become vulnerable to external intrusions (a description of a tournament in 1342 said: 'multi nobiles fuerunt graeviter laesi et aliqui mutilati' – ['many nobles were seriously wounded and others maimed']) (Murimuth, quoted in J. Vale, 2000).

A step towards the state's monopoly of legitimate violence is therefore the regulation of such tournaments, which became especially necessary as the tournaments 'urbanized', for instance in the German towns of Lübeck and Lüneburg in the 1240s and 60s, spreading west towards Lille, Douai and Bruges. Lower patriciates were now enabled to demonstrate chivalric abilities. However, there is a marked decrease in the violence of tournaments in records from the thirteenth to the fourteenth century. At the same time, an aestheticization of the tournament took place (J. Vale, 2000). This development is in line with Elias's analysis of the increasing control of the state over private violence. In medieval times, however, physical violence was only in certain cases recognized as punishable. Wife beating, for example, was far from being called 'domestic violence'. These things indicate that a growing autonomy of the state existed but had not yet crystallized the way it has in modern times. Several interrelated structural changes took place from the fourteenth century on that strengthened it and thereby equally strengthened the state's monopoly of legitimate violence. These were most of all the development of nationalist sentiments (especially in France and in England), the increasing urbanization and the onset of a new societal hierarchy through the rise of an economic class of merchants in the early Italian Renaissance. With these developments, the medieval societal hierarchy, as rooted in a divine cosmic order, slowly gave way to a class system in which mobility was less based on heredity than it was on economic success (although these, of course, are always interrelated). The definitive victory of state over church came, with Becket already having been killed in England in 1170, in the early fourteenth century, when the church became divided. Pope Boniface in harsh tones declared *Unam Sanctam*, the supremacy of church rule over the state, but was seized by Philip IV of France. Whereas the church used to carry out tasks like education, the keeping of birth- and death-records and the caring for the ill, these functions gradually became state-regulated. Philosophically, the popularity of Aristotelianism contributed to the primacy of the state. Marsilius of Padua was the first to unequivocally declare the subordination of the church to the state. Two centuries later, Machiavelli did not even care to discuss ecclesiastical governments because they were too little 'political' for his taste. The rise of nationalism as well as the rise of the sovereign nation state was spurred by the 100-year war, which ended in 1453. Around the same time, a diversion of economic routes was in place that favoured western Europe and especially the Italian city states. From this time on, the view of man begins to change significantly. Not surprisingly, in the early Italian Renaissance, Roman humanism is revived. It has become clear that the bounds of the feudal order can be transcended by fortunate individuals, that is, by individuals in possession of the *virtù* to seduce *Fortuna*. The fifteenth century truly is, as Huizinga said, the *Herfsttij* of the Middle Ages. A new respect grows for the civilian, for the entrepreneur. While the knight's life was full of risk and presupposed a 'hohe muot' ('high courage'), a new way of *riscare* implied another view of man (von Martin, 1931: 75). Class gradually began to replace estate. The new humanism is also found in thoughts on legal theory, for instance in More's *Utopia*, where a 'respect for equality' is propagated. These changes have had their effect on criminal law in general. The state increasingly became the autonomous sphere by means of which society organizes itself politically. As such, the criminal increasingly becomes a person not solely injuring another person, nor sinning against God and injuring the divine authority of the king, but he becomes a person injuring society as a whole. Thus, Grotius states that 'acts which "neither directly nor indirectly affect human society, or another human being", are not to be punished, but left to God' (quoted in Kelly, 1992: 238). As we have seen, the transition from Augustine to Aquinas meant a change in the nature of punishment towards reformation. In Hobbes, this is more explicitly so, as he says that the punishment of a crime is an evil inflicted by public authority, on him that hath done, or omitted that which is judged by the same authority to be a transgression of the law; to the end that the will of men may thereby the better be disposed to obedience

(Hobbes, 1969: 277)

In Hobbes, as for instance in his contemporary Pufendorf, the conservation of society becomes the main goal of criminal justice. Later accounts further stress this preservation of society. Locke, for instance, speaks of

the preservation of the whole [society, W.S.], by cutting off those parts, and those only, which are so corrupt that they threaten the sound and healthy, without which no severity is lawful. And this power has its original only from compact and agreement and the mutual consent of those who make up the community

(quoted in Kelly, 1992: 240)

Locke, however, only speaks of 'crime' in relation to crimes of property, but such crimes were often equally defined as violence. In the low countries, a breach of someone's right of some sort was usually referred to as 'gewelt' (Berents, 1976: 19, 82). An equation of 'violence' with 'physical force' was yet to be fully developed, and did not arise until the autonomy of the secular state was achieved by means of a monopoly of legitimate violence. Now, while Foucault claims that 'state power appropriated the entire judicial procedure, the entire mechanism of interindividual settlement of disputes in the early Middle Ages' (Foucault, 1994: 43), this clearly is an overestimation of the power of the early medieval state. The early Middle Ages saw private duels as uncontrollable by the state. The fourteenth century 'trailbastons' were still a somewhat desperate attempt by the state to control criminal prosecution and legal proceedings by means of an early form of trial by jury. It was not until the pacification of Europe in the middle of the seventeenth century (most notably the peace of Westphalia in 1648) that the appropriation of the judicial procedure by the state was complete.

The state's monopoly of the legitimate use of force: Potestas vs violentia

While Luhmann (1995: 109) has said that this pacification meant that the control of violence ceased to be of utmost importance, one might say that it was instead more directed internally as a constant keeping-in-check of private violence, and thereby ever as important in maintaining the then newly established autonomy of the state. The system of class had largely replaced the transcendent order of earlier times, where the worldly political community was rooted in a *civitas Dei*; while Hobbes's Leviathan was still a 'mortal God' under the 'immortal God' (Hobbes, 1969: 176), both were thoroughly uncoupled in practice. The class system now was the dominant mechanism of allocation of social positions. Elias describes how this change was executed violently in the French Revolution, where an old nobility, whose rank no longer coincided with its power, was replaced by a civil society (Elias, 1975: 403–4). And Sieyès propagated that the third estate was nothing but should be everything. If anything, the state that accompanied this civil society was cut loose from the church. The centralization of physical violence and the autonomy of the state are intricately linked, as it is inconceivable for such a state to endure in the absence of a monopoly of legitimate violence. With the increase of the state's appropriation of physical violence, violence became subject to strict regulation. In the absence of a state, violence cannot be treated as illegitimate, as is expressed perfectly in Hobbes's 'state of nature' (Hobbes, 1969: 278). It is the existence of *potestas* that defines *violentia*. Given the change from divine order to a system of economic classes, physical violence needed to be regulated much more strictly, as any physical violence might disturb the economic process which was now more than ever at the heart of the social body. Moreover, as the units of the modern society became individual citizens (for Montesquieu, all are equal under law), anyone could be illegitimately violated, yet all counted as economic units of production.

Urbanization involved another impetus to keep physical violence in check, since a higher concentration of people is thought to – under certain circumstances – produce more private violence. Yet the centralization of violence was, by the end of the eighteenth century, far from complete. Precisely because of the existence of a class system, some were deemed more equal than others. The paradox of early modern society is that everyone is an individual, while there are different kinds of individual. Violence of the lower classes, which was abundant in cities, was quickly punished, whereas, as Muchembled has argued, this mostly concerned the physical and less sophisticated ways of interaction of traditional people rather than destructive physical violence (Muchembled, 1991: 159). Physical violence occurred mostly among people doing hard physical work. But that is but one side of the coin. For violence by the upper class was mostly not defined as such; that is, it was not defined as *violentia*. As one researcher says, 'what distinguishes these fights from other forms of violence we have examined is that no one in them had legitimate authority; instead, authority was claimed by virtue of a code of conduct, property, status, or class' (Amussen, 1995: 26). That violence and its recognition is often related to class has also been found in anthropological research (cf. Halbmayer, 2001: 50). In early modern Europe, this was expressed mostly through laws designed to counter unwanted behaviour by the lower classes, such as drunkenness and prostitution (cf. Muchembled, 1991; Sugarman, 1992: 305–6). This led to a fine-tuning of relations in the trias violentiae, as can be inferred from Adam Smith's *Lectures on Jurisprudence* (in what somehow sounds as an anticipation of Marx, though with different valuation):

> when [...] some have great wealth and others nothing, it is necessary that the arm of authority should be continually stretched forth, and permanent laws or regulation made which may protect the property of the rich from the inroads of the poor [...]. Laws and governments may be considered in this and in every case as a combination of the rich to oppress the poor, and preserve to themselves the inequality of the goods which would otherwise be soon destroyed by the attacks of the poor, who if not hindered by the government would soon reduce the others to an equality with themselves by open violence
>
> (Smith, 1978: 208)

The label of illegitimate violence also became a means of purging society from other unwanted individuals. Whereas witchcraft used to be persecuted due to its allegiance with paganism in general and even the devil in particular, the early modern English definition of witchcraft allots a central place to 'violence', as 'witchcraft accusations depended, not on the pact with the devil, but on specific acts of *maleficium*, or harm, done by the witch' (Amussen, 1995: 27). Eighteenth century England saw violence 'as a way to discipline or punish those by whom they felt wronged' (Amussen, 1995: 27). That included legitimate and illegitimate (non-legal) forms of violence. In fact, 'what is essential for the social meanings of violence is the process by which the legitimate uses of violence by the state were mirrored throughout society, revealing the extent to which violence and punishment were imbricated in each other' (Amussen, 1995: 31). The monopoly of legitimate violence of the state was not yet fully developed, as physical violence, as a way of disciplinary measure or punishment, was tolerated outside the state. The state was, in fact, as yet unable to fully control private physical violence; in the seventeenth and eighteenth centuries its laws were, in practice, negotiated and reconstructed (cf. Sugarman, 1992: 306; Brewer and Styles, 1980). This 'tolerance' of private physical violence has gradually decreased. The nineteenth century marks the height of what Foucault has called the 'disciplinary society'. A stricter focus on inclusion of the individual and a control over his *vis* was institutionalized by means of disciplinary tools such as Bentham's panopticon. The prison, Foucault says, transforms the criminal from adversary of the sovereign into a deviant an abnormal enemy of the social (Foucault, 1975: 307). More and more, (legitimate) physical violence is sucked out of society and absorbed by the state. This process was related to a semantics of physical force as a negativity. Discipline became a meticulous control over the body. No room was to be left for spontaneous outbursts of physical force. This coincided with an industrial revolution which needed disciplined workers, workers who would keep on working after receiving a pay cheque. Alternatives for physical violence would emerge in the form of sports (Elias, 1986) and humour. As Peter Gay has shown, the nineteenth century saw a vast increase in humour as a way of conveying hatred. The cartoon emerged, often depicting violent scenes no late-twentieth century newspaper would dare publish (Gay, 1993).

Throughout western European history, then, the autonomization of the state has coincided with an usurpation of legitimate violence by the state. This was facilitated by a changing semantics of violence, one according to which private physical violence was *violentia*, which was opposed to legitimate *potestas*. The binary code 'legitimate – not legitimate' became crucial in the recognition of something as 'violence'. This development was facilitated by a growing humanism, which also penetrated the law. Paradoxically, one way to legitimize the punishment of murder became the idea that the murderer put himself in God's shoes. The modern state's monopoly of legitimate violence thus grew out of a secularization of the state, but the violent individual was punished precisely because he or she apparently still thought the place of God could be taken: murder 'virtually *usurps God's sovereign Authority* [...] and it does the *highest Injustice* to Man ...', wrote Charles Chauncy (1754: 5). If anything, the state became a secularized transcendence hovering over individuals bound together by contract. Thus, a medieval warrior nobility was gradually replaced by a sovereign state under which the individual had less possibilities at hand to avail himself of physical force without reprimand.

The symbolic formulation of this historical transition is given by Bodin and Hobbes. The change from a violent 'state of nature' to a sovereign in possession of a monopoly of legitimate violence can be read at once as a caricature of a general historical development and as a legitimation of that development. The state became the people's means of moral protection against themselves. This arrangement was based on the natural laws embedded in reason. Non-legitimate violence was thus banned to the realm of the irrational, the non-reasonable even. In the following centuries the use of physical violence ever more became a sign of lack of civilization. It became a sign, as it still is in many countries, of an 'underclass'. The individual resorting to physical force is an abnormality by the nineteenth century, an abnormality, nonetheless, that can be amended. The roots of English sociology lie in such 'social ameliorism', the attempt to change certain abnormal *individuals* as a response to existing *social* problems. This is a semantics that has extended into the twentieth century. The state's monopoly of legitimate violence has never been greater than it has been in this century. It is only in the twentieth century that vigilante movements and public lynchings finally disappeared (cf. Davis Graham and Gurr, 1969; Tolnay and Beck, 1992). Normation of behaviour and sanctioning of breaches of norms have been appropriated by the law, the only exception being probably a sphere of crime with its own internal violence. This has happened in each case of a growing autonomy of the state. It did so not only in the west, but for instance, as late as the end of the nineteenth century, in Japan as well (Mills, 1976: 525).

The definition of violence: In aide of the state?

Weber's definition of the state therefore has to be seen as a historical particularism that applies only (as was no doubt Weber's only intention) to a modern state that exists relatively autonomous vis-à-vis a civil society. The increasing appropriation of physical violence by the state has led to several paradoxes. To begin with, the appropriation by the state of a huge potential of violence has had enormous violent effects in the form of colonization and world wars. It is hard to maintain that, after having acquired a reservoir of violence, modern states didn't use it as well. In connection to this, sociologists like Giddens (1984) and Bauman (1998) have justly observed that the decrease of private violence went hand in hand with a far-reaching militarization that has brought about a sophistication and a technique of violence. Bauman thus holds that 'the civilizing process is not about the uprooting, but about the redistribution of violence' (Bauman, 1995) Paradoxically, the state has become both the most potentially 'violent' modern institution, and the most frustrated victim, as in modern times a violent crime first and foremost offends not God or king, but the state. Moreover, the subject of what used to be regicide is no longer a king that apparently fell out of grace with God or the gods; it is the 'innocent victim' of the political individual, and his or her death is first of all punished because it is unlawful, because it offends the state, like any murder (Scheffler, 1997). A more problematic paradox is that all violence cannot be legitimate. In other words, the state cannot succeed in gaining a true monopoly of violence, eradicating all private violence, since then it would become obsolete. Legitimate violence therefore exists by virtue of the existence of non-legitimate private violence. One might therefore say that without private violence, the state would lose its core function, and that the practice of the state would imply explicitly working towards its own destruction, at least insofar as it is based on the intended dissolving of all private violence.

Both these paradoxes are de-paradoxized by means of a normativity that exists in the modern semantics of violence. According to this 'ethic of violence', the state's violence, which is legitimate, is deemed 'good', whereas private, illegitimate violence, is 'bad', 'evil' even. This leads to the almost exclusive reservation of the term 'violence' for cases of private violence (Lindenberger and Lüdtke, 1995: 20; Collins, 2008: 2). As Bauman has said:

> one category of coercion is called 'enforcement of law and order', while the nasty word 'violence' is reserved only for the second. What the verbal distinction hides, though, is that the condemned 'violence' is also about

> certain ordering, certain laws to be enforced – only those are not the
> order and the laws which the makers of the distinction had in mind
>
> (Bauman, 1995: 141)

By only speaking of violence in case of private physical violence, the state
thus legitimizes itself – or at the very least: it avoids questions of legitimation. The semantics of action and reaction (discussed in Chapter 8) are of aid
in this process of autonomization of the state. The violence of the state is
justified by being merely a 'reaction' against a spontaneously 'active' private
violence. This semantics allows the active violence of the state, as well as the
question of the legitimation of the violence of the state in general, to remain
a blind spot both to itself and to most of its environment. For the common
sense notion of violence – that of intentional physical hurt imparted by
one person upon another – is quite simply, by and large, the contemporary
state's definition of violence. But it took a long time for this to crystallize.

All this has severe consequences for the social scientific definition of violence. In essence, the issue comes down to this: do we reify and thus scientifically legitimate the state's definition of violence or do we take a reflexive
stance and come up with a definition that breaks with common sense? It
is thus a bit too rash to say, as Randall Collins does, that 'violence' has to
do with the tension and fear of physical engagement, and that talk of 'symbolic violence' is rhetorical and confuses the issue. Collins takes a notion of
violence that is highly historically particular and highly contingent to be a
self-evident reality. He thereby forgets his own rule which holds that 'sociology is to a large extent the art of reframing other people's observations'
(Collins, 2008: 32).

Defining violence in sociology

We are in the paradoxical position of writing a sociological history of the
semantics of violence, while still in need of a definition of violence. Taking
stock of the development of the historical connotations of violence and of
the social functioning of the concept of violence, which can be shown to
be meaningful only as a binary opposition between *potestas* and *violentia*,
should give us clues if we are to come up with a definition of violence that
captures some kind of 'essence' of violence without falling into the trap of
essentialism. One might, then, wish to abstain from defining violence at all.
Violence can, on that count, be regarded as an 'essentially contested concept' (cf. Scheper-Hughes and Bourgois, 2004) and all we can do is indeed
take stock of the historical variations in its connotations and in the reactions it stimulates. Yet that would obliterate all possibilities of critiqueing
common contestations of violence. It would reduce social theory to but
one voice in the choir, which would be condemned to speaking in everyday terms, thus forsaking the fundamental principle which Bauman has

termed 'defamiliarization'. It would make sociology an ally of the outcome of contestations over the definition of violence, and, in short, it would turn sociology into an ally of the state, once the state has a firm hold over the definition of violence, as it has in the modern age that marks the strongest semantic differentiation between *potestas* and *violentia*. Sociology will have to deal with the fact that the language in which one speaks of violence is not without violence itself.

In sociology, Pierre Bourdieu has always stressed the interwovenness of language with practices of power and, moreover, with symbolic violence. Agents are equipped with certain linguistic dispositions, some of which are, given a certain social field, legitimate while others are not. The basis of the, according to Bourdieu, arbitrary differences between legitimate and non-legitimate uses of language lies in a field of positions of relative autonomy in which classifications and (linguistic) dispositions are the stakes of a continuous power struggle (see Schinkel, 2003). No definition of violence can therefore be oblivious of *the violence in and of language itself*. It is important that the intricate connection between violence and power that was found in the etymology and historical semantics of violence is retained in defining violence. To define violence will then always have the character of a Münchhausen-like action: one has to find a definition of violence using language, which is itself not free from violence. *The definition of violence will therefore always be coloured by violence itself.* In part, this is why violence, as stated in Chapter 1, has a tendency of being misrecognized. Language betrays us here. What Husserl (1976b: 372) has called the 'seduction of language' is doubly misleading in the case of violence, since language itself is a violent tool by means of which certain things – certain violent things – can be omitted from the definition of violence by allusion to the familiarity and the conceptual realism present in most use of language. The very existence of a certain concept of violence seduces us into thinking that there is no violence outside the denotation and connotation of that concept. The aptitude to misrecognition of violence can be seen as an intrinsic feature, an aspect, of violence, so to speak as an *illusion naturelle* (Malebranche) or as a 'well-founded *illusio*' (Bourdieu). With this in mind, we can survey some of the ways in which the definition of violence has been approached in social science.

The social scientific way of defining violence actually comprises three strategies. The first is to give an empirical definition of violence specifically suited for pragmatic purposes in one case, or one aspect of violence, which cannot be transferred to other situations in order to be deployed for other purposes in other cases or aspects of violence. By 'empirical definition' I mean here a stipulative definition that describes or sums up the empirical features of the members of the class of acts called 'violence'. This is a viable strategy for most empirical research. Of course, as soon as such definitions start to take on universal forms, we have to stop taking them seriously.

A second strategy is to sum up a number of acts that count as a connotation of violence. This strategy operates on a level of reflexivity that allows for the fundamental problems of defining violence to be avoided. It is useful in research where it is not necessary to develop a more than commonsensical notion of violence, but its main problems are (1) a neglect of other than physical forms of violence, (2) a neglect of other than non-legitimate forms of violence and (3) a neglect of the productive power of violence.

Finally, a third strategy is to not sum up anything at all, but silently presume the existence and knowledge of such a list. This is where Bauman's 'embarrassed silence, and other signs of shamefacedness', mentioned at the beginning of this chapter, come in. And this is probably the dominant social scientific strategy in dealing with violence as a research object. It is for instance noted in the *Oxford Handbook of Criminology* (Maguire et al., 1997: 859) that 'the conceptual issue of "what acts count as violence" does not cause too many difficulties for criminologists in practice *because they usually ignore it*' (italics in original). One way around this is of course to define violence circularly, such as in the definition of 'violence as "that which violates or causes violation and is usually performed by a violator upon the violated"' (Schiff, 2003: 162; compare Garver, 1968). More sophisticated analyses, such as Randall Collins' micro-sociological theory of violence, can also adopt an evasive strategy when it comes to defining violence. Collins for instance states: 'once we look, we find that violence is an array of processes that all follow from a common situational feature of violent confrontations' (Collins, 2008: 8). As noted earlier, Collins apparently knows a priori what 'violent situations' are. He can do so only on the basis of common sense. He then comes closest to a definition when he states 'violence is a set of pathways around confrontational tension and fear' (Collins, 2008: 8). But clearly, not all 'pathways around confrontational tension and fear' can be assumed to be the stuff of violence. In fact, one could just as easily come up with the definition of 'non-violence' as 'pathways around confrontational tension and fear'. Collins therefore indeed seems to opt for a strategy of non-definition, building on the commonsensical definitions of violent situations.

Problems of empirical definition of violence

But each empirical definition of violence, whether logically sound or not, is necessarily one-sided. As an extended example, I shall discuss David Riches' definition of violence as 'an act of physical hurt deemed legitimate by the performer and illegitimate by (some) witnesses' (Riches, 1986: 8). In discussing Riches' definition I cannot do justice to all empirical definitions of its kind, but this definition is both much-used and characterized by certain features shared by many other definitions of violence. It is a highly influential definition from the field of anthropology, and Riches' definition has been praised for being abstract enough to allow for cross-cultural comparison (Schröder and Schmidt, 2001: 4). Riches expressly considers the

Anglo-Saxon term 'violence' by using as a starting point the 'language of ordinary people' (Riches, 1986: 2). Violence, on the one hand, is always of contested legitimacy (Riches, 1986: 11), yet it is, according to Riches, also the terrain of consensus regarding its presence by those involved.

While this definition has definite advantages, its disadvantages are four-fold. A first is that it is exclusively focused on acts of *physical* harm. The restriction to 'physical hurt' is arbitrary and cannot be adequately grounded, not even in ordinary language. A second disadvantage is that the initial focus on ordinary language leads to a neglect of forms of violence through the medium of ordinary language. Language, as discussed earlier, is a play-ground of violence itself, not in the least because interests are at stake in the denomination of certain acts as violence and the simultaneous linguistic disguise of other violent acts. The question always is: who are the 'ordinary people', and what is their language, and from what social processes and clas-sifications does that language originate? Out of these first two problematic features of Riches' definition arise additional difficulties. The focus on ordi-nary language and the consequential restriction of 'violence' to physical vio-lence lead to two related characteristics ascribed to violence by Riches. One is that violence is recognized as such by those involved (Riches, 1986: 10). Yet the structure of ordinary language can be such as to blur the visibility and thereby the recognizability of certain other forms of violence. A third problem arises out of Riches' incorporation of the concepts of legitimacy and illegitimacy in the definition of violence. This assumes that the per-former of violence always deems violence legitimate, while (some) witnesses always deem it illegitimate. This clearly need not be true. Some performers may regard their violence as illegitimate, and, moreover, this may even be a reason for performing it. Besides, it is very often the case that the only wit-nesses present, being, for instance, friends of the performer, do not regard the violence as unacceptable at all. The criteria to speak of violence, namely (a) that the performer feels it is legitimate, and (b) that the witnesses deem it illegitimate, are far too restrictive. These are characteristics of some cases of violence, but hardly of all. A fourth disadvantage concerns the idea that violence, as 'an act of physical hurt deemed legitimate by the performer and illegitimate by (some) witnesses', requires 'violence' to be an *act*, which is problematic for a few reasons. First of all, the question becomes *which acts* count as 'violence'.

To take the simple case of physical violence, when two persons fight, one can ask what actions one wishes to call violence. Does a blow delivered by a 'performer' to a 'victim' count as violence? But where does the action of that blow begin and end? Does only the moment the performer's fist hits the victim's face qualify for being 'violence'? After all, a movement of the performer's arm that is in all but one respect exactly like such a blow, but which stops right before the arm would hit the victim's face, cannot be called 'violence' according to Riches' definition, since it is not an act of physical hurt. It would then automatically follow that in the case of a blow that does hit that face, only that part of the action where the face is actually hit – where the blow is 'delivered' – can be called an act of violence. Of course one might see the whole movement of the blow an action, but the point is that there is a lack of a substantial criterion on the basis of which to decide where violence as an 'action' begins or ends. For another blow, would that be another 'act of physical hurt deemed legitimate by the performer and illegitimate by (some) witnesses'? And the victim hitting back, would that make him a 'performer' of an act of violence against what is now a 'victim'? Secondly, when violence is seen as an act, what sense does it make to speak of a 'violent action' instead of 'violence'? Is this common use of ordinary language simply a pleonasm? Or should we take from it the clue that 'violence' is something other than an action, which, nonetheless, can consist of 'violent actions'? I believe this is the case. The position that 'violence' is an act appears to be untenable. When the micro-relations of a violent situation are considered, it becomes highly problematic to regard 'violence' as 'an act' of some sort. That is true for cases of physical violence, but all the more so for cases of what is called 'structural violence'. This kind of violence, which will be elaborated upon below, cannot be characterized as an act. In all cases, I propose that violence is seen as a process, which consists of actions that recursively follow each other and that cannot be wholly singled out without losing the identity ('violence') of the process as a whole. Violence is a process characterized by fluidity. One reason to assume this, lies in the fact that the opposite view, where violence is considered as individualized packages, as 'acts', is untenable. I thus propose to conceive of violence as a process, and to keep this connotation when use is made of the notion of a 'situation of violence'. Since a social situation 'is' not, but *takes place*, a situation of violence has the character of a process. This will be elaborated upon in the next chapter.

In thus reviewing the pros and cons of Riches' definition, I have taken one authoritative definition as an example. The same could be done to various definitions in other fields, such as Norman Denzin's symbolic interactionist definition of violence as 'the attempt to regain, through the use of emotional and physical force, something that has been lost' (Denzin, 1984: 488) or Raymond Geuss's political philosophical definition according to which '[violence] is [...] best understood by focusing on adverbial expressions such as "to act violently". Violence, that is, refers to a particular *way* of acting or operating. I act "violently" if I inflict pain on other humans, or if I act in a way that *would* inflict physical pain or injury on others, were they to happen to be in the path of the action in question' (Geuss, 2001: 21). But the list of definitions is, of course, too long to review them all and for the sake of argument, I claim that the general objections raised here apply to many differing empirical definitions of violence. One definition is crucial to include here, however, since it would appear at first sight to overcome various problems that many empirical definitions have. Johan Galtung's definition of *structural violence* is intended to overcome some of the shortcomings of restricted definitions of violence. As his is the first comprehensive formulation of a less restricted definition of violence, the next section is devoted to a discussion of Galtung's concept of structural violence.

Galtung on structural violence

Galtung defines violence as '*the cause of the difference between the potential and the actual,* between what could have been and what is' (emphasis in original) (Galtung, 1968: 168). This definition has become quite famous, and I believe there are two reasons for this. First, Galtung comes up with a notion of structural violence as a specific form of violence that has been innovative and therefore widely discussed. Second, Galtung's discussion of violence is conceptually meticulous. It is one of the most thorough analyses of the phenomenon. Now, violence as the cause of the difference between the actual and the potential has been further explicated by Galtung as follows: 'Violence is that which increases the distance between the potential and the actual, and that which impedes the decrease of this distance' (Galtung, 1968: 168). And he elsewhere adds that violence concerns not only the cause of the difference, but also the cause of maintaining the non-decrease between the actual and the potential (Galtung, 1968: 172). A further requirement to speak of violence is the unavoidability of the actual: 'When the actual is unavoidable, then violence is not present even if the actual is at a very low level' (Galtung, 1968: 169) In short, for Galtung violence is an *influence*, something which constrains human action and human being.

He then distinguishes six dimensions of violence: (1) physical vs psychological violence. Physical violence is characterized by somatic hurt. Within the category of physical violence, Galtung further distinguishes between 'biological violence', 'which reduces somatic capability (below what is potentially possible)', and 'physical violence as such' (Galtung, 1968: 169). An example of the latter is the imprisonment of a person or the uneven distribution of access to transportation. Psychological violence, 'violence that works on the soul', includes lies, brainwashing and indoctrination, but also threats. All of these decrease mental potentialities. (2) A negative and a positive approach to influence. Like 'negative' and 'positive' freedom, one can speak of negative influence and of positive influence as violence. The first includes cases of punishment that lead to decreased potentialities, whereas the second refers to rewards that have that result. Both are called 'violence' by Galtung, because in both cases, the effect is decreased potentialities. An example of the somewhat counter-intuitive form of positive violence, is the rewards given to consumers in a consumer's society, which 'is reward-oriented, based on promises of euphoria, but [...] also narrows down the ranges of action' (Galtung, 1968: 170). According to Galtung, such violence is more manipulatory and less overt than negative forms of violent influence are.

(3) An object hurt vs no object hurt. Galtung states that there are cases where no object of violence exists, such as when a group of people throw stones around, or when nuclear arms are tested. However, he does state that such occasions usually amount to the threat of physical violence, which is a form of psychological violence. The same applies, according to Galtung, to the destruction of material things. (4) A subject acting vs no subject acting. This distinction refers to the agency of violence. And here, Galtung makes an important distinction: 'We shall refer to the type of violence where there is an actor that commits the violence as *personal* or *direct*, and to violence where there is no such actor as *structural* or *indirect*' (Galtung, 1968: 170). His concept of *structural violence*, as opposed to *personal violence*, has been innovative in research on violence. It enables Galtung to speak of violence, as an avoidable negative influence on a person's potential, even in cases where a performing subject is absent. A major reason for structural violence is the uneven distribution of resources. According to Galtung, structural violence exists when people are starving 'when this is objectively avoidable' (Galtung, 1968: 171). He therefore also refers to structural violence as 'social injustice'. (5) Intended violence vs unintended violence. This distinction derives its relevance from the question of guilt, which, in Judeo-Christian ethics and Roman jurisprudence, has been more relevant than the matter of consequence of action. When the distinction between intended and not intended violence is not made, one is not only unable to distinguish intended instances of personal violence from unintended instances thereof, but one will also have a hard time recognizing structural violence for what it is. One may, as Galtung (1968: 172) says, 'be catching the small fry and letting the big fish loose'. (6) Manifest violence vs latent violence. This is the final distinction Galtung discusses. It partly concerns the observability of violence, for manifest violence is violence, personal or structural, that is observable. Latent violence is, however, not simply to be equated to unobservable violence. Rather, by 'latent violence', Galtung intends a situation, 'so unstable that the actual realization level "easily" decreases' (Galtung, 1968: 172). With these six distinctions, with the covering distinction between personal and structural violence, and with clear-cut definitions of these concepts, Galtung's take on violence has been sufficiently elaborated on.

Galtung's definition has two strong points that I particularly wish to stress. (1) His is an 'extended definition' of violence (compare Bourdieu, 1994: 107, 188; 1997: 98–9; Barak, 2003). Galtung puts it like this: 'we are rejecting the narrow concept of violence – according to which violence is *somatic* incapacitation, or deprivation of health, alone (with killing as the extreme form), at the hands of an *actor* who *intends* this to be the consequence' (Galtung, 1968: 168). One might argue that a common definition of violence is even more restricted than somatic 'incapacitation', since 'violence' is very often quite simply equated with intentional direct physical hurt. Violence as *intentional direct physical hurt* is probably the archetypical form of the narrow, yet highly common, conception of violence. As such, it is equally 'pre-conceptual' as the popular notions of a circular trajectory of the earth around the sun, and of the idea that atoms are ball-shaped material substances. Galtung has his specific reasons to reject it in favour of a broader, more inclusive notion of violence. This has to do with the context of Galtung's article. It was published in the *Journal of Peace Research*, and its context is indeed that of 'peace research'. Though his article has probably gained most of its recognition due to the definition and classification of violence that is put forward in it, its actual topic is peace. In Galtung's article, the definition of violence is merely a step towards a definition of 'peace'. He rejects the narrow conception of violence on account of it leading to a rejection of too little when the ideal is peace. So many things that are in contradiction to peace would go undetected. That is why, according to Galtung (1968: 168), *'an extended concept of violence is indispensable'*. Although the concept of structural violence has found its way into the canon of social science, there is, in general, little sympathy for the extended concept of violence per se. At least, when it comes down to the practice of research, there seems to be relatively little support for it. One exception is the concept of symbolic violence, as coined by Pierre Bourdieu, which will be discussed in Chapters 3 and 8. A commonly heard critique of the extended concept of violence is, for instance, reflected in the 'violence'-entrance in the *Routledge Encyclopedia of Philosophy*, where it is stated with respect to Galtung's definition and the extended definition of violence in general.

This style of proposal faces several difficulties: it is confusing, politically unhelpful and evades a central problem about violence. It is confusing because people do not ordinarily mean by 'violence' any and every form of social injustice, they mean such things as beating people up or torturing them with electrodes [...]. Moreover, the expansive sense of violence does not help with an agenda of social reform, because it encourages the cosy but ultimately stultifying belief that all social evils are really one and hence will yield to the one solution [...]. It is therefore preferable to operate with a concept of violence which is both narrower than that of structural violence and less morally loaded than [...] it

(E. Craig (ed.), 1998: 616)

I can think of three factors that are relevant in the rejection or embrace of the extended concept of violence. One is that it is believed the extended concept constitutes an inflation of the meaning of violence. This, however, means that such a meaning is *a priori* present, and the absence of this, or the search for it, was actually the reason for defining violence. The extended concept of violence can only constitute an inflation of the meaning of 'violence', when that meaning is silently presupposed to be identical with some kind of non-extended concept of violence. Proponents of the extended concept can reply to advocates of such a more narrow definition that their concept of violence constitutes a loss of meaning. Other factors therefore have to be at stake in the embrace or rejection of an extended concept of violence. A second factor is that of a certain economy of thought. The extended concept is harder to operationalize, and is therefore often rejected in research. Especially when research is funded by government, there is no room for reflection beyond the narrow commonsensical notion of violence government institutions usually entertain. A third factor of relevance here is the political views of the social scientist. Or rather, his view of the political. Those who advocate a value-free (in the sense of Weber's *Wertungsfrei*) notion of social science, and believe that research can and should at all times be 'neutral' with respect to its research-object, are prone to dismiss an extended definition of violence as an example of ideology incorporated in social science. Proponents of the extended version, on the other hand, are more prone to see the exclusion of extended meaning to the concept of violence as an ideology that is silently presupposed in social science. Reasoning along these lines, to advocate a narrow definition would in fact mean to be politically non-neutral, since it reifies existing commonsensical social constructions of violence, which are violent themselves in that they reproduce relations of power that are ideologically supported by the misrecognition of certain forms of violence (e.g., structural violence). The best one can then do, is to closely tie the concept of violence to the concept of power and to include as many consistent meanings into the definition of violence as possible. My sympathy lies with *some form* of this latter argument. That is why I believe Galtung's extended concept is a strong point of his definition.

(2) A second strong point of this definition is that it is relatively unbound to the presence of a violent subject. Especially the category of the intentional subject is stripped of its dominance in the concept of violence: 'We shall refer to the type of violence where there is an actor that commits the violence as *personal* or *direct*, and to violence where there is no such actor as *structural* or *indirect*. [...] whereas in the first case [the] consequences can be traced back to concrete persons as actors, in the second case this is no longer meaningful' (Galtung, 1968: 170–1). This conception of the violent subjectivity is both a precondition and a consequence of the extended concept of violence. A break with the exclusively 'subjectively intentional' view of violence is valuable for two reasons. One, it breaks with a dogmatic notion of the subject as an autonomous agent whose intentional actions can be traced back to this cognitive unity. This is a highly one-sided view of man – it is even, although it pretends to be a universal and a-historical representation of man, a socio-historically constructed view (cf. Foucault, 1966; Luhmann, 1997; Sloterdijk, 1998). I will adhere not to a tradition of social science in which this subject is the identity that is the source of action, but to an alternative tradition which stresses the negation implied in every identity, and

therefore the decentralized place of the subject. A second advantage of the non-centrality of the subject is that it paves the way for the observation of structural violence as a form of violence in its own right. Structural violence cannot be traced back to one or more individuals. Instead, it derives its momentum from the relative autonomy of the structure – which I no more than roughly delineate at this point as the more or less patterned nexus of diverse actions and communications – vis-à-vis individual actions and communications. This view is consistent with Durkheim's definition of a social fact in general. A sociological perspective on violence indeed cannot omit structural forms of violence from its view, as forms of violence where it does not make sense to speak of an intentional violent subject.

There are a number of shortcomings of Galtung's definition of violence. I will only discuss those shortcomings that are related to the context of Galtung's definition, as these are the most fundamental. They are fourfold, and all spring from a one-sided humanist view underlying that definition.

First, Galtung's definition is humanistically idealistic in that it refers not simply to a difference between the actual and the potential, but to a *lower* actual than the potential. This becomes apparent in the preliminary definition which is the basis of his final definition, and after he has presented this definition, which is in itself neutral. At times his formulations are, in this respect, neutral: 'the net result may still be that human beings are effectively prevented from realizing their potentialities' (Galtung, 1968: 170). This is consistent with violence as the *cause of the difference* between the actual and the potential, or, as he also states: 'Violence is that which increases the distance between the potential and the actual' (Galtung, 1968: 168). Galtung speaks of that difference in terms of the realized actual being *lower* than the potential, since 'higher than potential' is an impossibility. His preliminary definition is that '*violence is present when human beings are being influenced so that their actual somatic and mental realizations are below their potential realizations*'. And further on: 'when the potential is higher than the actual [...] and when it is avoidable, then violence is present' (Galtung, 1968: 168, 169). All the examples Galtung gives, point in the direction of an undesirability of a lower actual than was potentially possible. My critique on this presupposition is that it is quite conceivable that the potential is much more undesirable than the actual. At least, when 'potential' and 'actual' are not *a priori* 'humanistically' coloured, that is equally possible as its opposite. My point is, however, not to say that when the actual is lower than the potential, and when the potential is more undesirable, there is no violence. One can maintain, with Galtung, that any cause of the difference between the actual and the potential is violence, but then it follows that this holds independent of whether the actual or the potential is more desirable. Moreover, it needs to be pointed out that even when the actual equals the potential, and even if this is desirable not only from the point of view of the individual, there may be violence. Since the full realization of the potential may have been brought about by violent means. A young child's intelligence might be stimulated to reach its full potential by means of violent practices at private schools. This example indicates that Galtung's definition is flawed in conceptualizing violence as the cause of the difference between the potential and the actual. Galtung might respond to this by saying that, in the case of the above example, other potentialities are not realized as a result of the violent realization of one potentiality. But this rebuttal is flawed in that it presupposes an unrealistic idea of the potential.

Second, Galtung's notion of the potential is flawed as a result of its conceptualization within the same naively humanist framework. Now, as Galtung (1968: 169) himself says, 'the meaning of "potential realizations" is highly problematic'. Especially when mental aspects of human life are concerned, Galtung says, consensus regarding potential realizations is difficult to obtain. Although by no means satisfactory, his solution to this problem is to take as a guide 'whether the value to be realized is fairly consensual or not'. He gives the example of literacy and Christianity, where literacy is held in high regard almost everywhere, yet the value of being Christian is much less widely agreed upon. He therefore wishes to speak of violence when the level of literacy is lower than potentially possible, but not when the level of Christianity is lower than potentially possible. And he concludes by saying that 'we shall not try to explore this difficult point further in this context' (Galtung, 1968: 169). This, however, is more problematic than Galtung himself notices. Although his definition of violence does not immediately depend on ordinary language and common sense in general, it does so in the second instance. For in – 'humanistically' – relying on consensual views of what is valuable or desirable, the blind spots of common sense and ordinary language are smuggled into the definition of violence. Thereby, certain forms of violence will be unseen. What is valued and held in high regard in a certain social system is always a socio-historical construction that is related to positions of power. With Bourdieu, we might say that such preferences are always the products of a struggle over legitimate schemes of classification. That is to say, it is very well possible that there is a certain amount of violence incorporated in the preferences people have. With Galtung, such violence might be termed structural violence. Yet it is precisely this type of structural violence that is unseen in Galtung's definition of violence. To interpret his examples otherwise, the 'universal' value of literacy is, one might argue, a 'Western' claim that perhaps performatively becomes true in a world where illiterates are made dependent on literates for their survival. That is the world Galtung speaks from. If the reply to this is that it reeks of a kind of value-relativism inherent in a rather radical social constructivism, the answer must be that it is Galtung himself who links the definition of violence to a public consensus regarding what is valuable, with all the ontological relativist consequences for the notion of violence that this has, as can be inferred from a brief discussion of his second example. For, as for

Christianity, there have been times when being Christian was universally valued, and when non-Christians were even hardly regarded as people at all. According to Galtung, one would have to say that in those days, a lower Christianity than potentially possible constituted a kind of violence. In the end, Galtung's definition of violence is weakened by its recourse to a general consensual agreement on what is valuable, since such an agreement can be violent itself. To use it in a conceptualization of violence is a kind of begging the question.

A third disadvantage of Galtung's definition also springs from an all too humanist background. Consider the following again, yet seen in light of another aspect: 'when the potential is higher than the actual [...] and when it is avoidable, then violence is present'. Galtung only wishes to speak of 'violence' in case of the actual being lower than the potential, where the actual is avoidable. Yet thereby, he reintroduces the subject into the definition of violence, as something that is always present when violence occurs. Whereas he further on presumes that there are cases of violence in the absence of a violent subject, he actually cannot do without such a subject in his definition. For to say that 'a life expectancy of 30 years only, during the Neolithic period, was not an expression of violence, but the same life expectancy today will be seen as violence according to our definition' (Galtung, 1968: 169), is to presume that, in the end, all those who did not do anything to avoid this low life expectancy, are somehow 'guilty' of structural violence. Although Galtung does not mean to say that these are in fact violent subjects, his assumption that violence is a difference between the actual and potential that is potentially avoidable, does not fully do justice to the structural aspect of structural violence. He only goes so far as to include the possibility of the absence of subjectively *intended* violence, but the idea of the *avoidability* of all forms of violence is unwarranted. It springs again, from an all too 'humanist' notion of man and of the social, according to which man is essentially free if he chooses to be so collectively within a sociality that is man-made and therefore does not possess a relative autonomy with respect to human beings. Galtung believes in the avoidability of all violence because the context of his work is that of peace research, which is informed, or motivated, by a certain activism, a will to change the world into a more pleasant place. He therefore has to assume that violence is avoidable, since if it weren't, peace activism would be a frustrating activity. But *structural* violence, as Galtung (1968: 170, 173) himself says, is 'built into the social structure'. It is therefore not directly controllable, manipulable or avoidable. A social structure is not controllable by human beings, since it has a degree of autonomy relative to these human beings. When the reply to this sociological truism is that political action can change social structure, the twofold answer is that (a) policy interventions always have unintended consequences that at times run directly counter to what was hoped to be realized by them. These unintended consequences cannot be avoided; it is not simply a question of studying harder at possible outcomes. It is rather a case of uncontrollable complexity of the social, which cannot be 'predicted' in some form of *mathématique sociale* (Condorcet) or *physique sociale* (Comte), since such a prediction is itself a social fact that changes what it applies to. In the case of policies to counter violence, the unintended consequence may be violence, in some form or other (cf. Portes, 2000); (b) political action may change social structure, but in that case the only correct description of reality is that a political structure changes an(other) social structure, or that a social system (politics) changes an(other) social system. To conclude, Galtung's assumption that violence is, by definition, something which is avoidable, is a major weakness of his conception of violence.

Concluding remarks

The crucial problem to be dealt with has been designated in the beginning of this chapter as a problem of the paradox of defining violence. That is to say that any empirical definition of violence will necessarily have its blind spot, which runs the risk of being an ideological recognition of violence as a result of a social scientific non-recognition thereof. This problem has also been discussed in Chapter 1 where it was said that even a fractured realism constitutes its own act of determination through negation. And if one were to respond that, in defining violence, one doesn't run this risk of reifying certain forms of violence, one apparently possesses a definition of violence prior to defining violence, which is paradoxical all the same, albeit less reflexively so. The points discussed in this chapter are to be taken into consideration when defining violence, to which the next chapter is devoted.

3
The Definition of Violence – Part II

A definition of violence

The ontological perspective

Violence can be defined empirically in numerous ways. What happens then is that certain empirical events are said to constitute 'violence'. Each of those definitions will probably uncover aspects of violence, but none of them wholly captures what violence amounts to in social process. In searching for a definition of violence, the first move is to get out of the paradox of simultaneously seeing and not seeing, of highlighting aspects and at the same time blotting others out. I therefore define violence *ontologically*, and I define it as *reduction of being*. I now need to explain what it means to define violence ontologically, and precisely what it is that makes the definition of violence as reduction of being preferable over against alternative, perhaps almost always more commonsensical conceptualizations of violence. In order to explain this definition, I draw on a number of sources in philosophical and sociological thought.

In much of the tradition I will discuss, the notion of violence as reduction of being is implicitly and at times even explicitly present. This is therefore not an entirely new definition, and I intend to show that although its conceptual systematization has been lacking until presently, it has deep roots. Philosophically, one might call it a radicalization of Enlightenment-anthropology; sociologically, it is a radicalization of symbolic interactionism. Each time this definition of violence has come up in the history of thought, it has not been carried through to the end. It is often dealt with inconsistently. This is due to what can be called *biaphobia* – literally, a fear of the force of life, analogous to what Nietzsche called 'denial of life'. I will understand it as a scholastic fallacy leading to the misrecognition of violence. Since the reduction of being that is violence is essential to all (social) life, this fear of violence is indeed a denial of life. Even in an extended definition like that of Stuart Henry, which explicitly refers to the reduction of a person, it is maintained that 'acts of violence, then, are acts that make others power-less to maintain or express their humanity, that is, that deny their ability to make a difference' (Henry, 2000: 20). It is thus assumed that there is any way of being human without reducing human being. I will question that assumption. First, however, some clarification as to the *ontological* character of this definition is required.

The difference between an ontological and an empirical level of analysis is best explicated in Heidegger's terms, as the difference between the ontologi-cal and the ontic. This difference, which goes by the name of the 'ontologi-cal difference', is the basis of the ontology of *Sein und Zeit*. It is my intention to interpret the same ontological difference as a way of analysing what 'happens' ontologically before we can speak of empirical events that we nor-mally classify as 'violence'. Heidegger introduces the ontological difference in order to distance himself from a Western metaphysical tradition (roughly starting with Parmenides, Plato and Aristotle; culminating in Descartes, Kant and Nietzsche) that has sought to think of Being in terms of being(s), or that has reduced Being to a 'highest being', a 'first mover'. According to Heidegger, what has thereby been forgotten is Being itself (*Seinsvergessenheit*). But, as Heidegger says, there is something more, although this really 'is' not a 'something'. What has been forgotten is that it actually is the being of ontic beings that should be the focus of thought. This being of beings, which Heidegger writes as 'Being', is what an ontology is concerned with. What *is* this Being? It *'is'* not, since that would make it a being in the ontic, or 'empirical' sense (Heidegger, 1993: 6).[1] Being is always the Being of (a) being. There *'is'* no such 'thing' as Being, independent (in a non-ontic sense) of beings. For Being is to be seen as the Being of beings, the naked 'that' of the Being of a being. Or, it might be termed the *happening* or *process* of being, the unfolding of being, when all these terms are not themselves taken to refer to ontic beings of some sort. A flawed analogy would be to say that when I am walking, there is me, moving, walking, but there is also the walking itself; or in another example, there is me, violating, but there is also the violence itself, which, though it can only be distinguished ontologically, 'is' not factually. I am a being, and therefore I can speak of the Being of me as a being. To this being, which we ourselves are, Heidegger refers to as *Dasein*. Man, as a being, is Dasein (literally, 'there-being'; Mulhall, 1996). Before he realizes himself in real, ontic states of affairs, he always already *is* a being. His 'Being' refers to this always already being a being. Next to speaking of man as an ontic being, for instance as a man, a farmer, a father of children, one can say that that being is a being. Then, one can speak of his Being in the ontological sense. Heidegger's *Sein und Zeit* is mainly concerned with the ontological structure of man as a being, of Dasein. As such, his project can be compared to Kant's in that he tries to find (transcendental) conditions of possibility of the ontic (empirical). *That* a person looks towards the future is possible because he or she, ontologically, is thrown into a world in which he or she has past, present and future.

A similar ontological *a priori* is what my definition of violence as 'reduction of being' is meant to be. Whatever ontic shape violence assumes, it always 'is' a reduction of being. I have hereby given a preliminary sketch of only the nature of my definition of violence. In order to further explain it, I will draw more on the work of Heidegger and (other) phenomenologists, including reference to what has been said in Chapter 1 about Husserl's views on the noematic perception of spatial objects. What was said there was the basis for the epistemological outlook I have termed 'fractured realism'. Every observation consists of a necessary selection of certain aspects of reality, which are highlighted and make up what is seen, at the equally necessary cost of excluding other aspects. Unselected aspects remain in a backgrounding horizon, awaiting possible future observational selection. The premise here is that reality is infinitely rich and complex. Finite beings necessarily have to come to what Luhmann calls a 'reduction of complexity', which at the same time does not do away with complexity, since it saves a horizon of alternative aspects that would, if selected, constitute a different reduction of complexity. Every observation therefore has its blind spot, and no observation captures the whole of reality. What Husserl in the end calls 'world' (*Welt*) cannot be observed as a whole. Reality is rich and cluttered, opaque. I now want to apply these premises to (inter)action. It immediately needs to be stressed that this does not concern an incorporation of Husserlian phenomenology in the analysis of violence. The Husserlian model of aspects in acts of consciousness, as briefly outlined in Chapter 1, will be taken as a model for social action in which actions towards others are said to highlight aspects of the being of those others. Actions, too, are reductions of complexity in the sense that the actually performed action is but one contingent possibility out of a horizon of possibilities. The object of action, or that space of reality that is affected or changed by it, thereby gets equally reduced; it is reduced to 'something to do so and so with', whereas it 'contains' many alternative ways of dealing with. In Chapter 1, an aspect of a phenomenon was defined as 'the selective highlighting of a certain relational identity'. Here, an aspect can be less epistemologically taken to be the same relational identity, but not one that is observed, but rather acted upon and thereby highlighted in practice. It equals the meaning Heidegger highlights in the term 'phenomenon', as 'that which shows itself in itself' (Heidegger, 1993: 31). This means the other exists in social practice in the form of the aspect of his or her being that is selected by the actions of an ego. With respect to the social situation as a whole, the highlighting of an aspect in social practice at the same time means that actions are thus shaped that *social practice itself* assumes the form of (or stands in light of) the relational identity of the aspect in question.

One might compare this to the way Harrison White speaks of identities seeking footing in social process in and through control over other identities (White, 2008). That process of identities controlling identities which appear only in and through the very same social process is not without violence. Actions elicit re-actions that are triggered by the 'definition of the situation', which is the aspect in light of which practice exists. Any action reduces the other to but one aspect of his or her being, and this selection of aspect allows the other to be in social practice. At the same time, this selection is co-constitutive of the selection in light of which the social practice as a whole unfolds. That is to say that if I violate another person, that person is not only reduced to what he or she at that time is in the social situation in which he or she exists, but social practice itself now stands in a certain relational light. That means that the whole practice of reducing the other reduces the situation to but one possible aspect, since it could have been a different situation. Consciousness is not a prerequisite for this social process in which any action is always also a reduction.

Violence, ontologically defined as reduction of being thus pertains to the reduction that has always already taken place prior to any ontic social state of affairs between subjects. This definition can be further developed by putting forward two claims, which are elaborated upon below: (1) violence is that aspect of the social which consists of a reduction of the ontological aspect-horizon of a being (Dasein), (2) violence is an aspect of the social that is always at work in a more or less highlighted sense. That is, it is an aspect that is, qua, aspect, always present (in a non-ontic sense), but the degree to which this aspect is actualized as effective in practice differs. Ontically, violence therefore is a sliding scale.

Violence as reduction of being

These claims need substantiating. I will start with Heidegger's ontology of Dasein, and then deal with successive insights from a tradition that followed in Heidegger's footsteps.

Every human being (Dasein) can be ontologically characterized by possibility (Heidegger, 1993: 42). That is to say that before any ontic realization of a being, that being 'is' the sum total of unrealized possibilities. Furthermore, being-in-the-world is always already a being-together (Heidegger, 1993: 118). If we see a person (Dasein) as a being that is ontologically characterized by possibility, each ontic realization of ontological possibilities constitutes a reduction of complexity. It is possible to reintroduce as a characterization of Dasein Husserl's concept of a *horizon* here, when that is in no way regarded too technically, that is, in the sense of a limited set of well-defined alternatives. Nonetheless, ontologically, that person can be regarded as a horizon of alternative ontic states of being. This horizon is to be seen as an ontological *a priori* without beginning or end. Ontologically, a person is always, in Levinas' terms, an infinite Other. This person, like any person, is a being-together with other persons (*Mitdasein*). Although Heidegger clearly recognizes this, he soon falls back into a story of a Fall (*Verfall*) into 'das Man' over against an 'authenticity' (*Eigentlichkeit*) of Dasein, which turns ontology into deontology. Heidegger then states that Dasein first and foremost listens to public opinion, does what everybody else does. Although he explicitly says he does not undervalue this inauthentic being, his tone and concepts betray a preconceptual dislike (in his terms, a certain *Vorgriff*). However, we are here concerned with an ontological definition of violence that is as 'neutral' as possible. Man, fundamentally understood as being-social, as being-with, being-together or being-with-others, always exists in relation to other beings. As such, Dasein is constantly exposed to others, and their influence shapes its being. In part, this is what is called 'socialization' in sociology. This way of being-in-relation is not solely an existence of (ontological) freedom. Precisely when ontology adequately incorporates the social, the simultaneous effects of freedom and constraint that the encounter with the other entails are highlighted. Every influence Dasein undergoes reduces its being in the sense that it is not free to be whatever it could want to be, but it is that which the coming together of the influence of others on it and its influence on them allows it to be. A subject is precisely this: Dasein in sociality, always already under the influence of others. I therefore use the concept of 'subject' in a literal sense (the Latin, not the Greek): a subject is sub-ject, always subjected to others. Heidegger's *Geworfenheit* therefore always already means *Unterworfenheit*.

At the same time, however, a subject always subjects others – as identities control other identities that control them (White, 2008). This reciprocal subjection, or reduction, is crucial to the understanding of violence as reduction of being. To be a subject is to be reduced *to* a subject. That is to say, a subject is an ontic being whose ontological horizon has been reduced to certain aspects that are highlighted in his being-subject. As soon as there is existence of an ontic being, a reduction of being to the being that that being is at that moment has taken place. At any time, a selection has been made of certain aspects out of a horizon of possible ways of being, while other aspects remain unactualized. *Violence is precisely that aspect of human interaction which consists of a reduction of being, of selection of ontological aspects and simultaneous non-selection of others.* Precisely because, as Galtung emphasized, a being is potentially many things, though, *pace* Galtung, these can be normatively good or bad ways of being, any way of being necessarily means a reduction of being. The question of violence now hinges on the potential to realize potential, that is, on *the possibility of changing the aspect of the other*. The aspect of the social that entails the reduction of being in any social interaction can only be identified within a second-order observation. To the first-order observer, this aspect has always already been highlighted, albeit it is not necessarily in a subjectively experienced way, since the subject itself is already a product of a reduction of being.

That any interaction entails a selection of some aspects of being of those involved in interaction and non-selection of other aspects, that is, that any interaction involves a reciprocal reduction of the ontological horizon of those involved in interaction, can be illuminated by the example of an interaction between professor and student. The professor is a professor to a student. He or she is not usually a friend, lover or neighbour of the student. In their interaction, the student reduces the other to a professor, whereas the professor is much more than that. In order to interact, however, a selection that is relevant to the situation of interaction needs to be effectuated. The other is thereby necessarily reduced to less than he or she is. In the end, both are constrained by the need to regard the other as professor or student, and this causes some things to be banned from interaction. What needs to be emphasized immediately is that the ontological negation present in social interaction is not purely a negativity. For two things become apparent when violence is considered in this way. First, *violence is an aspect of all (human) being and (inter)acting.* Second, *violence is not a priori to be regarded as negative, as solely constraining.*

If the only way to be is to have always already been reduced to but a few of many possible aspects of being, this reduction of being is necessary for anyone to be. Therefore, violence is an aspect of every situation. It is positive in that it is constitutive of sociality, since only the reduction of being that violence is, lets beings be what they are, while they 'are', in the ontological sense, always much more. If this is what 'violence' amounts to, then how does this have anything to do with the way violence is predominantly conceptualized? To explain this, I return to the concept of the ontological horizon. That horizon may be more or less reduced in the sense that in any selection of aspects, a host of alternative aspects is kept ready at hand. This reduction, this violence, can therefore be seen as a sliding scale. This should be a premise that clears the conceptual mist that may exist relative to common notions of violence in the social sciences to a certain degree. While all interaction necessarily involves a certain violence – since a reduction of being is necessary for such interaction to exist – there are grave differences between this everyday reduction of being and the reduction of being that takes place in cases where the more commonsensical notion of violence applies. Consider again the example of the professor and his or her student. The student reduces the professor to 'a professor', since he or she cannot interact with him or her while acknowledging the whole potentiality of the professor's being. He or she has to 'deal with' the professor in a certain manner that conforms to behaviour appropriate to professor–student interaction, and as a result, many aspects of the professor's being remain unselected. The student does not interact with the professor primarily in light of the aspect that the professor is a man or a woman, or in light of his or her being someone's lover, and so on. Likewise, the professor reduces the student to 'a student'. The only way to consistently conceive of violence is to regard this elementary reduction of being as violence too. But although the violence of the professor and the student is a certain violence, it is not a violence that is 'grave' in the sense that it strikes one as being particularly violent in the commonsensical negative or destructive sense of the term. But this would be better formulated as follows: the aspect of violence hardly becomes highlighted in this professor–student interaction, although it is always to a certain degree highlighted, that is, actualized as a situational precondition. What is this 'certain degree'? What is the difference between this violence and the violence that is highlighted to such a degree that it becomes the dominant aspect of interaction, that it, in other words, becomes that in light of which the situation unfolds itself? This difference might be said to be located in the extent to which the ontological horizon of alternative aspects of being is allowed to co-constitute the interaction. As discussed in Chapter 1, a horizon of negated, unselected aspects is not merely cast aside, forgotten, but it remains at hand, and co-constitutes the interaction together with the aspects that are selected. So the professor treats his or her student primarily as a student, but co-constitutive of this are the non-selected aspects of the student being a man or a woman, someone's friend, someone's lover, a son or daughter, with a certain life-experience, and so on. Although at any time it is not possible to see the student in light of all these aspects – since the list is infinite – many are co-constitutive of the interaction between professor and student. It is crucial, however, that this is not yet what determines the level of violence in interaction. It would be mistaken to say that the aspect of violence is highlighted to the extent to which the ontological horizon of the other is co-constitutive of interaction. For a student might kill his or her professor precisely because of 'all' the things that the professor is. The ontological horizon of the professor is then co-constitutive of the interaction between professor and student, yet violence is present to an extreme extent. So the crucial question really is whether or not the ontological horizon is kept at hand in the sense that, as Wittgenstein says, a *change of aspect* is allowed to occur. Can the other be seen in light of any aspect of his or her being, or can alternative aspects of being not be actualized?

In other words, there is an inverted symmetrical relationship between the extent to which the aspect 'violence' is highlighted in interaction and the extent to which the ontological horizon of the other in interaction is kept at hand in the interaction and a different selection is possible, along with the aspect(s) that are selected. In yet other words, one can say that violence is relatively little present in interaction so long as the interacting actors are prepared to 'change the aspect' of the other. Professor and student are in most cases prepared to do that, to change the aspect of the other when interaction requires this, to see the other in a different light. They then retain the richness of the other's being. When they do so to a lesser degree, a

more severe reduction of being takes place. The further the ontological horizon of the other is reduced, the more violently the other is treated. In the
extreme case of the student killing the professor, the ontological horizon,
the infinite array of aspects of being of the professor is shrunk to only one
aspect: the professor is now merely an object, he or she is reduced to his or
her pure material being, to mere *res extensa*. No other aspects of his being
are highlighted or are allowed to become highlighted. Out of his ontological horizon, nothing can be selected anymore. In the situation in which the
student murders the professor, a change of the aspect of the professor is a
negated situational possibility. Although it is highly likely that the ontological horizon of the professor is still co-constitutive of this reduction of his or
her being to but one unchangeable aspect – since in most cases someone is
killed because of certain aspects of his or her being the killer would rather
not see – this horizon is not kept at hand and a change of aspect does not
take place when the professor is indeed killed.

One advantage of defining violence ontologically as reduction of being
is that *violence can now be seen as a sliding scale*. It is now possible to distinguish between more and less severe forms of violence based on a substantial
criterion, instead of an arbitrary one. It has never been a matter of doubt
that killing a person constitutes a more severe form of violence than bullying a person does, but the difference has been primarily based either on
intuitive classification, or on relatively arbitrary hierarchies, often juridical
in origin, that lacked a precise conceptualization of when and why violence
takes a more serious shape. In the terminology put forward here, the question becomes: 'to what extent does the ever present aspect of violence in
interaction become highlighted?'. The answer lies in the extent to which the
other is reduced in his being. One of the most drastic reductions is that to
pure matter. This is an aspect that is always co-constitutive of (inter)action,
since the other would not be that other if he weren't always also a material
thing. Yet he or she is always more than that. Any (inter)action that fails
to display the readiness to acknowledge this 'surplus of being', to allow the
other to be seen in a different light, that is in light of other aspects, can be
characterized as severely violent. A substantial reason for doing so is given
with this definition of violence.

Another advantage this definition has, concerns the 'when' of violence.
When do we ordinarily speak of violence? Existing empirical definitions
have great problems here, since if violence is, for example, seen as intentional physical hurt, then when does 'violence' actually occur? When does
it set in? The moment A hits B? But what *is* that moment? Has it set in
as soon as A raises his hand, or does it not set in until his hand forcefully
hits B's face? And does it only last as long as the contact lasts? Or is 'violence'
the label we pin upon the whole social situation in which such events take
place? Does it, as the ethnomethodologists say, define the situation? But
what would then be the 'beginning' of this situation? And its end? And is

there, within this situation, no difference in the degree of violence before A hits B, and during this action? If 'violence' is the definition of a situation, then does it make sense to even speak of levels or degrees of violence? Does it make sense to differentiate, within a violent situation, between more and less violent moments? When violence is regarded as reduction of being, the answer to such questions would be that there is a certain degree of violence in every situation to begin with. In a 'violent situation', then, the reduction of being is an aspect of the situation that becomes strongly highlighted or 'urgently present' in the foreground of (the horizon of) the situation (it then becomes plausible to say that violence starts to 'define the situation'). It remains highlighted to that 'violent' degree for as long as either A or B, or both, act in relative oblivion of their respective ontological horizons, in the sense that these may be co-constitutive of the aspect(s) that are selected and are thus constitutive of the situation, but can only to a limited degree be changed for another selection of aspect(s). The limit, or extreme case of violence is reached when no such change of aspect is allowed for. As soon as A and B are prepared to change the aspect of the other the fight ends, and violence no longer is an aspect that is highlighted, brought to the foreground, of the situational horizon. In the 'afterwards I felt sorry'-argument,[2] which perpetrators of violence often make (cf. Presser, 2003), it becomes apparent that they are able to see their former opponent in light of more than their mere status of 'enemy', which is the only thing they could see them as in the heat of the situation. So with respect to the questions of the degree of violence and the 'moment', or temporal fixation of violence, considerable conceptual clarity is gained when violence is defined as reduction of being.

The productivity of violence – on biaphobia

Durkheim has said that 'a very intense social life always does a sort of violence to the organism, as well as to the individual consciousness, which interferes with its normal functioning' (Durkheim, 1915: 227). While I agree with the recognition that there always is 'a sort of violence', I would add that this is endemic to *all* social life, and that this violence is always a part of and a necessary condition of the 'normal functioning' (whatever that is exactly) of a person. To paraphrase Nietzsche's *Zarathustra*, it comes down to not seeing only one face to Dasein (Nietzsche, 1979: 310). The *productivity* of violence has to be acknowledged. Or, in other words, we must change the aspect in thinking about violence in such a way that a consistent conceptualization becomes at hand according to which violence is not *a priori* seen as a destructive negativity. A comparison is in order here with the question whether freedom can exist alongside rules that regulate behaviour. The answer is of course yes, since the rules are constitutive of freedom. Only the rules of chess provide the freedom to play chess, they are a necessary precondition for it. Violence is productive in a similar fashion: it is an ontological precondition of ontic being. Only when the aspect of violence becomes highlighted in a one-sided fashion, that is, where other aspects of interaction are, in a practical sense, undervalued, is it possible to say that violence becomes a negativity in the sense that it destroys instead of produces (this is of course irrespective of the normative 'positivity' or 'negativity' of both productive and destructive violence). Similarly, only when a regulatory frenzy exists and rules grow rampant can there be a conflict between rules and freedom.

The productivity of violence is a forgotten aspect of violence. Especially in the humanistic tradition, violence has been one-sidedly seen in light of its destructive aspect. Even though Seneca says that the wise person is not surprised at the omnipresence of aggression, 'since he has examined thoroughly the circumstances of human life (*condicio humanae vitae*)' (quoted in Nussbaum, 1993: 100), this wisdom only pertains to the idea that 'shit' quite simply just happens, and that there is little one can do about it but withstand the negativity of it. In more 'idealistic' versions of humanism, from Erasmus to Condorcet, Turgot and Comte, through to Galtung, Ricoeur and Habermas, one finds the attempt to therefore eradicate all violence. The Leitmotiv here is summarized by Erasmus' statement that only to man 'nature' has given 'the use of speech and deliberation, both pre-eminently suitable to nurture and nourish benevolence, so that not in man too, all would be accomplished solely by physical force' (Erasmus, 1969: 14; my translation). Two recent extended definitions of violence, subsequently brought forward by Henry and Barak, suffer from the same ill. Barak (2003: 26) defines violence as 'any action or structural arrangement that results in physical or nonphysical harm to one or more persons'. Henry (2000: 19) defines it as 'the use of power to harm another, whatever form that takes'. While being extended relative to the dominant legalistic definitions, these definitions share with such commonsensical definitions a one-sided focus on harm. Destructiveness is said to be a defining characteristic of violence. Yet this humanism can be critiqued on the grounds that it has not been humanistic enough. It misrecognizes the *conditio humanae* by *a priori* excluding from it something it misrecognized as being purely destructive. With reference to the paragraph in Chapter 2 on the etymology of violence, I will call this view of violence as a pure negativity and as being solely destructive *biaphobia*. It is a specifically scholastic and intellectualistic fallacy found in much humanist and Enlightenment thought. A critique of this humanism that highlights both its relevant insight into the nature of violence and its biaphobic moment allows for a further clarification of the definition of violence.

That violence, in all its manifestations, is a counterforce that disturbs human community is a tenacious prejudice. The very formation of the concept of *humanitas* (in the second century BC) grew out of dissatisfaction with the rather militaristic notion of *homo romanus*, which became *homo humanus*, a concept popularized greatly by Cicero (cf. Landmann, 1982: 22).

The ideal of the *homo humanus* was furthermore opposed to *inhumanus*, which replaced the no longer usable notion of *barbarian*. Violence was associated with the latter *inhumanus*, virtue with the *homo humanus*. With Roman humanism, as noted earlier, the notion of *vir*, the true man, is stripped of its more forceful connotations in favour of its moral overtones. It would remain as such until Machiavelli, who lived in a time of Italian revitalization of Roman (historiographic) humanism, recombined the two. The separation between violence and true humanity is of course also a basic dogma in the thought of the Enlightenment. Yet at the perimeters of that thought, Freud too opposes *Lebenstrieb* and *Destruktionstrieb* – not insignificantly first elaborated upon in *Zeitgemässes über Krieg und Tod* – as analogous to Eros and death. But why place the destructive instinct on the side of death (in the sense of being opposed to life)? It is human life that is characterized by it as much as it is under the influence of the opposite urge. The fact that violence and sociality are not diametrically opposed not only holds with respect to the necessary everyday reduction of being of which I have argued that it would be consistent to include it in the conceptualization of violence. It also refers to situations in which the aspect of violence is much more brought to the fore – situations, therefore, to which the commonsensical notion of violence applies. Social science has often seen violence in light of a certain moral aspect, though there is at the same time a wide consensus within social science that that is not the aspect it is supposed to select as an object of research. Only when the social is *a priori* seen as a harmonious *and* (these are not opposites) non-violent realm of human being-together, can violence be biaphobically conceptualized as something which runs counter to that being-together. But when this implicit social scientific morality is cast off, it becomes necessary to say that even extreme forms of violence establish a connection, a relation. Violence most of the time *brings people together*. When the simplified situation of A and B fighting is considered once more, violence is to be seen as the dominantly highlighted aspect of the togetherness of A and B. They could be together working or playing, and they can be together in violence – since these are always only aspects of a social situation, the only difference is the degree to which such aspects are actualized or highlighted.

Strictly speaking, the first social scientific observation, which is always a second-order observation, can, with respect to violence, only be that it is a form of sociality, of human being-together. This may be a truism, but this axiom seems to be rarely remembered in the study of violence. Now, it is very well possible that violence bring people together in a 'positive' or constructive way. Reports from war mention the special bond that enemy soldiers develop when dug into opposing trenches, for instance during World War I (cf. Derrida, 1995: 17–18). On a more 'abstract' level, it is relevant to point out that the very basis of whatever 'order' is said to exist within the societal system is based on a reservoir of violence, a threat, that is called the state's 'monopoly of legitimate violence' (or, as this may be reformulated in accordance with the dominant semantics of violence: the state's legitimate monopoly of violence). Constitutive of the *polis* is the *polemos*. Added to this is the idea in social theory that the 'constitution of society' is based on the exclusion of an alterity, therefore on a certain violence, which is said to be a 'normal' social fact (cf. Durkheim, 1937; Laclau and Mouffe, 1985; Schinkel, 2009). It shows indeed the normality of violence as constitutive of sociality. There is nothing inherent to 'violence' in general that opposes it to a relatively homoeostatic social system; it is an integral part of social life that has a basic constitutive function in that life. Heidegger (1953: 117) demonstrates how the *polis* refers not only to the 'city' or 'state', but to the place of being in general. The constitutive connection between *polis* and *polemos* thus similarly exists at all levels of the social.

Humans past humanism

Prior to the inconsistency due to its biaphobic moment, the humanist tradition does contain a certain knowledge about violence. It has understood the reduction of being, although it has recognized it as present only in extreme cases, and, as I have argued, this brings with it the arbitrariness of cutting the realm of human (inter)action in two at a certain point, and this is not based on a substantial argument. Yet it is enlightening to consider how extreme cases of violence have been conceptualized in this strand of thought, in order to then expand this understanding beyond biaphobia to forms of violence not recognized as such in the humanist tradition. Forms of extreme violence have been primarily understood as forms of *dehumanization*. That violence can be seen as dehumanization or depersonalization can be argued on the basis of many examples. American soldiers have, for instance, been trained in dehumanizing the enemy since World War II, when only 15–20 per cent of the men actually dared to shoot a visible enemy. The result was that 55 per cent actually fired during the Korea war, while 90 per cent did so in Vietnam (Berger, 1977: 122; Grossman, 2003). In extreme cases of violence, the dehumanization is often precisely what prompts perpetrators to their actions and simultaneously justifies them due to the adiaphorization it entails. In a similar way, Auschwitz-atrocities have been explained. The incarcerated were no longer regarded as people; they were, in other words, reduced in their being to an extreme extent. The same thing happened when certain American soldiers in Vietnam killed anyone they encountered because all they thought of was 'bodycount', a technical term replacing 'human beings' and euphemizing their reduction of being.[3] One perpetrator in the My Lai massacre (1968) argued: 'I was ordered to go in there and destroy the enemy. That was my job on that day. That was the mission I was given. I did not sit down and think in terms of men, women and children. They were all classified the same, and that was the classification we dealt with, just as enemy soldiers' (quoted in Muncie and

McLaughlin, 1996: 304). During that war, enemy soldiers were referred to as 'gooks', which enabled a dehumanization. In the documentary *First Kill*, one American former soldier says that the standard reply of a soldier to the question 'why are you here?' was 'to kill gooks'. When a former soldier asked 'but why did you kill those kids?', the answer was 'because of bodycount'. A similar notion of dehumanization has been used to describe practices of torture: 'Torture is a deliberate attempt to destroy and dehumanise, conducted by people who are in a situation that allows no empathy whatsoever with their victims' (Sironi and Branche, 2002: 547). Pictures of the acts performed by US soldiers in the Iraqi Abu Ghraib prison very clearly indicate various techniques that morally facilitate torture. The Iraqis were hooded, so that their face could not be seen – the face, as will be discussed below, which is highly relevant in the moral appeal a person exerts upon another. Next to this, the prisoners are naked most of the time, which equally separates them from regular human life. When naked, not facing their guards, and huddled up together, sometimes even stacked in pyramid shape, it becomes all the more easy for the torturers to not have to see them as human beings. The way violence is given shape thus facilitates its legitimation and thereby, in a strange tautology, its occurrence.

Similarly, Randall Collins (1974: 419) has described 'mutilation' as 'punishment not by death, but by life at its lowest level'. 'Life at its lowest level' would then be the epithet of an extreme reduction of being. Such extreme reductions of being are tied to a notion of humanity that is performatively violent. Nazi's didn't consider Jews to be human beings, and to emphasize this, they dressed them in striped rags, shaved their heads, underfed them to then be strengthened in their concept of 'the Jew' even more by reference to the 'inhuman' smell their prisoners in concentration camps gave off. During the colonization, which the French called the 'mission civilisatrice', a hierarchy of humanity was a presupposition according to which blacks were at the bottom of classification which whites headed (cf. Lindqvist, 1996). The same took place in the Rwanda massacre when Hutus and Tutsis clashed (initially driven apart for convenience by Belgian and German colonizers). One example is that of a woman playing dead, reporting her neighbour, a participant in a slaughter of many, bending over her, saying 'does this thing still live?'. Anthropological data similarly indicate that many people's definition of 'human being' is restricted to the designation of that people alone, while everyone else is regarded as non-human. For example, the Yukpa people of north-western Venezuela separate *Yu'pa* (people) from *Yuko* (enemy), where '-pa' means 'a group of the same class' and '-ko' means 'a group of another class' (Halbmayer, 2001).

An all too human 'dehumanization'

The dominant philosophical and social scientific traditions of thinking about violence have always in one way or another been intricately bound up with commonsensical notions of violence. That does not mean they have not seen violence along the lines of a reduction of being at all. They in fact have, and termed it 'dehumanization'. This negation of the being of another being is, however, not restricted to such 'beastly acts' as severe physical violence. In fact, as Dostoyevsky notes, animals rarely engage in 'beastly acts of violence' when compared to humans. Related to the notion of dehumanization is that of a denial of existence, which, for instance, allows Dante to say that 'violence may be done against the Deity, in the heart denying and blaspheming him' (Dante, 1996: Canto XI). On a more 'worldly' note, according to Carl Schmitt the essence (*Wesen*) of the political lies in the friend–enemy opposition, which he bases on the negation of the existence of the other (Schmitt, 2002: 27). I argue that such a negation of the otherness of the other will always necessarily have to take place. This is what the humanist tradition has never wanted to realize. It is informed by a biaphobic will to eradicate all violence, while it cannot escape the performance of violence itself. In order to come to a further clarification of the definition of violence as *all* reduction of being, I will agree with Heidegger that 'humanism' has not been 'human' enough. Extreme violence may be a dehumanization, but dehumanization is an all too human process. Randall Collins has even said that 'torture and mutilation are distinctively human acts; they are indeed advanced human acts' (Collins, 1974: 422). This is because the torturer or the mutilator 'could not even attempt his arts without a capacity for taking the role of the other' (Collins, 1974: 422). Lesser forms of violence – (inter)action in which the aspect of violence is not highlighted in an extreme sense – are in fact 'all-too-human'. For it is human to reduce human beings to but a few aspects of their being. Every 'humanization' is at the same time a dehumanization. Every dehumanization is still, albeit in extreme cases in the smallest possible respect, a humanization. The humanist idea of the human being which does not acknowledge the aspect of reduction of being in every letting be, is a humanism that is not humanistic enough because it places the all-too-human dehumanization outside the realm of the human. To Zygmunt Bauman's Kantian statement that 'the pure gift is the recognition of the *humanity* of the other' (Bauman, 1990: 91), the sociological qualification would be that 'sociology posits that social agents do not perform gratuitous acts' (Bourdieu, 1994: 150; my translation). With respect to the humanism of his times, Heidegger writes that it sees the human in terms of 'value'. Yet it is precisely such a 'value' that makes Dasein an object – an object of (e)valuation (Heidegger, 1949: 41).

Humanism reduces human beings to 'things', precisely in its attempt to formulate a 'positive' idea of the essence of the human, which excludes violence. That is what makes this humanism violent *and* what makes it human. Heidegger has laid bare the biaphobic inconsistency in the humanist tradition, but on another level, Heidegger himself displays biaphobia. The critique of this humanism should not be that it objectifies man in its very attempt not to do so, but rather that this objectification is not recognized as a necessary and constitutive part of the *condicio humanae vitae*. For contrary to whatever hopes Heidegger might have had for a future *Lichtung* in which an Eckhardtian *Gelassenheit* is expanded throughout society in the moral realm, the sociological claim I wish to put forward is that human life *always necessarily* entails a reduction of being. While Heidegger's comments on humanism serve to highlight what one could call (at least when that tradition is viewed in light of the aspect of violence) its biaphobic inconsistency, Heidegger in the end merely withdraws to another biaphobic position in still maintaining the idea that a non-reduction of Dasein is a possibility. This inconsistency can be overcome with the positions of subsequent writers, commenting on Heidegger.

Subjects and objects: Violence as *Verdinglichung*

First, it is relevant to state that, drawing on Heidegger's exposition of the biaphobic inconsistency of 'humanism', violence can be conceptualized in other words as that aspect of human (inter)action which consists of the simultaneous subjectification and objectification of a (human) being. Reducing the ontological horizon of the other to a few selected aspects is, when that horizon is kept ready at hand in the possibility of aspect-change, the everyday violence that is constitutive of all human being-together. In reducing the other in interaction with him or her, the other becomes a subject and an object at the same time. Only in extreme cases of violence has this reduction of being been recognized and classified under the notion of 'objectification'. With respect to the Nazi concentration camps, for instance, Hannah Arendt (1968: 438) has spoken of a way of 'transforming the human personality into a mere object'. Primo Levi's 'question' 'If this is a man' thus pertains to the extreme objectification of a human being. When Levi describes his first roll-call in Auschwitz, he mentions that 'the officer asked *"Wieviel Stück?"'* (Levi, 1965: 22). The prisoner of the concentration camp therefore is characterized by Levi as 'a man whose life or death can be lightly decided with no sense of human affinity, in the most fortunate of cases, on the basis of a pure judgement of utility' (Levi, 1965: 33). In Marxist literature, *Verdinglichung* has always been understood as a reduction of human beings to mere objects – objects that were or are even fetishized themselves (cf. Horkheimer and Adorno, 1944). In a similar vein, Paul Tillich has said that 'a profound insight has been developed in modern literature, namely, that one of the fundamental expressions of sin is to make the other person into an object, a thing' (Tillich, 1959: 210). To a certain degree, however, no one escapes objectification, since to be a subject, to be able to *be*, is to have always already been reduced. To put it in the form of an obvious platitude, one cannot be, at one time, all that one *can* be. A reduction, an objectification, has always already taken place.

Sartre has extensively written about the everyday objectifications that are the 'stuff' of violence. In his existential ontology, a rupture is experienced by a *cogito*, a being-for-itself, and the Other: 'Between the Other and myself there is a nothingness of separation' (Sartre, 1969: 230). The Other is the no-itself: 'Others are *the Other*, that is the self which *is not* myself. Therefore we grasp here a negation as the constitutive structure of the being-of-others' (Sartre, 1969: 230). The 'Other' is the negation of the for-itself, and this is only possible, according to Sartre, as the experience of an *object*. Just as the being-in-itself is nihilated in order for the being-for-itself to be, the Other can only be conceived as 'objectness' (*objectité*). Being-for-itself necessarily objectifies the Other, and it is objectified by the Other itself (Sartre, 1969: 236). For the Other is a negation of the self as *cogito*, since it *is not* self, but Other. When posited as a subject, the Other is an object of my thoughts (Sartre, 1969: 229). This objectification of the Other is necessary, according to Sartre, because self-consciousness can only appear as self-consciousness for an Other. The Other is the 'one *who sees me*', and to whom I appear as an object. Being-for-itself needs from the Other a recognition of its being (Sartre, 1969: 237). The inherently conflictual relationship between self and Other is due to the fact that both self and Other rely on each other in order to recognize themselves as being-for-itself (compare Hegel, 1970: 147). And they do so, in Sartre's terminology, as 'objectness'. Subject and object become, in a sense, conflated categories: 'The peculiar possibility of apprehending myself as an object is the possibility belonging to the Other-as-subject' (Sartre, 1969: 296). This, in turn, is only possible because the Other is an Other-as-object. There is no escaping this simultaneous subjectification and objectification. It becomes especially apparent in the phenomenon of shame, but also in love, since love, according to Sartre, is also the enslavement of the Other, specifically as freedom. Sartre's conclusion, famously stated in *Huis Clos*, is that 'hell is other people' ('l'enfer c'est les autres'). Here, however, Sartre succumbs to biaphobia. Sociological reason permits an analysis of subjectification and objectification in more neutral terms, or at least in terms endowed with more nuance. These can be said to be two aspects of one ecstatic structure of being (Dasein) as being-together or being-with-others. What Sartre quite accurately points out to be the objectness of self and other corresponds to sociological notions concerning the *classifications* by means of which the other is perceived (cf. Durkheim and Mauss, 1963), which include the fact that 'the classifier classifies himself' (Bourdieu, 1996: 467). The Parsonian–Mertonian role set entails a similar reduction of the subject subjected to others, which always works both ways. Sartre saw violence as basic to being-for-itself, but he did not appreciate the positivity that this violence of everyday life always is. Only when the other is reduced in his being in the sense that he is not allowed to exist in light of other aspects of his being than those that are at one point in (social) time highlighted, does violence turn from primarily constitutive to primarily destructive to the being of the other. This difference is merely a matter of scale: the extent to which the other is reduced – and there is no not reducing the other – equals the level of violence towards the other, or rather, *between* self and other. It is to be stressed that this reduction is always a reduction in the double sense of a reduction of the ontological horizon of the other to certain aspects, and a reduction of the possibility of aspect-change. A higher level of violence is described by Sartre as exercised by the sadist. The sadist is involved in a purely instrumental utilization of the other: 'the sadist treats the Other as an instrument in order to make the Other's flesh appear' (Sartre, 1969: 402). Here, there is no changing the aspect of the objectness of the other. The other cannot be considered to be some-thing other than the *thing* he is conceived to be by the sadist. The sadist, or in general, the person we call 'violent', in a practical sense takes the objectness of the other at one point in (social) time to be the whole of the being of the other. To the killer, the only selected aspect of the being of his victim is the latter's objectness in a literal sense: his materiality, the *res extensa*, which is in fact always transcended by a horizon of aspects of being. The killer is not oblivious to that horizon and it may very well provide the motive for his actions, but he simply ignores it and refuses to make it count above the aspect that is actualized. Yet the very fact that we can and always need to reduce the other to but relatively few aspects of his being indicates that the other is always more than what he, at any given time, 'is'. The commonsensical notion of violence applies to cases of violence where this ontological 'fact' is omitted from interaction as a constitutive force.

Sartre's existential ontology is written entirely from the perspective of the *cogito*. Yet violence is not restricted to situations between 'self' and 'other'. We can find in Michel Foucault's work a more sociological account of subjectification and objectification. Foucault shows how humanist efforts to 'socialize' people actually led merely to a new kind of subjectification. In the end, it even led to the subjectification of man as 'man', a human being, endowed with universal value, a knowing 'subject' over against a world of soulless objects to be known to man. Thereby, this subject is at the same time an object among other objects, as De Lamettrie and others argued. This objectness becomes incorporated into the human subjects by means of various disciplinary techniques. The human sciences then become the 'disciplines which will [...] treat men as objects'. It is not Foucault's intention to show that processes of subjectification are a specifically modern product, but rather that, in modernity, these take a new and more immanentized, even incorporated shape. In his study of the rise of the prison, he claims that a panoptic model was born in the eighteenth century. For our purposes, it is interesting to note that this model was accompanied by a discourse that sought to get rid of the excessive violence of pre-modern punishment and torture. Foucault, however, sees in the coming of a disciplinary society simply another kind of violence, based on a more meticulous control over social subjects. This control was effectuated through classifications that were devised to subject individuals into disciplined subjects of society. This was a society that sought to discipline and to include, instead of to avenge and to exclude. A criminal code was developed that was able to do this. Control became control over the body of the inmate; space and time become socially constructed parameters of the body of the prisoner. Especially in his earlier work, Foucault relates this development to the rise of modern capitalism. It has often been argued that workers have had to be 'socialized' into the role of capitalist production workers (Foucault, 1975). Foucault sees in the rise of panoptic discipline the development of what he later called a dispositive – a power–knowledge constellation – in which the individual was subjected as a *homo economicus*. For Foucault, knowledge and power are correlatively bound together. Power has the effect of control and subjectification, which at the same time amounts to objectification. As Foucault says, 'my objective [...] has been to create a history of the different modes by which, in our culture, human beings are made subjects. My work has dealt with three modes of objectification which transform human beings into subjects' (Foucault, 1982: 208). He thus distinguishes certain modes of objectification that are not directly relevant here, except for the sheer fact that these modes of *objectification* produce *subjects*. The fact that the ways in which people are subjectified are historically relative – they differ in each *episteme* or dispositive – means that each cultural construction of 'man' reduces man to something less than he actually 'is'. Foucault thus provides a historical analysis of the shape of violence. He is, moreover, interested in the imma- nent societal processes that are at the heart of the most basic concepts of 'man' and 'human being'. He thus says in *Surveiller et punir* that discipline is a technique of power that produces individuals (Foucault, 1975: 172).

From the point of view of the avoidance of biaphobia, the genealogy of the modern subject put forward in this work has the advantage of involving the recognition of the *productive* aspect of power. Power is not simply something (certain) people have and use to suppress others; it is rather immanent to the field of relations those people constitute. In *L'Histoire de la Sexualité*, Foucault coins the term 'the tactical polyvalence of discourse' to indicate the duality inherent to processes of subjectification (Foucault, 1976: 132ff.). These do not simply concern a relation between a master and a slave, but the productivity of power means that while homosexuals, for example, are subjectified to fit a certain violent vocabulary, the same vocabulary provided them with a means of emancipation. Both aspects characterize the discourse of homosexuality: while homosexuals are medicalized and thus disqualified as belonging to a social region of 'perversity', that discourse at the same time allows them to emancipate; it allows for a discourse-in-return to exist (Foucault, 1976: 134). A similar productivity of violence is found in the normalization that takes place in the procedures of discipline (Foucault, 1975: 187).

What Foucault's work highlights in exemplary fashion is that dehumanization is constitutive of humanization. Only from a 'humanistic' point of view – a view which is not human enough – can one condemn dehumanization as being wholly destructive and negative. While Foucault writes on power, the ontological perspective on violence developed here can be elaborated in a similar way with a view to the social productivity of the reduction of being. To define violence as a reduction of being is to move past a biaphobic deontology that sees only one aspect of violence – its destruction – and to allow for the constitutive aspects of violence to be highlighted.

We must therefore reinterpret the humanist–Marxist critique of *Verdinglichung* and regard it as a necessarily Janus-faced social process. This critique has in fact not recognized its own violence in presupposing the objectification of a human *subject*. This subject is the product of a process of *Verdinglichung* or objectification itself (Nietzsche, 1979 III: 487). The subject is a *simplification*, or, in other words, a reduction. It is always more than a 'subject', and has been reduced to this. This reduction is what *enables* the subject to be, and whatever more it is than a subject, it can only be it as subject. It is not surprising that at the basis of Kant's moral philosophy is the synthetic practical *a priori* to always consider every human being also as an end in itself. The definition of violence I put forward here explicitly entails the idea that, while Kant's concept of 'humanity' may yet be a biaphobic construct, it does recognize that people are instrumentalized and that morality depends on the degree to which the other is always at the same time regarded as an end in itself, which would be the degree to which an aspect-change is allowed for. Kant's notion of 'humanity' is the totality of the ontological horizon. Yet since that totality is necessarily reduced in social practice, violence is not *a priori* to be regarded as immoral.

When violence is taken to be a social process that is ontologically characterized by a reduction of being, no other part of Heidegger's ontology is more suitable to elucidate this than the most 'practical' discussions in that ontology, that is, those that deal with the everyday 'care' of Dasein for *objects*. Heidegger refers to material things mostly as *Zeug*, 'equipment', that which the Greeks called *pragmata* (Heidegger, 1993: 68). *Zeug* is first and foremost 'something to ...' (do this or that with). Heidegger calls this way in which objects are cared for by Dasein in everyday practice *Zuhandenheit* (readiness-to-hand). A hammer, for instance, is first of all a 'hammerthing', something to hammer with, like my pen is ready-at-hand as a thing to write with. In this everyday mode of caring for objects, Dasein does not reflect on the object any further, it does not become present-at-hand. That means it does not become a consciously thematized 'object' over against a knowing, observing 'subject'. This is indeed the use of the concepts of 'object' and 'subject' I wish to make here. These do not refer to consciously thematized entities, as they do in the intellectualistic tradition. Rather, they appear in social practice in a co-evolutionary fashion. Only the second-order observation of such practice, as is the meta-theory of violence I am engaged with in this chapter, can meaningfully speak of objectification and subjectification as constitutive of that practice. The first-order observation of the practical behaviour (*das praktische Verhalten*) in which Dasein deals with things has its own insight (*Sicht*) that is ontologically fundamental (in the sense of *ursprünglich*). *Zeug*, or things to ..., appear in a certain sight (*Umsicht*). This means that they are seen in a particular *light*. In the terminology I have put forward, certain *aspects* of the thing(s) are highlighted. Heidegger stresses that this way of caring for objects is a form of 'counting on' (*rechnen mit*), which is at the same time a not counting on what is not appropriate at a certain time. These non-appropriate (non-usable) aspects are, however, preserved (*behalten*) (Heidegger, 1993: 356), like aspects of a Husserlian horizon of a material object. The reality of social practice is very similar to the way Heidegger speaks of caring for things. There are various ways in which a person 'deals' with another person. These are ways of letting the other be in social practice. Ways of the other's being that are not selected are preserved and can in their turn be selected. In a certain sense, the other is always already reduced to some form of human being-ready-at-hand. I treat my fellow passengers on the subway most of the time as *res extensa*, matter to move around. That is not a conscious and certainly not a reflexive way of engaging in the social practice of moving around on the subway; it is rather a consequence of certain semi-autonomous subsystems that are part of 'me' and that register and coordinate below the level of consciousness. That is already the way it is for the simple reason that a human being's information-processing capabilities rely for the most part on subconscious routines, and only to a very small degree on conscious feedback. Constitutive of my moving around on the subway is always the ontological horizon of any passenger. For I avoid looking this 'matter' in the eyes for more than half a second. Only when I am intent on killing subway passengers do I totally shut out their ontological horizon in the sense that the possibility of a change of aspect in suspended. That horizon is then still co-constitutive of my selection of the aspect of the passengers as soon-to-be-murdered by me, since I don't want to kill empty matter, but people whose material being is but one aspect of their being, for one because they are beings that value their material being. Yet in that case, which could, for instance, be a case of terrorism, I do not allow alternative aspects from the ontological horizon of those passengers to become highlighted through selection, that is, through change of aspect. This is where this interaction differs from less violent everyday interaction, like the non-murderous ride on the subway, which is nonetheless also characterized by a reduction of being that has always already taken place.

Levinas' counterargument and its biaphobia

Philosophical discourse, especially in the last century, has repeatedly circled round questions of the other and of letting the other be. A crucial question is whether or not the reduction of the being of the other has indeed *always already* taken place. Eric Weil, for instance, pays attention to processes of instrumentalization and objectification as violence. Yet he suggests that this only happens as the result of a process of violence intended as an organized counter-violence against (the danger of) intra-societal and inter-state forms of violence. This response consists of an organization of social life which brings about the reduction of the person to a 'thing'. The scientific conception of man objectifies everything, including humanity. This involves a subjectification through which people think of themselves in rationalized scientific terms (Weil, 1967: 82). The idea that, to a certain extent, reduction of being through a simultaneous subjectification and objectification always takes place, has been more fundamentally attacked by Emmanuel Levinas. It is relevant to consider how Levinas intends to escape this, and how he can be said to fail to adequately do so.

Levinas' argument in *Totalité et Infini*, on which I will focus here, is that philosophical thought has been primarily oriented towards 'totality'. It has thought of people first of all in terms of an 'I', Heidegger's 'Dasein' included. And while Heidegger intended to escape objectivism, he fails to do so, according to Levinas, because he treats fellow men as secondary to Dasein. 'Mitdasein' is only being-with for Dasein. Furthermore, Heidegger's main interest is Being itself, which is, to Levinas, nothing but a substitute totality of being or an equivalent to a 'highest being'. Heidegger allots primacy to the relation between being and Being (*la priorité de l'*être *par rapport à l'*étant), thereby subordinating the relation to the other (*la relation avec* quelqu'un *qui est un étant*) to the relation between Dasein and *Sein* (Levinas, 1974: 15–16). Yet Levinas stresses that it is the relation to the other that is the *ethical relation*. Heidegger's ontology is therefore characterized by violence – which is, significantly, something Heidegger explicitly recognized. In this metaphysical tradition, then, the conceptualization of the world is at the same time the appropriation of the world. In a similar vein to Horkheimer and Adorno commenting on 'understanding' (*begreifen*) that it is a violent way of appropriating (*greifen*) (and like Habermas' critique of *vernehmen*), Levinas states: 'Western philosophy has most often been an ontology: a reduction of the other to the Same (Levinas, 1974: 13; my translation). This reduction of the other as a theme for an 'I' is a negation of the alterity of the other that is anterior to all negation. And it reduces the other to a neutralized object, in the horizon of sameness. It is indeed the Husserlian notion of a *horizon* that is attacked by Levinas when that concept is used in an ontology of human being to denote the totality of the being of such a being, as I have used it here. This ontological horizon, another form of classical idealism to Levinas, is part of the 'economy of the same' by means of which the alterity of the other is appropriated and placed within the horizon of an 'I', reduced to the same. The other, in Levinas' view, always escapes such objectification. His philosophy is an ethics in the sense that he sets out to think of the other only as alterity, an alterity that is principally not appropriable. The true metaphysical other is other with an alterity that is not representable and that is prior to 'all imperialism of the Same' (Levinas, 1974: 9). Likewise, the other does not limit the same and nor does it therefore reduce the 'I'. If it would, it would not be the wholly other. To Levinas, then, the absolutely Other is (the) other (*L'absolument Autre, c'est Autrui*). Here, he intends a pure alterity that cannot be reduced to the same, despite all efforts to do so by Western ontological metaphysics. Over the Other, or the Stranger, 'I' have no power (*Sur lui je ne peux pouvoir*). Levinas therefore radically rejects the phenomenological tradition, and he would probably have rejected what has been said above concerning the reduction of being that necessarily occurs and that is constitutive of social life. To Levinas, the other remains fundamentally Other. Knowledge of the other will have to accept *inadaequatio*. If it doesn't, the result is injustice. It is precisely the experience of severe injustice which prompts Levinas to place the other beyond totality into an ethics of *infinity*. Yet the question is whether or not, in doing so, he has remained within the logic of appropriation after all.

To a large extent, Levinas' analysis runs parallel to what has been said in this chapter, since Levinas recognizes the omnipresence of an effort to appropriate the other, to reduce the other in an objectification. His analysis radically differs from the above, however, when he claims that because the other essentially escapes the grasp of the 'I', there is a possibility of not objectifying the other and of the 'I' not being objectified by the other. Like Sartre and Heidegger, Levinas retreats to a biaphobic position. In his case, like in Heidegger's, this is expressed by the retreat to a last resort of non-appropriation. For Levinas, it is the *face* of the other that resists appropriation or possession. While the face is a thing like other things, it is also something more: it always breaks through its thing-like form (Levinas, 1974: 172). The face of the other escapes us, it reminds us of the infinity of the alterity of the other. The ethical is the epiphany of the face of the other, yet it is also only the face of the other through which one can violate the other. The transcendence of the face of the other *calls* upon the 'I' to respect the alterity of the other. Whereas murder, also in Levinas' terms, is the total negation of the being of the other (Levinas, 1974: 168, 173), the face of the other has as its *expression originelle*, the first word: 'thou shalt not commit murder' (Levinas, 1974: 173). But murders are committed, and while such complete reductions of the other are not common in everyday life, less severe negations are a necessary precondition to that life.

Were Levinas to effectively escape the language of 'ontological imperialism', this could hardly be maintained. Derrida, however, has demonstrated that he does not escape from it. The point Derrida's deconstruction of Levinas' ethics can make plausible that is relevant here is that Levinas' attempt to develop an ethics based on the (biaphobic) possibility to not reduce the other fails, and in fact coils back into the (onto)logic of reduction of being. Derrida summarizes Levinas' attempt, for instance by saying that 'this thought calls upon the ethical relationship – a nonviolent relationship to the infinite as infinitely other, to the Other [...]' (Derrida, 1978: 102). Yet Derrida sees in Levinas' critique of especially Heidegger a certain violence as well. This has to do with 'the necessity of lodging oneself within traditional conceptuality in order to destroy it' (Derrida, 1978: 139). Levinas' attempt never leaves the logic of what it intends to surpass. The very use of the words 'infinite' and 'Other' presupposes that a negation of the finite exists, which is precisely what Levinas opposes (Levinas, 1974: 9). However, the only possible positive infinity is a negation of finite spatiality. And while Levinas accords to *language* the special place of being the relation between the same and the other, Derrida notes that precisely for that reason, the other bears the trace of the same, since it is locked in the logic of language, the logic of *difference* vis-à-vis the same (Derrida, 1978: 143). The problem is to *describe*, with the language of ontology, an infinitely other that would necessarily escape such a language of the same. Because Levinas accords infinity to the alterity of the other, yet does so through ontological language, he has a problem similar to that of a negative theology that still names what is essentially unnameable (and what is 'essentially' here?). Language is the very structure of inside–outside, and any beyond language is therefore characterized by the inside it necessarily negates to 'be' beyond. 'The other cannot be what it is, infinitely other, except in finitude and mortality' (Derrida, 1978: 143). The other can only be an other as an ego, which is the only thing that can be an alter to an ego. The other therefore is Other '*in my real economy*' (Derrida, 1978: 157). Levinas intends to depart from the economy of the same, but fails to do so. While he places violence solely on the level of ethics, he fails to recognize the ontological violence necessary for any being to be either other or same. Levinas' eschatology too, 'is not possible, except through violence' (Derrida, 1978: 162). We can conclude with Derrida:

> this transcendental origin, as the irreducible violence of the relation to the other, is at the same time nonviolence, since it opens up the relation with the other. It is an *economy*. And it is this economy which, by this opening, will permit access to the other to be determined, in ethical freedom, as moral violence or nonviolence
>
> (Derrida, 1978: 160)

What Derrida here states comes down to the necessity of the reduction of the being of the other in order to be in-relation-to the other. This violence, which is ever present, has a positivity to it, it is *enabling*. Without it, being-in-relation, or being-social, would not be possible. Derrida thus moves beyond Levinasian biaphobia.

Yet Derrida has his own biaphobic moment. For he makes a somewhat strange move when he wants to rescue Heidegger from Levinas' violence at the end of his deconstruction of Levinasian ethics. Here he says that '"to let be" is an expression of Heidegger which does not mean, as Levinas seems to think, to let be as an "object of comprehension first" [...]. The "letting-be" concerns all possible forms of the existent, and even those which, *by essence*, cannot be transformed into "objects of comprehension"' (Derrida, 1978: 172). Yet here, Derrida seems to part with the earlier argument that violence is always, in a sense, present in the relation between ego and alter. Whereas Levinas' 'infinite other' is violated because it *cannot* appear in relation to ego – it is, after all, infinitely other – Heidegger's 'letting-be' (*Gelassenheit*) is characterized by exactly the same violence. It seems, then, that after deconstructing Levinas' biaphobic escape from an inescapable reduction of being, Derrida seeks a similar escape route. He himself has shown the impossibility of this. His argument has been focused on the social relation between 'self' and 'other'.

While this argument has been more 'purely philosophical' than that of Foucault, the result is very similar. One might formulate it alternatively within the bounds of sociological theory: social beings operate under the pressure of selection, of reduction of complexity. If no aspects are selected the other is not allowed to be, which is a reduction itself. That is how I feel a fundamental insight is gained when violence is defined as the reduction of being. Violence is always present, yes, but all is not violence. The *level* of violence, the degree to which 'violence' is highlighted as an *aspect* of a certain *praxis*, or – in frozen perspective – social situation, is precisely the degree of reduction of that horizon and of the possibility of a change of aspect(s). This involves the basic reduction of an ontological horizon by means of selection of aspect(s) *and* the reduction of the possibility of aspect-change. The latter is therefore the reduction of the possibility of an*other* reduction of that ontological horizon. To be is to be reduced, objectified as a subject, by both self and other. Sociology has often presupposed this by positing some kind of order or social structure. This presupposition introduces violence as an ever-present object of research, as Durkheim's intuition indicates. The same in fact goes for the opposite presupposition, that of social chaos.

Conclusion: Nine advantages of defining violence as reduction of being

The definition of violence as reduction of being is placed within a tradition of thought in which the theme of violence has gradually become more pertinent as a subject of discourse. I believe there is much to be gained by conceiving violence this way. Since violence is a negation of aspects of being, the study of violence – at least when it is concerned with violence between people – has to hook up with a social philosophical anthropology when it is in search of a definition of violence. I have used the phenomenological model, in an adapted form, and I have indeed used it as a *model*, not as a one-on-one representation of being-in-relation. One might think that this definition of violence is an 'abstract' one. However, in reality the more abstract notions are those taken-for-granted concepts that are hardly given consideration beyond their use in research. Seeing violence as a reduction of being allows for certain connections to be seen. That is, it gives deeper insight in what happens when we speak of 'violence', and it solves many problems that are a result both of not defining violence and of defining it 'empirically'. As a summary of this chapter, I will review the advantages of this definition in light of the strong points of the empirical definitions that have been discussed earlier.

(1) The definition of violence as reduction of being transcends the difficulties of empirical definitions. These difficulties have been identified under the general heading of aspect-blindness. Though only four definitions of violence have been discussed, I have argued that any empirical definition of violence necessarily highlights but a few relevant aspects of violence while it blocks access to other aspects equally relevant to an understanding of violence. Since the definition of violence as a reduction of being is ontological, not ontic or empirical in character, this problem is overcome. Of course the problem remains when observing violence empirically, but still two things have been gained. One, a fundamental understanding of the nature of violence. Two, and consequently, a much better assessment of ontic violence. There is now a much more consistent measure that can be used in the empirical observation and recognition of violence. Whereas empirical definitions in the end draw borders that are necessarily *arbitrary*, in order to delineate what counts as violence and what doesn't, the ontological definition allows for a *substantial* demarcation-criterion of violence to be utilized. Phenomena that have a similar ontological structure can now be grouped together under the generic label of 'violence' on the basis of a shared substance. In short, the advantage of the ontological definition over the empirical definition lies in its possibility to overcome the aspect-blindness that the latter is always characterized by. In other words, since aspect-blindness is a reduction, in this case of the ontological horizon of 'violence', *the ontological definition of violence is less violent than the empirical definition*. Indeed, in the remainder of this book, whenever I come across social scientific aspect-blindness, this will be characterized as a kind of social scientific violence itself. That will not be done because it concerns an inadequately studied research object, but because that research object happens to be violence, the recognition and misrecognition of which automatically involve certain violence themselves.

(2) In the paragraph on 'ways of defining a concept', two methods of defining a concept have been briefly discussed. Both find resonance in the ontological definition of violence, since this definition involves a substantial characteristic, an 'essence' of all violence, while it at the same time allows for contextual factors to be incorporated. A boxing match is a good

example here. All empirical definitions struggle in accommodating such a social practice in a definition of violence, with the result that it is either seen as violence, or perhaps as a special case of violence, or not at all seen as violence. These are clearly inadequate ways of conceptualizing a boxing match in light of violence. Regarding it as a special case of violence displays the conceptual inadequacy of such definitions, which is due to their lack of substance. Totally separating it from violence, on the other hand, is due not to the merits of a contextual definition that identifies a boxing match as a social setting in which it is inappropriate to speak of violence, but rather to the rigidity and aspectual one-sidedness of an empirical essentialist definition. A third option would be to consider it as a kind of 'legitimate' or at least 'legitimated violence', but this prefix is equally without substance, since no defining characteristic of violence is conceptualized in order for the boxing match to be classified as any kind of violence, legitimate/legitimized or not. When violence is ontologically defined as reduction of being, a much more substantial, and less arbitrary account can be provided for the special case of the violence of a boxing match. It is then possible to say that there is a relatively high degree of violence implied in such a match, since, within the ring, opponents reduce each other to little more than an opponent they need to physically wreck. However, on the total scale of severity of violence, it is not to be equalled to a fight between two men outside the context of a boxing match. Why? Because the boxers only reduce (the ontological horizon of) the other to the degree prescribed by the context of the boxing match. That means they will allow for a change of aspect of the being of their opponent. After the match, they shake hands and walk away. Only when the match 'escalates' and the players engage each other in an irregulatory fashion, when the referee is pushed aside, as sometimes happens, a more severe reduction takes place, in which aspect-change is blocked further than it is in a regular match, and therefore a more severe violence sets in. With the help of the ontological definition of violence, conceptual dilemmas such as that posed by a case like this can be more adequately dealt with.

(3) Because 'violence' is no longer relatively arbitrarily delineated, as it is in any empirical definition, the problem of a rigid classification of 'violence' and 'non-violence' is overcome. Empirical definitions of violence constitute a reduction of the reduction of being that violence is. Violence is then reduced to a quasi-ontological form that, to paraphrase Parmenides, either is or is not. The ontological definition of violence regards it as a *sliding scale*: violence is as severe as the reduction of an ontological horizon that entails a reduction of the possibility of changing the aspect within that horizon. Therefore, to call someone a name constitutes a lesser violence than to throw sticks and stones at him or her. To kill a person is an extreme violence in which only the material aspect of someone's being is highlighted, without the possibility of a change of aspect. Yet to bully a person day in day

out can be of similar severity, since it often leads to reduced mental and physical health and sometimes to suicide or criminal behaviour (cf. Smith and Brain, 2000: 3), and it therefore constitutes a significant reduction of being. It shows a complete lack of respect for the richness of a person's being. The possibility of aspect-change is a crucial element of violence. A raging mad person is frighteningly dangerous because he or she is perceived as having only one thing on his or her mind. Such a person is too 'determined' (without conscious control), and determined to reach an unpleasant end, to come to a change of aspect. For the same reason, a group of people is more threatening than an individual. The group has a larger potential of reduction of being. A group of people unanimously marching the streets is more threatening than an individual, because it is more apparent that they pursue one goal and that a change of aspect is highly unlikely. By a similar token, a procedure is violent, since it objectifies, reduces, without conscience, without the possibility of a change of aspect. The more autonomous procedures are, relative to people, the more violent they usually are. That is one reason why one might object to a judicial 'Legitimation durch Verfahren'. The conceptualization of violence as a sliding scale does justice to the idea that there can be more or less violence, without, however, quantifying the 'more' or the 'less'. It has this advantage for instance via-à-vis a philosophical definition of violence, such as the one espoused by Hent de Vries in *Religion and Violence*. According to De Vries (Vries, 2002: xvii), violence refers to 'any cause, any justified or illegitimate force, that is exerted – physically or otherwise – by one thing (event or instance, group or person, and, perhaps, word and object) on another'. Such a comprehensive definition of violence may capture the omnipresence of violence, but fails to qualify that the *intensity of force* differs. There is a delicate balance between going beyond the commonsensical notion of violence and meaningless comprehensiveness ('if it's everything it's probably nothing').

With respect to the point of extreme cases of personal violence, something needs to be briefly articulated. I have, in this chapter, on occasion spoken of murder, or more precisely, of killing another person as an extreme form of violence. Since the definition of violence is now sufficiently elaborated upon, I should like to answer two residual questions. One is the question concerning, so to speak, the 'end' of the sliding scale of violence. Is to kill a human being the most extreme form of violence? Secondly, what about the subjective intent involved in many cases of violence? Is it entirely irrelevant for determining the degree of violence what the intention of an actor is? I will address these two questions in one compound answer. The reduction of a person to mere matter is indeed one of the most extreme reductions of being, since a change of aspect is not allowed to take place. But why would to kill a person be any more violent than to kill an animal or an inanimate object? There is no doubt that to kill a human being, and, moreover, to kill a human being purposefully, is more violent than to accidentally kill a human being or than to kill, accidentally or not, an animal or plant, or to destroy an inanimate object. The reason for this is entirely compatible with speaking of violence in terms of a situational aspect that pertains to the reduction of being. For to kill a man accidentally is no doubt violent. A far greater violence is it, however, to kill a man purposefully. In both cases, a change of aspect is not allowed for. But in the first case, unlike in the second, *the possibility of allowing a change of aspect is itself not allowed for.* If, by accidentally pushing a button causing someone standing next to me at the rim of the Grand Canyon to be catapulted into death, certainly his or her being has been reduced and certainly there has been violence to a high degree. But crucial to the degree of violence is not only that reduction itself, but also the reduction of the possibility of changing the aspect of a person. I had no way of knowing violence would be the result of my moving my hand, which then accidentally triggered the tragic events that followed. Therefore, there was no way of allowing aspects of the being of the person in question to be selected, or, for that matter, not selected. The point of this is *not* to say that the degree of personal violence therefore depends on the subjective intention of a violent actor. It is imperative that this is not the case, for this would reintroduce into the definition of violence all the problems that the conceptualization of reduction of being is capable of overcoming. While it is certainly true that it would be impossible to speak of violence in the absence of any kind of subjects, the stuff of violence does not reside in any subject. What is meant here is that a more extreme degree of violence lies in the reduction of aspects that are potentially highlighted within a given situation. That is to say that my intentional reduction of a person to mere matter is not only a reduction of his being to but the material aspect thereof, but it also is a reduction, a violation, if one will, of alternative aspects of that person's being that are allowed to be co-constitutive of the situation but that are not allowed to be fully highlighted, that is, to be selected. An example that illustrates this is the torture of a human being. In torture, alternative aspects of a person's being are co-constitutive of the selected aspect, but in a wholly distorted way. Let's, for the moment, presume that torture takes place with no ulterior motive or purpose, but wholly for the sake of torture itself. In such a case, the being of the tortured person is reduced to the material aspect only, as in the case of murdering that person. However, torture is a more sophisticated way of reducing a person to that material aspect than killing a person is. For in torture, the only aspect that is allowed to be selected is the material aspect, whereas other aspects, and in particular what, for want of a better term, can be called the 'spiritual aspect' of that person is co-constitutive of the situation. However, this co-constitutiveness is not the way in which aspects of a person are usually co-constitutive of interaction, even of the interaction in which a person is killed. Rather, the spiritual aspect is remained at-hand in a distorted way, the aspect itself is already reduced. For what happens here is that the spiritual aspect, or the aspect of consciousness, is remained at-hand in such a way that the reduction of being that does not allow that aspect to be selected is explicitly fed as input into the mind of the tortured person. The explicit negation of the possibility of a change of aspect is the specific form of reduction that characterizes torture. The tortured person is not only reduced in his or her being, *he or she is also reduced to the experience of the difference between negation of being and non-negation.* Precisely because a person is always more than what he or she is allowed to be, an intentional reduction of being is more violent than a non-intentional reduction of being. In the case of an intentional reduction of being, a negation of the being of a person takes place against the background of a non-negation of being. In the case of accidental violence, such a background does not exist, since no aspects were allowed or not allowed to be selected. The use of the notion of 'intention' is meant to indicate a certain agentic direction of practice which is never fully realized since it meets with other influences bearing different directions. The practice or situation is always a resultant of such directions. In accidental violence, the absence of intention is therefore the absence of alternative situational possibilities. Intentional violence is violence resulting from the actualization of such situational possibilities; accidental violence is an autonomous breach of the autonomy of the social situation, which consists of actions eliciting each other. The explicit interactional reduction of being is a reduction of being that actualizes the situational possibility of reduction of being. In the case of accidental violence, there is only reduction of being, and there is not: reduction of being against a background of non-reduction. The most extreme forms of violence are actualized in situations which allow for a change of aspect of the being of the other, and in which this possibility is subsequently not actualized. This is why it is possible to say that torturing a person for a certain period of time can be just as extreme a form of violence as killing a person is. One might argue that, in case of torture, a situational change of aspect remains a hypothetical possibility, and that torture, therefore, is still a lesser form of violence than murder. However, during the process of murder, that is, during the extreme reduction of a person, such a change of aspect is still a hypothetical possibility. It ceases to be such a possibility the moment the other person is actually murdered, but then the violence ceases to exist as well – at least in the form in which it did exist, since it is always possible to violate a dead body. In the phenomenology of a situation of torture, a change of aspect is present only as an absence. So this ultimate hypothetical possibility – which already exists as the possibility of external occurrences disturbing the process of violence – of changing the aspect is no criterion for the severity of violence. In fact, no general *prima facie* rule for the severity of violence can be given. This is, after all, not a *mathématique sociale*. However, it can be maintained that, for each form of violence, the intentional form – by which, again, is not primarily meant a subjectively experience intention – is always more violent than the accidental form. Yet it is to be stressed that this only allows for personal forms of violence to be compared; it does not entail that structural violence, which is always 'unintentional', is always a lesser violence than intentional personal violence. Structural violence is altogether situated beyond the category of intention.

Furthermore, the above conceptualization of extreme forms of personal violence also makes it plausible that and why killing a human being is more violent than killing a non–human being. Finally, the result of consistent application of this conceptualization is that forms of structural violence which are not 'avoidable', in Galtung's terms, can be rated as less severely violent than forms of structural violence which can be avoided. While most examples I have given – and will give in what is yet to come – in this chapter pertain to highly simplified situations of a few people interacting, violence is equally present in relations with non–human beings and in relations without distinguishable actor-agency. An example of the latter is structural violence. While Galtung's interpretation of structural violence is flawed in his idea that such violence, by definition, is avoidable, the great insight he has given is that where the possibility of such avoidance does exist, a greater violence is at stake.

Now, without quantification, it is a general truth that, on the sliding scale of violence, the possibility of a change of aspect therefore determines the severity of violence of a social practice. Jack Katz gives some examples that highlight this in exemplary fashion. An American soldier interrogating a Vietnamese peasant woman with the use of physical force during the Vietnam war suddenly stopped doing so when, as Katz (1988: 7) says, 'the interrogee violated the esthetics and the moral stance underlying the ongoing dynamic'. The woman defecated in her pants, and this changed the aspect of the situation in such a way that the soldier was able to see the woman in a different light, to change the aspect of her being. The result was that the soldier could now ask himself 'I'm beating up this girl, for what? What the fuck am I doing?' (Katz, 1988: 7). Another example from the same war is that of a soldier driving a truck through a group of Vietnamese. Only when he stepped out of the truck to see a kid stuck between the wheels staring 'back at him with an absolutely level stare' did he walk away (Katz, 1988: 7). An accidental occurrence can thus cause extreme violence to end by changing the aspect of the situation in such a way that the violent person, in his or her actions, comes to a change of aspect of the person(s) he or she violates. In this example, 'silence and spatial equality broke the momentum' (Katz, 1988: 7). When the aspect of the violent situation changes, it can become possible to see the other in light of more than its physical aspect. Violence is then 'turned down' on the sliding scale. More aspects of an ontological horizon remain ready-at-hand as possible selections. People know this change of aspect is what it's about in such situations. The plea of the person about to be murdered that emphasizes 'I have children' is meant to change the aspect of that person. To make the killer see him or her in a different light, in light of the relationship with his or her children. The killer is requested to act upon more than the material aspect that he or she is intent on exclusively reducing the victim to. That means the killer is requested to not just allow for other aspects to be co-constitutive of the selection of the material aspect of being, but to also allow them to be selected through a change of aspect. Interestingly, research shows that in the case of remorse by an offender of violent crime, such a change of aspect is performed. Remorse is accompanied by a 'humanization' of the victim of the violent crime, and remorseful offenders try to find out many details of the personal life of their victim to indicate how much of a person, a human being it is or was that they violated (cf. Presser, 2003).

Another consequence of seeing violence as a sliding scale is that it becomes possible to regard the 'threat of violence' in a much more realistic way. What usually eludes us when we speak of the threat of violence is the violence of such a threat. The linguistic separation between 'threat' and 'violence' is an expression of a supposed ontological separation. Only when 'violence' is strictly conceptualized as 'physical violence' can this be warranted. Yet it is crucial to regard a threat of violence as characterized by a certain amount of violence itself. The law usually recognizes this, as becomes apparent for instance in the United States Code, which defines 'crime of violence' as 'an offense that is a felony and [...] has as an element the use, attempted use, or threatened use of physical force against the person [...]' (U.S. Penal Code, Section 924 (c) (3), title 18; quoted in U.S. Department of Justice, 1995: 2). A 'threat of violence' reduces a person to a significant extent, that is to say to the extent that the threatened person's possibilities of being are reduced in accordance with the possibility of the exertion of a violence greater than the violence of the threat of violence. A qualification that needs to be added here for the sake of conceptual clarity is that a threat of violence only amounts to violence when the object of violence is another person, not when the object is only a material object. This might seem a superfluous qualification, since no one threatens a tree to cut it down, but this only shows that threats are forms of violence specifically targeted at people, or maybe at animals as well. Violence in general, however, is not limited to sentient beings, since one can violate an inanimate object or a tree and speak of a reduction of its being. This line, which is connected to an increasingly theoretically significant sociology of objects, will not be further pursued here. To return to the violence of a threat of violence, it has to be emphasized that such a threat is not only 'violence'. The point is that it can be seen in the light of an aspect of violence, in that it consists ontologically of a certain reduction of being – one that is more significant than the reduction of being in the absence of a threat of violence in a given interaction. That is why Hobbes writes on the nature of war that it 'consisteth not in actual fighting; but in the known disposition thereto, during all the time there is no assurance to the contrary' (Hobbes, 1969: 143). And like Hobbes (1969: 114) says that 'reputation of power, is power', the threat of violence can legitimately be regarded as a form of violence itself, that is, it can be seen in the light of the aspect of violence as constituting a greater violence than a situation without such a threat and without any other form of unusual violence (compare Aron, 2003: 50; Schinkel, 2009). This breaks open the rigid conceptual structure of conventional social scientific discourse, which usually assumes a subject A, the perpetrator (at least as soon as a threat of violence is transformed into 'actual' violence), intentionally inflicting physical hurt upon subject B, the victim of violence. Here too, a change of aspect is facilitated when violence is defined as a reduction of being. The separation between perpetrator and victim is relevant as a mechanism of attribution of agency. Sociologically, however, the study of violence entails that both 'perpetrator' and 'victim' are necessary preconditions for a process of violence. The victim is never external to violence, and in some cases the presence of a potential victim is what incites, and thus in part causes violence. Either way, it is the *in-between* of the subjects that is the space of violence; the social process is never attributable to a perpetrating subject. Such a reduction of the process-character of violence may take place within the legal system, and then the observation of violence highlights a specific aspect of violence, but this observation has its specific blind spot.

On a different plane, it can be stated that the very label of 'victim' exhibits a certain amount of violence. That is to say, the label of victim has an aspect of violence that can become significantly highlighted if that label becomes an automatic classification of certain subjects involved in violence. While the label has analytical purposes of distinguishing between the agencies of cause and effect, it can in another sense be a constraining classification. In case of sexual violence, for instance, Barry has remarked that 'victimism denies the woman the integrity of her humanity' (Barry, 1979: 45). For a similar reason, Badiou rejects an ethics based on the idea that human beings are predominantly potential victims of evil (Badiou, 2002). As Barry says, 'the assigned label of "victim", which initially was meant to call awareness to the experience of sexual violence, becomes a term that expresses that person's identity' (Barry, 1979: 45). Yet a person's identity is never exhaustively represented in a label that necessarily constitutes a reduction of such an identity. The ontological definition of violence as reduction of being, according to which it is possible to regard empirical cases of violence as positioned along a sliding scale of violence, allows for a consistent conceptualization that can explain, on substantial grounds, just why and how the threat of violence and the label of 'victim of violence' are violent themselves. In addition, the view of violence as a sliding scale solves the problem of the ontological limit between 'violence' and 'non-violence'.

(4) The insight that this definition provides in defining violence itself as one *aspect of a situation or social process* is a fourth advantage. First of all, this

allows a broadening of the narrow focus on subjects and their intentions. Secondly, it enables an escape from an all-encompassing 'definition of the situation' that leaves little room for anything else taking place in social practice. As for the first point, it is clear by now that violence cannot be reduced to subjects. To do this is to do violence to the reality of violence. Violence is the very subjectification and objectification that precedes the situational existence or appearance of a sub-ject. *Before one can speak of a subject, there has been violence.* Violence is, so to speak, the 'end' or 'point of contact' of the relation between subjects. *Violence is the shape of the surface of the subject, which touches the relational between of subjects-in-interaction.* As for the second point, while any practice stands in a certain light, or while, in other words, one aspect of social practice is always highlighted as defining, other aspects are present and co-constitutive of that practice. When I consider violence to be a necessary aspect of all social practice, that does not allow anyone to make the assumption that I say 'violence is everywhere'. Rather, it is that aspect of a social situation, practice or process that concerns the reduction of being of the participants therein. It is therefore possible to say that *violence is the political aspect of any situation*. It is an aspect that is, in most situations, relatively little highlighted. That is why usually we don't become consciously aware of the aspect of violence in a situation in which a waiter brings a person a coffee. The violence that this situation entails, the reduction of that person to 'a customer', and the reduction of the waiter to 'a waiter' is certainly there, but it is only productive for both parties. As soon as the person shouts at the waiter, and especially when he or she hits the waiter, for instance out of dissatisfaction over lack of service, a more drastic reduction takes place, and in the social situation which then exists, the aspect of violence is conspicuously highlighted, since the actions of this social practice are now not geared towards a non-violent goal, the pursuit of which is accompanied by a small amount of violence, but reduction of the other becomes an explicit means and purpose of the actions at the same time. Violence is then moved to the foreground of the interactional horizon. It becomes that towards which the actions of the participants are directed. The waiter is hit, and forgets all about his responsibilities and duties as a waiter – he or she wants to get away, or perhaps retaliate. Violence now sticks out due to the fact that it has significantly increased. A bystander is now likely to predominantly see the situation in light of the aspect of violence. Nonetheless, even then, that is only one aspect of the situation.

(5) A fifth advantage of the definition of violence as reduction of being is that it is able to incorporate the long-standing semantics of the respective etymologies of 'violence' and *Gewalt*. Most of all, the strong connection between these terms and the concept of power has been emphasized. Additional connotations are those of force, control and honour or reputation. These find resonance in the connection between reduction of being and the identity of a person that is constituted by a simultaneous

subjectification and objectification. Every reduction of being in social interaction is the establishment of a relation of power in which the parties or persons involved are reduced to a certain identity that is conceptually analogous to the notions of honour and reputation that are found in the etymologies of violence. The party in interaction which we commonly describe as 'the most powerful' is that party which establishes the greatest reduction of being of the other parties involved. While this party is then 'the most honoured' party, all others are endowed with a certain reputation, and identity as well. Besides this, it is also to be said that the dominant party in interaction is still reduced in its being due to the fact that in any interaction, both the powerful and the powerless are necessarily reduced in order to 'be' powerful and powerless. Violence is always at the same time an externalization of the self and an appropriation of the other by the self. Power and violence are not, as Hannah Arendt says, each other's opposites (Arendt, 1970: 56, 87), but they are different aspects of the same process. Arendt's argument is made with respect to politics. She claims that a powerful state is a state that does not need to resort to violence. Only a weak state knows violence, both in its own assertion as in the private use of violence by its citizens. This argument, however, foregoes the violence of a powerful state because it is exclusively concerned with violence as 'physical violence'. Violence is a relation seen in light of the aspect of reduction of being; power can be regarded as the relation seen in light of potential being, which includes potential reduction of being.

(6) This definition accommodates a view of the process, of the flowing or 'liquid' character of the social. Violence is a process that takes place *in* interaction but is not reducible *to* any empirical event that can be isolated from that interaction. It is the continuous shaping of the ontological horizon of those involved in interaction, and it designates the way the subjects in interaction are able to *be* in interaction. It is only through the interaction that the identities of the subjects involved in it appear as simultaneous subjectifications and objectifications to themselves and to the other(s). There is thus no longer the simultaneous vagueness and rigidity of a notion of violence as something which starts here and ends there, but which, at closer inspection, cannot really be pinned down after all, since all the problems discussed in this chapter and in the preceding one (where does it begin?, where does it end?, where 'is' the violence in a situation called 'violence'?) then resurface to haunt the social science of violence. Hence the popularity of the strategy to not define violence at all but silently presume a (pre-ontological?) understanding of it and hope no one will be a bad sport and start asking questions. A focus on reduction of being, on the other hand, is a focus on the in-between the subjects-in-interaction. Tracing back 'violence' to a perpetrator only, wholly misses the actual violence itself, which always takes place *between* what we tend to call perpetrators and victims. To allot to violence, even to personal violence, a subjective intention to violence is no longer

a necessary condition for being able to speak of violence in social science. A person is violated if he or she is accidentally reduced in his or her being. Such unintentional (personal) violence – let's suppose, for sake of argument, that 'accidental' equals 'unintentional' – is, however, situated lower on the sliding scale of violence. It is crucial to understand why intentional selection of the aspect of violence of a situation amounts to a more violent situation than an unintentional selection of that aspect does. First, that is due to the fact that 'non-intentional violence' is unlikely to last as long as 'intentional violence'. When I accidentally push someone, a reduction of both our being has been established, though more so in case of the person I push than with respect to my being. When I accidentally push someone, the action of my pushing the person does not allow for some aspects of my being to be selected, since the action of pushing, even when unintentionally or even unconsciously performed, entails a certain selection that momentarily excludes alternative selections. As for the person I push, it is obvious that the action reduces him or her. However, I am unlikely to subsequently hit this person after having unintentionally pushed him or her. That means I will be prepared to change the aspect of that person the moment I become aware of my unintentional act. In accordance with the definition as explicated here, this therefore constitutes a lesser violence than an intentional reduction of being of another person does. However, unintentional violence might yet, in some freak case, last long. The most important difference between intentional personal violence and unintentional personal violence therefore lies in the possibility of the possibility of a change of aspect. The possibility of a change of aspect of the other determines the level of violence, that is, the degree to which the aspect of violence in a social situation is highlighted during the unfolding of that situation. Yet specific to a situation of unintentional private personal violence is that the possibility of allowing a change of aspect is not allowed for. It is therefore no problem to provide a consistent and substantial account of unintentional violence with the help of the definition of violence as reduction of being. This, however, only implies (as the somewhat uneasy terminology of '(un-)intentional personal violence' indicates) to personal forms of violence, and it is not to be thought of as implying that structural violence, in which violence is by definition not subjectively intended, is always a lesser kind of violence compared to many forms of private violence. Rather, the concept of 'intention' is to be conceptualized differently then. I do not believe it is necessary to speak of 'collective intentionality', but I think that it is useful instead to assume that institutions, too, possess the possibility of changing the aspects of individual persons. This possibility is related to the steering capacities of institutions and it is the possibility of such institutions to accept input from their environment. It is often formalized in rules and procedures prescribing such possible inputs. The degree to which institutions possess this possibility of changing the aspect of individuals and utilize it is a measure of the level of structural violence they exert. Forms of structural violence that can be traced to a definite set of institutions can therefore be treated as analogous to intentional forms of private violence.

(7) This definition furthermore recognizes the fact that violence always has reference to persons as whole identities. If a person hits another person on the arm, he does not hit or violate that arm, but the whole person. Only an identity as a whole is the object of violence. Through violence, a person as a whole is objectified in a certain way. Violence is that aspect of a human being which concerns the negation of aspects of the human being that is essential to the human being. That is part of the reason why the study of violence needs to ally with an anthropology of social philosophical signature.

(8) The definition of violence as reduction of being is able to highlight the aspect of productivity of violence. There is a tenacious reflex in Occidental thought in general and its social science in specific to one-sidedly regard violence as a destructive phenomenon. This research attitude, which, as far as I can tell at this moment, is present in all definitions of violence, can be termed *biaphobia*. To counter it, two presuppositions of the definition of violence as reduction of being can be put forward. (a) The destructiveness of violence is but one aspect of violence. To focus exclusively on this aspect ignores the aspect of productivity of all violence. Violence can, as Riches one-sidedly stresses, be goal-directed. It can bring desired states of affairs into being. And, as has been argued extensively above, it is the enabling precondition of interaction per se. (b) Violence is to be seen as a sliding scale. The destructive aspect of violence becomes more highlighted, or actualized, when violence, as an aspect of interaction, becomes more highlighted. In other words, the further violence moves up the scale, the more its aspect of destructiveness becomes obvious. However, that still does not mean that the aspect of productivity is then less highlighted. Destructiveness and productivity are not mutually exclusive, but rather observer-relative. The most obvious example of this is the inter-state violence of war. War destroys as well as produces, establishes. That is why Machiavelli, Kant, Hegel and many others assumed that a war can sometimes have a positive, morally cleansing effect on a culture threatening to perish. At the level of the social system as a whole ('society'), violence is an indispensable way of procuring order, be it by uniting or by dividing, both of which, when consistently executed, amount to stability. In everyday forms of violence, the productive aspect may be contained in the overcoming of resentment, or in the formation of a deviant identity when means to establish a non-deviant or 'normal' identity are unavailable. As Jack Katz reports, 'Here "survival" implies being deviant, and being deviant, or "bad", takes on the meaning of *being* in general' (Katz, 1988: 271). Of course it needs to be said that the non-deviant identity is equally characterized by a violence that has both a destructive and a productive aspect. It is therefore quite unrealistic to

juxtapose language and violence as each other's opposites or to assert that violence is the end of all communication, or that violence is the last resort after communication has failed (cf. Ricoeur, 1967: 87). Such a biaphobic theoreticism violates both violence and language. Violence is supported by language and language by violence. That is why Gadamer's 'wirkliche Gespräch', Habermas' 'herrschaftsfreie Diskussion' and the Rawlsian contract are and will remain counterfactual assumptions, ideals designed to eradicate as much as possible the violent aspect of social life. In the end, they do not escape the dialectics of Enlightenment, because such ideals, too, can only be upheld by a reductive effort. The possibility of highlighting the productivity of violence, which sometimes takes the paradoxical form of a violence that facilitates a reduction of violence, is a further advantage of the ontological definition of violence.

(9) The ninth and final advantage of this definition I wish to mention here is that it adds significant weight to the idea that there is more to violence than physical hurt. The conception of 'reduction of being' clearly provides home for an 'extended definition' à la Galtung. That means that it entails the somewhat counter-intuitive possibility of speaking of violence where John Doe probably wouldn't. My assumption, however, has been that the counter-intuitiveness of the definition is in itself irrelevant to its (heuristic) value. If (social) science would have to abide to common intuition, it would first of all become irrelevant, and second, unable to say anything concerning common sense that would not already be common sense. But there is another substantial reason to transcend common understanding of what violence is. First of all, it is to be clear in what sense violence as 'reduction of being' differs from the common perception of violence as intentional physical hurt. The basic difference here concerns the depth of understanding of the phenomenon. While the commonsensical notion of violence defines it merely by reference to empirical cases that have already been defined as violence in a similar way, this strategy clearly begs the question. It lacks a substance of violence, an answer to the question just *why* these events are classified as violence, what it is that *makes* them violent. When violence is seen as reduction of being, such substance is provided for. Accordingly, this definition does not refute the common understanding of violence. Where the common intuition of violence applies, this definition is almost certain to apply as well. However, because it does so on the basis of an intrinsic criterion of demarcation, the opposite situation, being that it identifies violence where the common perception does not, is an equally legitimate possibility. It claims that the reason violence is recognized in some cases – which are usually those of intentional physical hurt – is due to the experience of a reduction of being that is not reflexively recognized as such, since one would have to be a social scientist or perhaps a philosopher to reflect on it in such a way, like one needs to be a physicist to reflect on matter as energetic particle waves, or a psychologist to reflect on aggression

as sublimated sexual desire. Violence as reduction of being is thus a second-order observation of a process which may or may not be recognized as violence by a first-order observer. This therefore allows reductions of being not commonly perceived as violence to be recognized as such. Examples are Galtung's concept of structural violence and Bourdieu's concept of symbolic violence.

An element of social epistemology is sufficient reason to put forward this second-order observation, or as it has been called in the opening frame of Chapter 2, this meta-theory of violence. For any semantics of violence is itself infected with violence. Violence, in that sense, is the archetypical distortion of pure representation. The first-order observation of violence suffers from this more than the second-order observation, because of its substantial lack of artificial second-order reflexivity. Precisely because the observation and non-observation of violence is a matter of power and violence itself, the definition of violence cannot be left at the hands of the first-order observer, who is too pre-reflexively immersed in the social, or who may in some cases even have a stake in the non-observation and non-recognition of violence. Sociologically, it is relevant to uncover the socially productive negation (for instance the 'practical *negations*' and 'the *collective misrecognition*') (Bourdieu, 1993: 74, 81) of the social world if a genuine understanding of violence is to be gained.

Private violence, state violence, structural violence

In the above, the concepts 'private violence' and 'structural violence' have been used although not adequately conceptually distinguished. This needs to be done in relation to a third kind of violence, which is state violence. These three forms of violence will, throughout this book, be regarded as ideal-typical forms of violence. Private violence will be understood as the reduction of being exerted by individuals or groups without state authority, although not necessarily recognized as illegitimate. The notion of state violence designates all reduction of being emanating, in the end, from the state and backed by its authority and monopoly of legitimate violence. Structural violence concerns all reduction of being not exerted by a locatable agent, but emanating from the differentiation of the social system as a whole. In Chapter 8, these forms of violence will also be conceptually linked to each other by means of the concept of the *trias violentiae*.

Two questions

Two questions remain: (1) does the definition of violence not defer the problem of the objectivity of the observation of violence from first order to second order?, (2) does this definition itself escape violence? To the first question, the answer is that this is in part the case, but that this is not a problem at all, but a merit of any scientific conceptualization. The advantage of a scientific definition of a certain phenomenon or process lies in the deeper understanding that it yields relative to commonsensical understanding or practical knowledge. Does this definition, then, incorporate all aspects of violence? It no doubt does not, but because it is an ontological definition, it does avoid the necessary negation of aspects of violence that takes place with the use of every (empirical) definition of violence as an ontic 'thing'. Yet, to turn now to the second question (whether or not this definition escapes violence), the answer will have to be that it does not, and that the ontological difference is itself characterized by a certain violence. While René Girard (1985: 171) have stressed the violence of Heidegger's ontology, that violence was self-professed (Heidegger, 1993: 327). Its sociological adaptation that I have put to work in this chapter is no different in this respect. The paradoxical character of this enterprise will be fully explicated in Chapter 9. For now, it suffices to say that there is no doubt that the violence of the definition of violence stands out in its productive aspect for the understanding of violence. The unenviable task (Galtung) of 'putting things straight' in social science (Bauman) by defining violence, constitutes a predominantly productive counter-violence against the predominantly destructive violence of not defining violence in a social science that claims to study 'violence'.

4
From Critique of Violence to Autotelic Violence: Rereading Walter Benjamin

Reflections on violence usually turn out to be more focused on class struggles, on a 'diagnosis of the times', than on violence. They sooner speak about causes of violence than about violence itself. Or they turn their attention towards violence as evil, thus sliding off to 'the problem of evil', this being rather 'the problem of God'. They reflect upon the issues of morality raised by violence, but not on violence itself. Or, as is the case in Walter Benjamin's *Zur Kritik der Gewalt*, they reflect more on law and justice than on violence. Though I will no doubt fail to do so, I want to approach a fundamental understanding of violence by taking Benjamin's text as a point of departure. Why this text, and why not any other that is supposedly about violence?

There is a sense of urgency in Benjamin's essay. The unsettling combination of destruction and constitution of order that is achieved by violence, is present throughout the essay. Violence becomes apparent as the pivot around which law is organized. But his text offers anchor points for yet another theory of violence, a fundamental theory of violence, one that intends to touch upon the *eidos* of violence. A theory that recognizes the *intrinsic* aspect of violence alongside its *instrumental* uses. For though Benjamin speaks about 'violence itself as a principle' (Benjamin, 1965: 29), and of 'the essence of violence' (*das Wesen der Gewalt*) (Benjamin, 1965: 63), in doing so, he is more interested in the possibility of a distinction between sanctioned and non-sanctioned forms of violence, and the consequences of this possibility for the essence of violence. As such, Benjamin never really arrives at that 'essence'. His 'critique of violence' is synonymous to 'the philosophy of its history', since only the idea of its 'end' can make a visibility of its temporal manifestations with the use of critical distinctions possible.[1] Benjamin's critique of violence thus unfolds itself as a treatise on law and justice, ending with the pessimistic hope of a messianism without a Messiah when he speaks of a 'divine violence' (*göttliche Gewalt*). If there is such a 'thing' as an essence of violence, it is bound to escape Benjamin in the distinctions he makes in order to capture it. His main – that is, his preferred – distinction is that between mythical violence (*mythische Gewalt*) and 'divine violence'. This is not a binary opposition, nor is it a distinction which can be dialectically turned into a synthesis of both, for it is the distinction between the domain of representation and the unrepresentable, between the demonic and the divine, between an omnipresent violence of, for and in the name of the law, and the possibly impossible possibility of its *Aufhebung*: a divine violence, which is pure (*die reine Gewalt*) and which ends the *Setzung* of law by means of mythical violence by once and for all realizing *justice* (Benjamin, 1965: 64). Why is the possibility of such a divine violence 'possibly impossible'? Because it is an *Aufhebung* which annuls itself qua *Aufhebung*: it destroys instead of preserves in synthesis, because it cannot be *aufgehoben* itself, and, most importantly, because it may never come – and even if it were to come, it would be unrecognizable (Benjamin, 1965: 64). Furthermore, it is possible to say that if it were to arrive, it would not even be able to manifest itself the way Benjamin describes it: as purely destructive. For it would – and Benjamin only hints at this, though he almost fears and resents it – immediately turn into mythical violence. Amid all of this, it is precisely the *pure violence*, violence in its most *pure form* qua violence, that is lost.

But Benjamin's text offers other paths than the one it ventures on itself. Precisely because Benjamin's is a *critique* of violence, the conceptual distinctions he makes use of are unusually explicit. These distinctions shed light on what Benjamin ultimately does *not* discuss: that pure violence, or that essence of violence he claims to philosophize on. I will first discuss Benjamin's distinctions in detail, in order to clarify them and to then move away from them. Derrida, who has critically discussed Benjamin's conceptual distinctions in *Force de loi*, would be apt to say that it is only possible to move away from these distinctions by way of differing in relation to them. It is indeed, as I will discuss, precisely the epochè of Benjamin's *Leitdifferenzen*, or the dissolving of their opposites, in relation to which I wish to speak about a more 'pure', perhaps 'original' violence. Since Benjamin's is a complex text, not only qua minimalistic style, but also because of the traditions it is rooted in, it is only by means of a careful analysis of *Zur Kritik der Gewalt* that a 'pure' or 'original violence' can perhaps be highlighted.

Zur Kritik der Gewalt

How does Benjamin come to a 'critique of violence', and does he even really come to it? He defines what a critique of violence amounts to right at the beginning of his text: its task is to come to a representation of the relation between violence and law and justice. For, he says, any *causa efficiens* only becomes 'violence' the moment it enters the realm of moral relations (*sittliche Verhältnisse*). Law and justice are the key concepts of that realm. Violence means a breach of moral relations, which are characterized by the centrality of law and justice. A first step is thus taken. Second step: the most fundamental relation in any juridical order is that between means and ends. Third step: violence can only be located on the side of the means, not of the ends. It is important that Benjamin does not hereby intend a critique that is based on the justness of the ends for which violence is a means, for that would not give a criterion of violence itself as a principle, but rather of the cases in which it is applied (Benjamin, 1965: 39). Such a more specific critical starting point has, says Benjamin, been blotted out by the tradition of natural law, which never sees any problem in the application of violent means to justified ends. As long as the causes are just, the use of violent means remain unproblematic. Benjamin's discomfort with this tradition leads him to turn to the alternative tradition of positive law, in which the justification of the means occupies a central place. Benjamin explains that natural law can critique any existing law only in light of its ends, while positive law can judge factual law only by means of a critique of its means. Their legitimacy or lawfulness becomes the overriding criterion. While positive law is blind to the absoluteness of the ends, natural law is blind for the relativity of the means. Because positive law does allow for a distinctive view of violent means – one that is able to distinguish between kinds of violence irrespective of the goals they are meant to further – Benjamin prefers, for the purpose of his study, the viewpoint of positive law. He adds, however, that it will become clear that a perspective outside of both positive law and natural law is what is really needed. This is what he intends to develop as his critique of violence. Still within the discourse of positive law, then, Benjamin adheres to the common distinction between legitimate (in the sense of lawful) and illegitimate (unlawful) violence. These, he notes, amount to a distinction between non-sanctioned violence and sanctioned violence. This distinction is not intended as a means of classification of violence. It is rather the consequence of the possibility of such a distinction for the essence of violence (*das Wesen der Gewalt*) that he is interested in. As a basis of this distinction, Benjamin says, there must function a hypothetical criterion of the existence or non-existence of a general historical recognition of the respective ends of both sanctioned and non-sanctioned violence. Ends that lack such a recognition are called 'natural ends' (*Naturzwecke*); those that are recognized as legitimate are called 'lawful ends' (*Rechtszwecke*). And yet, this remains a 'hypothetical criterion', since the ends as such are not really decisive here. Natural ends are all those ends of individual persons. Characteristic of the law is the condemnation of these, when they are pursued by means of violence. All these natural ends are to be replaced by lawful ends; no individual is allowed the use of violence in pursuit of natural ends (Benjamin, 1965: 34). The historical recognition of ends in the tradition of positive law first and foremost serves to preserve the law itself. And it is not the natural ends per se that the law perceives as a threat to its existence, but the very being of violence outside the law.

The monopoly of violence of the law (more precisely of the state) is in the self-interest of the law. The law first and foremost intends itself. Benjamin offers an example as 'evidence' of this conception of the law: the figure of the 'great criminal'. Whatever appalling ends his violence was directed towards, the people still feel sympathy for him, which is actually an underlying sympathy for something that threatens the law by contradicting it. Intent on showing that even in cases where a certain amount of violence is legitimate, the law fears private forms of violence – as I have called them – Benjamin gives another example. This is the example of the strike, which constitutes a form of violence that the law allows by way of exception. There is violence in the strike, since it is used as a kind of blackmail. The situation in which the law, with its monopoly of violence, allows for a certain amount of violence outside itself, de-paradoxizes the moment the strike turns into a revolutionary general strike. Then, the state will declare that the right to strike is being misused and, by way of exception, the exceptional case of the strike will be forbidden, as it now causes too much of a threat to the law. This shows, according to Benjamin, that violence is not something unfit to ground or modify juridical relations in a relatively stable manner. On the contrary, violence can provide the ground to a system of law, regardless of experienced injustice. It can be both law-establishing (*rechtssetzend*) and law-enforcing or law-preserving (*rechtserhaltend*). Benjamin gives another example to further elucidate this. The violence of war is an example of law-establishing violence. That is why, Benjamin says, war is usually ritually sanctified by a piece that marks an instauration of the juridical order. Yet in the days of general military service, this violence also becomes law-enforcing, since the subjection of individuals to military ends has become a lawful end (*Rechtszweck*). The distinction between law-establishing violence and law-enforcing violence is not 'pure'; Benjamin intends to show that the two are intertwined, at times occurring simultaneously. That is precisely the internal contradiction of the law. A duality is visible in the function of military violence, and in a ghostly mix (*einer gespenstischen Vermischung*) violence exists in the modern institution of the police (Benjamin, 1965: 43). The law in general appears in such a double moral light (*in so zweideutiger sittlicher Beleuchtung*) that one might even wonder, Benjamin says, whether at all there are non-violent ways to deal with conflicting interests. Benjamin wants to point out that the violence of the law is neither purely law-enforcing or -preserving nor wholly law-establishing. Any law-enforcement at the same time contains an aspect of law-establishment, of *Setzung* of law. This becomes most apparent in the 'highest violence', that which concerns life and death, as it appears within the law: the death penalty. Its meaning is not exclusively contained in its punishment of a breach of law, but it at the same time ordains the law, as can be deduced from the disproportionate punishment the death penalty often constituted in early juridical orders. Benjamin infers: 'in the exertion of violence over life and death, more than in any other instance of law, the law reinforces itself'. The modern institution of the police is another example of a mix between both forms of violence of the law (these are, says Benjamin, *aufgehoben* in the police). The violence of the police is law-establishing because it ordains regulations, and it is law-enforcing, because it engages in the lawful upholding of the goals that are defined as *Rechtszwecke*. This leads Benjamin to say that the modern institution of the police is the most dangerous kind of police. What Benjamin works towards is the idea that all violence of the law is characterized by the duality *rechtssetzend-rechterhaltend*. Furthermore, he wants to argue that all law is contained in a circular violent movement. All violence, he says, is, as a means, either law-establishing or law-enforcing. There furthermore is a conflation of these categories; both are often combined. The crucial point Benjamin makes is not this mixing of types of violence; it is rather the fact that the law is frittered with either kind of violence. Both natural law and positive law come together in the shared dogma that 'just causes can be reached by just means, just means can be directed towards just causes' (Benjamin, 1965: 31). Benjamin slowly works towards a critique of the violence of law and of law as such. Within the law, there is no resolving of conflict without violence. And it is the archaeo-historical perspective that is crucial here. What Benjamin writes, it slowly crystallizes, is a *Verfallsgeschichte*, a history of the demise of justice and language. In order to make this clear, we shall have to venture outside this text (without really leaving it) to provide it with the context Benjamin silently presupposes.

Messianism and violence

To see what is at stake in *Zur Kritik der Gewalt*, the text needs to be seen in light of Benjamin's ideas on language, history and messianistic theology. In the same way in which violence marks the transition, or perhaps the inter-penetration, between the theory of law and its *praxis*, there is a relation between language and action. In Benjamin's letter to Martin Buber, this becomes apparent at a relatively early stage in Benjamin's thought. In this letter, he explains why he feels unable to cooperate with Buber and his journal *Der Jude*. Benjamin is appalled by the enthusiasm many German Jews have with respect to the outbreak of the First World War. Most importantly, however, it is a certain conception of *language* Benjamin takes issue with. The instrumental view of language, in which language is an arbitrary tool which has a certain purpose, is a kind of language Benjamin conceives as demonic. Political action and language only come together in a wordless sphere (Benjamin, 1978: 127).

Crucial in the connection between language and (the history of) law is an understanding of what is at stake in Benjamin's early essay *Über Sprache überhaupt und über die Sprache des Menschen* (1916). In the metaphysics of language that Benjamin writes there, human language has its place among a natural language, which is a language of things (Benjamin speculates it can also be found in certain art forms) and a divine language, the language of God. Man stands above mere things in that he has received the gift of the language of names. This Benjamin draws from the first chapters of the book of *Genesis*. He furthermore postulates Genesis' paradisaical situation as the realm of an adamic language, which consists solely, or *purely*, of *names*. The Jewish theological background of Benjamin's though is apparent here. In Jewish thought, the *name* quite often takes a central place as the word and essence of God. The name of God is also the medium of the creation of the word (Scholem, 1960). The name is thus seen as the essence of language. Through naming, human language gains sight of the divine trace in the language of things. And through the name, therefore, the spiritual being of man 'communicates' itself to God. Through naming, man addresses God, the 'original' name, which remains unspeakable. Moreover, in the name, language addresses *itself*. It addresses itself through the name, since the name is the essence of language. The language of a human being is the medium through which it communicates its spiritual essence in the form of a name, especially as a 'proper name'. Man *names* nature, which addresses man in a nameless and mute language, a residue of God's word of creation. All higher language is translation of lower language; highest is the clarity of God's word, which is the unity of all language. This vertical axis of language is complemented by a horizontal axis, which has a diachronic structure De Cauter, 1999: 110). While the essence of language, and, one might say, the 'original' language has no object and no means – it is immediate in the double sense of being direct, unmediated and of not being a means to an end exogenous to itself – world-history is marked by language, by many languages in fact that have fallen from that essence.

Benjamin sees a general trajectory of human history. Again, Genesis is the inspiration. The paradisaical situation of a nomenclature that is in immediate presence with all things only lasts for as long as man resides in paradise. As soon as man was banned from paradise, he lost this pure language, and has forevermore tried to regain it. The Fall of man and his original sin mark the end of unmediated language. From a language of the name, which was able to pick up on the divine residues in things and to then address man's own spiritual being to God through the name, a language of words comes into being. Language has now become a means to an end external to the means. The word is a mere sign, a medium. This instrumental language has turned away from things, from their presence and their unmediated contemplation. Exemplary of this is the story of the confusion of tongues of Babel. Man's attempt to regain access to the divine is countered by God in a multiplica-tion of languages. God, the untranslatable name, condemns man to an endless task of translation in which every word is marked by its inadequacy, as is therefore every translation. The immanent magic of the name is lost. It is only to be found again in a messianic arrival. That is why, in the text

Die Aufgabe des Übersetzers, Benjamin ascribes a kind of messianic task to the translator. His is a task of restoration, of return to the adamic language. The diachronic analysis of the fall of language thus starts with the Fall of original sin. To understand how that Fall is at the same time a fall into world-history, and into the history of good and evil, or a history of the law, we must return to the beginning once more. In Genesis, paradise is pictured as containing both the tree of life and the tree of knowledge. The paradisaical situation is 'governed' by the tree of life, which exemplifies the unmediated relationship between God and all his creatures. As soon as the fruits of the tree of knowledge were eaten, the world changed, since it was now separated into two realms. The tree of knowledge is the tree of the knowledge of good and evil. The moment man gained this knowledge, his unmediated presence with the world was broken in two. The world was now divided into good and evil, the sacred and profane, the legitimate and the illegitimate, the pure and the impure. The tree of knowledge has meant a differentiation out of the undifferentiated world of the tree of life. Christian interpretations stress the idea that God had to expel man from paradise, for as man gained God's knowledge of good and evil, only the fruits of the tree of life would stand in his way of gaining a life as eternal as that of God himself. The Jewish mystical tradition Benjamin is situated in tends to stress the messianic restoration of paradise under the tree of life. From the moment of the Fall, all things stand in the light of the distinction between good and evil. What was one is now divided.

The Fall therefore marks the beginning of world-history. It is not a moment *in* history, but its very inauguration. Joining Kant – as Benjamin says philosophy should in his *Programm der Kommenden Philosophie* – Benjamin's 'critique' of violence becomes interwoven with a philosophy of history. He makes use of a tripartite distinction between kinds of history. After the pre-historical 'natural history', the Fall inaugurates 'world-history', which is followed by the history of God as a reunification of what had been separated in world-history. What we normally refer to as 'history' is this world-history for Benjamin, a history that starts with the Fall of man and that ends with the coming of the messianic divine history. In his *Theologisch-politisches Fragment*, Benjamin therefore says that only the Messiah completes history in the sense that he (sic) completes and ends the messianic relation itself (Benjamin, 1965: 95). This is why, as one commentator has said, 'Benjamin appears as a theologian *manque*, fighting to break out of materialistic categories, who finally forsakes the angel of historical materialism for the Messiah of Jewish theology' (Beiner, 1984: 423). Only in this light can Benjamin's rejection of Buber's invitation be truly understood. Buber's political *engagement* is based on an *instrumental* notion of language. Buber uses the journal *Der Jude* as a way of influencing political affairs. What that in fact amounts to is a use of fallen language within world-history to restore the Fall into morality. Yet only something from *outside* that history can inaugurate divine history (Benjamin, 1965: 95). The realm of God is not the *telos* of a historical *dynamis*; it cannot become a goal within world-history. Only a return to an unmediated language, and, in the moral realm, to an *unmediated justice*, can mean a restoration of the paradisaical situation. Benjamin therefore condemns the idea of historical progress. Progress remains bound to the logic of means and ends, the logic of mediation that is a result of a broken immediateness, which was the direct presence with the world of paradise. Progress would thus be the end of a world-historical future altogether. In the *Geschichtsphilosophische Thesen*, Benjamin says that progress lies not in the future, but in the past. A storm blows from paradise, and 'that, which we call progress, is that storm' (Benjamin, 1965: 85). The only possible progress lies in remembrance of the Fall. The historian's task is to save the past for the future. Benjamin accordingly attributes a 'weak messianic power' to each generation (Benjamin, 1965: 79).

It is therefore with a certain negativity that Benjamin approaches history, and, since world-history after the Fall is a history of good and evil, the history of the legitimate and the illegitimate – the history of the law. Yet this negativity, Marcuse has remarked, is at the same time a positivity in Benjamin's approach (Marcuse, 1965: 104). A reasonably accurate summary of *Zur Kritik der Gewalt* would be the following: since man's original sin, the world is divided into the legitimate and the illegitimate. The categories of the law are thus a result of the Fall of man. Both law-establishing violence and law-enforcing violence are categories of a logic of means and ends. Their demonic cycle will have to be broken by a messianic force that breaks into this logic from outside, thus bringing justice to the world once and for all. Only with this in mind can Benjamin's text be properly understood. We can now pick it up where we left it.

All law is contained in a circular violent movement of law-establishing and law-enforcing violence. Within the realm of law, a non-violent resolution of conflict is impossible according to Benjamin (1965: 45–6), since it at least leads to the threat of violence in case of a breach of settlement or contract. Neither can any parliament come to a non-violent political consensus, since any accomplishments of a parliament in the end amount to juridical decrees which are violent in establishment and enforcement. For Benjamin, then, even a last unmediated sphere of non-violent conflict-resolution, the sphere of language, has been appropriated by the law. Only late in its fall has the violence of the law entered this sphere. Benjamin infers this from the modern punishment of lie and deceit. It becomes apparent in this that the law acts in contradiction with its own violent nature, since while it used to violently counter private forms of violence, it now uses violent means to counter what are, according to Benjamin, non-violent actions (deceit) out of fear of possible violent responses (by the deceived). And so the 'pure means' of violence that is *rechtssetzend* are time and again complemented by a violence that is *rechtserhaltend*. The law does not serve lawful ends, but it first and foremost serves to conserve itself. This 'ghostly mix' between law-establishing and law-enforcing or law-preserving violence is a perversion. Law-enforcing (law-preserving) violence is threatening.[2] In a sociological jargon that still does not quite express what is at stake, one might say that the law is characterized by a kind of 'goal-displacement'. It has become its own goal, and even as such, it still functions as a *means*, as we shall shortly see. In *Schicksal und Charakter*, Benjamin already speaks of this problematic nature of the law as a 'leftover of man's demonic stage of existence' (Benjamin, 1965: 71).

Law has taken the place of justice. It is a leftover from a demonic stage in history. Benjamin also refers to the law as having a mythical structure. In his essay on language he refers to the 'mythical origin of the law'. This mythical origin both explains why the law has taken the place of justice, and why, as a 'leftover' from a demonic age, it still exists.

The law's mythical origin

Within both natural law and positive law, there is no way out of the problem that the violence of law tends to grow rampant in preserving the law itself in a dialectic of means and ends based on a violent *Setzung* of the law. Neither is there a non-violent settlement of human affairs. This leads Benjamin to reflect on wholly *other* forms of violence that do not fall within the realm of the bifurcated theory of law but cannot be excluded from world-historical existence (Benjamin, 1965: 54). This questions the shared basic dogma of natural and positive law: that just ends can be achieved by justified means, and that justified means can be used to attain just ends. According to Benjamin, reason cannot decide over the justice of ends and the justifiability of means. One can never know whether these can conflict with each other. Only God can decide upon the justness of ends. What is a just end in one situation can be unjust in another, albeit similar situation. The generalizability of the law conflicts with this. Problems of law are therefore, Benjamin says, in the end indecidable. So he intends to reflect upon the possibility of an unmediated kind of violence.

One such kind of violence Benjamin finds in the violence that accompanies anger, which is not a means, but a manifestation of anger. Such 'objective manifestation' can be found in Greek myth. In its 'original' form, mythical violence is purely a manifestation of the gods, not a means for their ends, but a manifestation of their being. Their violence establishes law, it does not punish infringements upon an already existing law. Benjamin gives the example of Niobe. This example shows that this mythical violence, which establishes a law, is not really destructive, since it slays Niobe's children yet not their mother, whom it leaves guiltier than before, as a mark of the difference between gods and men. It is for this reason that there is a similarity between the violence of the myth and the violence of the establishment of law. For law-establishing violence too is not a 'pure means'. Like the violence of the myth, it is ambiguous (*zweideutig*). It is not a pure mani-festation of justice, but it is *entangled with power*. Benjamin gives examples derived from the realm of state-law to show that, like the violence of the Niobe myth, law-establishing violence lingers on after the establishment of law. There, one finds the same act of drawing a border (*Grenzsetzung*) that one finds in Niobe's myth when his children are slain but their mother is condemned to a life of guilt under the threat of the violence of the gods. This drawing a border is (arche)typical of law establishing violence (*das Urphänomen rechtssetzender Gewalt überhaupt*), says Benjamin. Where borders are drawn, the opponent is not simply destroyed but, however big the power of the conqueror, 'rights' are accorded to him. Benjamin interprets this as drawing the vanquished party into a violent grip. Like the mother of Niobe's slain children, the vanquished party in a war remains in the grip of the victor. That is why a war is usually ritually ended with a 'peace'. Such a line, or border, is ambiguous in that it is supposedly the same for both parties, yet this line, which neither party may cross, is in effect more favour-able to the victor than it is to the vanquished. Benjamin illustrates this with an example that shows how 'mythical ambiguity' applies to all realms of law. He quotes Anatole France's satirical saying that it is equally prohibited for the rich and poor to sleep under bridges. The point being, of course, that this equality is ambiguous in that the law solely affects the poor, since the rich don't desire to sleep under bridges. Violence that is law-establishing is therefore called 'mythical' by Benjamin. It is not a 'pure means', it is not discarded the moment law is established, but it lingers on, this time even as an unmediated manifestation of power:

> The function of violence in the establishment of law is twofold, in the sense that law making pursues as its end, with violence as the means, *what* is to be established as law, but at the moment of instatement does not dis-miss violence; rather, at this very moment of law establishment, it specifi-cally and immediately establishes as law not an end unalloyed by violence but one necessarily and intimately bound by it, under the title of power. Law-making is power making, assumption of power, and to that extent an immediate manifestation of violence. Justice is the principle of all divine end making, power the principle of all mythical establishment of law
>
> (Benjamin, 1965: 56–7)

Justice is a messianic promise; world-history only knows law. A law whose violence of establishment lingers on because the law is a form of power, or better yet, it is an incorporation of power. This is where Benjamin's Judaic theological roots and his materialist background come together. He provides a theological archaeology of what Pascal, following Montaigne, has called 'le fondement mystique' of the law (Pascal, 1976: 63). The instauration of law is a violent matter of fate. Fate is ambiguous; it is violent since there is no higher authority to sanction and regulate it. As soon as law has been established, it bans all violence from the private sphere, though even then it is not safe, since there is, as Derrida notes, even something within the law that threatens it (Derrida, 1994: 87). This is what the example of the (revolutionary) strike is intended to show. In law, violence lingers on. That is why 'there is something rotten within the law' (Benjamin, 1965: 43). Power is a continuous manifestation of the inaugural violence of the law that has not been discarded, but keeps on serving lawful ends. Benjamin concurs with Sorel's 'metaphysical truth' that all law has always been the law of the powerful. And it will always be that, since, from the perspective of violence which alone can guarantee the law, there is no equality, only – at best – equally great violence. Violence is the privilege of the powerful. It is the crucial combination of historical materialism and Judaean theological messianism that allows for Benjamin to find a way out of this 'mentality of violence'. The law is necessarily bound up with violence. Benjamin says, in terms reminiscent of Machiavelli and Carl Schmitt, that the consciousness of the latent presence of violence in the law prevents it from degenerating (Benjamin, 1965: 46). But he then makes a last, crucial distinction in his 'critique' of violence.

Mythical versus divine violence

This distinction is the one between mythical and divine violence (*die Göttliche Gewalt*). It is coined by Benjamin to break the circle of the violence of law. Divine violence is a messianic figure intended first of all to think the end of that circle. Benjamin also calls it the *pure* violence. Because the mythical manifestation of immediate violence is identical to the violence of law, Benjamin says this violence shares in the problematic of the law's historical function, and its destruction becomes a task. It is as though this necessity to conceptualize a way out of the violence of the law becomes a moral imperative for Benjamin. For it is a task that spurs, for one last time, the question of a pure immediate violence. Over against myth, Benjamin places God. This move not only shifts the meaning of their respective forms of violence; it implicitly contains, as Derrida has noted, the opposition Greek-Jewish, and the moral hierarchy that Benjamin thus assumes to exist between these modes of thought. The Jewish addition is thought to be a way out and destruction of what the Greek tradition has bred in terms of the law, which asserts itself through a violence that coincides with the power of a status quo, which both theories of positive and natural law implicitly support. This is a tradition of drawing borders, a necessary consequence of all world-history, which cannot but distinguish what was undifferentiated in the beginning. Divine violence is therefore neither law-establishing nor law-preserving or -enforcing, but it is free of this violent circle of the law; it is law-destroying (*rechtsvernichtend*). And where mythical violence draws borders, divine violence destroys without limitations; where mythical violence bears guilt yet requites, divine violence does away with guilt; whereas mythical violence threatens, divine violence strikes, and while mythical violence may be bloody, divine violence is lethal without blood. While mythical violence is violence informed by a modern vitalism that cares about all individual life for the sake of life itself, a divine and pure violence cares only about the living itself.

Benjamin juxtaposes the modern vitalism inherent in mythical violence to a divine violence that cares not about taking one or two lives, not for the living in the plural (life), but for the living in the singular. The reason for this is that justice cannot be negotiated by means of life. Mythical violence is informed by the reasoning that more important than justice is a being, and its being itself. Because non-being of man in general is, to this vitalism, more fearful than the not-yet-being of the just man, Benjamin concludes that it reduces life to the level of plant and animal. And even if such life would be declared as holy as the life of man, its holiness would have to be something transcending the banal physical manifestations of its life. Man, to Benjamin, never coincides with his life, nor with any of his momentary characteristics and physical shape. Modern vitalism thus seems to be a last attempt at searching for the holiness that the Western tradition has lost, in the cosmologically impenetrable (Benjamin, 1965: 63). Mythical violence accordingly is the result of a fallen tradition in which a cosmological view is connected to the suspension of justice by existing powers. Mythical violence executes bloody caesuras that preserve those unjust balances of power. Divine violence is a messianic promise, or hope, to one day end this situation. The critique of violence has to be the philosophy of its history, for the very opposition between mythical violence and pure, divine violence would be unseen were it not for this philosophy. In other words, Benjamin proposes to see the history of violence in an alternative (cosmological) light, so that not only the distinction between law-establishing violence and law-enforcing (law-preserving) violence is seen, but also their difference vis-à-vis divine violence. There is, however, a final difference between mythical and divine violence, or better yet, a last difference that is infinite. According to Benjamin, only mythical violence can be known as such with certainty. Like the Messiah standing at the gates of Rome in drags, unrecognized, in Blanchot's story, divine violence remains unknown, even if it were to arrive (see Derrida in Caputo, 1997: 24). When pure, immediate, divine violence manifests itself is never quite possible to determine. It might manifest itself in all the 'eternal forms' that the *Mythos* corrupted by means of law, but one will never be able to tell when one has encountered it. Benjamin radically states that all mythical, law-establishing violence, and all law-enforcing violence that aids it, is to be rejected. All divine violence can be called sovereign, yet it is always, Benjamin says, insignia and seal, never the means of a holy execution. For whoever claims divine violence and uses it as a means to an end, takes it into the mythical sphere of instrumentalism.

Benjamin therefore poses divine violence as a way out of mythical violence and the violence that preserves the law, but since divine violence necessarily remains remote or at least not recognized, unknown, his is a (revolutionary) messianism without Messiah.

Perhaps like no other of his generation, Benjamin has embodied a messianic power. In the remainder of this chapter, I wish to address two issues. One, does Benjamin succeed in contemplating a way out of mythical violence in particular and perhaps even violence in general, or does he at least find a possible way out of the violence of the law? Two, does Benjamin succeed in contemplating a pure and immediate violence?

Is there a beyond violence?

One theme that seems to subsist throughout Benjamin's work is that of escaping from a fallen situation, and of *returning* to a paradisaical state that *is yet to come*. In particular, he has wanted to escape from violence (compare Benjamin, 1977: 9). He wants to write for revolution, but not for fascism (or for a fascist revolution). But is there not always, even after a revolution and even after a manifestation of divine violence, a fall back into the mythical categories of means and ends? What comes *after* the revolution, and *after* divine violence? Benjamin would perhaps reply that such questions are a result of thinking in world-historical terms, and that these are suspended 'after' revolution or divine violence. If, therefore, his view is to be attacked on the grounds that his historical scheme will be unable to shut out (mythical) violence, that scheme itself is to be critiqued. It is possible to do that in its beginning. The paradisaical situation knows no law, since the tree of knowledge of good and evil is untouched. The *origin* of the law is *founded* in that tree and the expulsion from paradise, the Fall, that is subsequent to man's 'consumption' of its fruit. This seems to shortcut the problem of the foundation and legitimation of law in a 'magical' way. This, however, is strangely paradoxical. For the fruits of the tree of knowledge were *forbidden*. *Before* the knowledge of the law, there was therefore a law.[3] Even this transcendent origin of the law is thus incapable of preceding the law. Seen in light of this aspect, Genesis concerns the adamic form of the tautology of the law and the ever-present problem of what Carl Schmitt has called – in the realm of the political – a state of exception. Even in paradise, law has to be founded by something outside the law, by a force, which is exempted from the law and in case of which therefore the very question of justice is suspended. This is the inaugural violence of the law, on the basis of which Genesis is law-preserving, or as Benjamin should say, corrupt. One might well maintain that the wisdom of Genesis lies partly in its aspect of being a foundational myth of the law, which shows the impossibility of a lawful foundation of the law. But for Benjamin's case, this means that recourse to the state of paradise as a state prior to world-history and its corruption by the law fails to be just that. In other words, Benjamin's attempt to think his way out of the violent circle of the law by means of positing a non-violent 'before' the law, fails. As such, Benjamin's philosophy of violence is not free from biaphobia, of trying to find a way out of violence while recognizing only a destructive, negative aspect of violence. Specific to his theory is that in Benjamin, biaphobia appears as messianism.

If his attempt to conceive of a 'before' the violence of law fails, then there is much reason to assume that the messianic way *out* of it is equally flawed, since it is based on the idea that it is not possible to forego the (to Benjamin) violent working of the law in that situation. Since, then, the messianic restoration is thought to be a restoration of a situation prior to the violence of the law, it clearly fails to be such when it is posited not simply as a way out of the violence of law into a situation of non-violence, but explicitly as a restoration of the paradisaical situation. But even if Benjamin's messianism were based wholly on a hope of a future state of non-violence (at least of the law, which therefore could not exist) and pure justice, even then one could have serious doubts as to whether such a thing would be possible through a form of divine violence in the way Benjamin conceives of this. For divine violence would exist wholly outside the sphere of means and ends. Yet it has a definite *purpose*: it seeks justice, and an end to the instrumentalism of the law. Would this violence then not be equally incorporated into an instrumentalist logic itself? And, moreover, would it not consequently need a violence to secure justice? A similar critique on the purity of Benjamin's divine violence comes from Derrida (1994: 89), who has stressed that divine violence is a pure performative act. And in 'Du droit à la justice', Derrida says that a performative speech act can only be just when it is based on conventions and other performative acts, which means it is always inherently violent (Derrida, 1994: 59). This is based, in Derrida's text, on a radicalization of the Kantian schism between theoretical and practical reason, and on the idea that a convention, a rule, would incorporate theoretical reason into practical reason, thereby violating it.

More directly with respect to divine violence, Derrida questions the possibility of a pure divine violence. The violent ambiguity that characterizes mythical violence is all the more present in divine violence, the occurrence of which is *indecidable*. No man can decide upon divine violence, no man can even know it. Only God, the wholly other, signs it, as Benjamin ends his text. But would not divine violence degenerate into mythical violence or law-preserving violence as soon as it had occurred? Because divine violence can only exist as an *other* of mythical violence and of law-preserving violence, can it wholly extinguish it? If it could, it would not *be* what it *is*, since it is only as difference vis-à-vis mythical and law-preserving violence. Moreover, would not a just order resort to mythical violence to safeguard justice? Divine violence is a means to an end that is an end of all means. Of course Benjamin is careful not to say this; divine violence remains nobody's means, remains signed by no-one but the wholly other. Yet here another critique, brought forward by Derrida, sets in. In the *Post-Scriptum* to his text on Benjamin, Derrida draws a comparison between Benjamin's text and the Nazi *Endlösung*. Benjamin's text gives rise, according to Derrida, to the frightening temptation of casting the Holocaust in terms of Benjaminian divine violence (Derrida, 1994: 145). This divine violence, which strikes without bloodshed, would then be that of the gas chambers, and Derrida is 'terrified' at this thought. This is surely an evocation of somewhat bad taste, but Derrida may yet be right that Benjamin's text is still very 'archeo-eschatological' (Derrida, 1994: 146). For to posit a divine violence, a violence to end all mythical and law-preserving violence, a violence that ends the injustice of the powerful but which cannot be known or recognized beforehand, is, to a certain extent, to invite a violence that claims to be divine but never will be. Is not the combination of historical materialism and Judaeo-theological messianism a 'ghostlike mix'? For it is that combination that forces something to arrive which *cannot* arrive, which is always to-come (*à-venir*). Derrida has therefore proposed a messianism without Messiah and without revolutionary underpinnings; one occasion on which he preaches this is the recent 'war on terror' and the supposed export of democracy. However, it can be argued that this hypo-critical hope for a future that never presents itself has in common with Benjamin's text a certain biaphobia, an unwillingness to bear violence, to consider violence in itself or to consider violence in light of its productive aspect. Benjamin's biaphobia becomes paradoxically apparent in his recourse to a violence to end violence. In doing so, he in fact takes recourse to the 'mentality of violence' that he critiques, but with biaphobic intention. This is the tragic of the biaphobia of the 'final effort' (*Endlösung, dernier effort*), which preaches paradise beyond violence *by means of* a last violent push, which in reality comes down to a predominantly *destructive* violence. Despite all biaphobic critiques of Machiavelli, his conviction that the greatest immorality lies (in my terms) in a politics of biaphobia – which does not possess *virtù*, the ability to do what is necessarily to be done in order for the political community to survive (cf. Machiavelli, 1997: 60, 64) – might be far less destructively violent than a revolutionary-theological divine violence, or, for that matter, than an in-different indecisionism of Derridean messianism. Benjamin's concepts in *Zur Kritik der Gewalt* are certainly not unusable for the purposes of fascism. Nor does Benjamin succeed in contemplating a way out of mythical violence in particular or out of (the) violence (of the law) in general. Related to this is the last question I want to espouse with respect to this 'strange text': does Benjamin succeed in contemplating a pure and immediate violence?

From biaphobia to autotelic violence

Right from the start of *Zur Kritik der Gewalt*, two things happen: (1) Benjamin announces he will speak of violence, and even of a pure violence; (2) Benjamin speaks not of violence but of justice. In order to overcome this inconsistency, Benjamin's conceptual distinctions need to be liquidated. Derrida's deconstruction of Benjamin's text has similarly focused on these distinctions, particularly with respect to the fact that Benjamin's text is a self-proclaimed *critique* of violence. Critique, says Derrida, is derived from *krinein*, to separate, and crucial in the (self)deconstruction of Benjamin's text is the impurity of its basic distinctions, its fundamental separations. The liquidation of Benjamin's concepts does not merely serve to demonstrate the purity of their differences, but seeks to make them altogether confluent. Benjamin's crucial distinction, the distinction that makes it possible to find a pure and unmediated violence, is the distinction between means and ends. Right from the beginning, Benjamin assumes that a cause (by which he no doubt means a *causa efficiens*) only amounts to violence when it encroaches upon moral relations (Benjamin, 1965: 29). As has been argued in Chapter 3, this is already a biaphobic way of speaking of violence. From the start, therefore, *pure* violence is left out of Benjamin's focus. After confining violence to the realm of the law, Benjamin continues by stating that the most elementary relation of a juridical order is the relation between means and end. And he furthermore states that violence can only be found in the realm of means, not of ends (Benjamin, 1965: 29). Violence is confined to the realm of means within the framework of moral relations sanctioned by law. Now, as noted, Benjamin abhors the categories of means and ends. Situated in violence exclusively on the level of means, then, is a result of a biaphobia that season but the destructive aspects of violence. True, divine violence is contemplated in light of a productive aspect, namely that of the production of justice, but this productive violence is first of all the product of a scholastic intellectualism, and, secondly, it is contemplated as a way to end all actually existing violence in the realm of the law. It is, therefore, biaphobia which informs Benjamin's critique of violence. And it is the subsequent distinction between means and ends, and the localization of violence at the side of the means that he was of Benjamin's view of a pure violence. According to this view, violence, as Hannah Arendt has said, is 'instrumental by nature' (Arendt, 1970: 79). Since Benjamin critiques all instrumentalism because of its destructively violent origin and consequences, he in turn disapproves of all violence in the realm of law, which is instrumental. To escape from means and ends, he posits an immediate violence that is messianic in nature. But there is a much less violent way of contemplating the end of the means.

The end of the means: On autotelic violence

There is something rotten in the categories of means and end, something which appears the moment those categories become confluent and disappear. If Benjamin seeks a pure, immediate violence that is itself not law-establishing, autotelic violence would appear to be a more realistic category that divine violence. 'Autotelic' is derived from *autos* (self) and *telos* (goal), and thus denotes that which is its own goal.[4] Autotelic violence, therefore, is a violence that is its own goal, of violence in which means and end are conflated. If there could ever be such a thing as a wholly unmediated violence, autotelic violence would have to be that most 'pure' form of violence, perhaps as the most original manifestation of violence. If I were a Platonic conceptual realist, I would say that autotelic violence is the Form or the Idea of all phenomenal violence. Biaphobia has prevented autotelic violence from being highlighted in many a treatise on or critique of violence. Benjamin's critique of violence suffers from the same ill that so much of the philosophy and social science of violence suffers from: *it claims to be concerned with violence when in fact it is not; it claims to discuss the nature of violence when in fact it reduces and thereby violates it.* As for Benjamin, a true 'critique of violence' would need to endure the possibility of autotelic violence, perhaps even as a condition of possibility of all violence. Only when means and ends are made confluent by positing the possibility of an autotelic violence, only then have Benjamin's categories been liquidated. And Benjamin's text needs to be liquidated because it violently misrecognizes violence itself. The distinctions Benjamin makes on the first page of this text obscure his view of a pure, immediate violence from the start (cf. Gasché, 1994: 198–200). Autotelic violence is precisely that immediate violence, though it is not 'pure and immediate' in the sense that divine violence is thought to be by Benjamin, since it does not destroy in the name of the living itself or in the name of justice, but inasmuch as it destroys it does so merely in the name of itself. And in its destruction, it also produces, but it only re-produces itself. Autotelic violence seeks nothing but its own autopoiesis. Only autotelic violence can possibly be said to be a 'pure' form of violence, since it does not seek to replace the law by a mythical alternative, nor does it seek to inaugurate justice as the end of the law; it only seeks to destroy law, and to destroy justice. At one point in Benjamin's text, the idea of an autotelic violence seems to shine through. When Benjamin (1965: 35) speaks of the 'great villain', he assumes that the sympathy of the masses for this person is a sympathy for something that contravenes the law. But it may well be that this sympathy is a sympathy for pure violence, for violence for the sake of itself. Then, fear and fascination are equal measures of its impact. They are responses that share an underlying realization of a dreadful nothingness, an apocalyptic feeling of a maybe, the end. One might wonder, using Benjamin's categories in *Das Kunstwerk...*, whether the experience of autotelic violence is an *Erlebnis* or an *Erfahrung*, or whether it perhaps conflates these categories as well.

Autotelic violence and 'pure' violence

Autotelic violence does not intend to be law-establishing; it merely seeks the destruction of the law and the simultaneous reproduction of itself.

Because of its boundless destructiveness vis-à-vis the law, it is the most threatening violence to 'law and order'. This is mirrored in the responses of the law to cases of violence which appear to be spurred by nothing but the *will to violence*, where exterior motives, reasons referring beyond violence itself, are absent. In such cases, where the law strikes harder than usual, the self-preservation of the law that Benjamin sees as its sole goal is indeed highlighted as its primary motive. Where violence for the sake of itself escapes the grip of the state, the state is threatened most in its autopoiesis. For autotelic violence not only defies the law in recognition of another law, an alternative law; it is at odds with *any* juridical system, and any such system is threatened by it. Where the law is undermined most severely, law-preserving violence strikes the hardest. Law-preserving violence will there be, as Benjamin says it will be, mixed with law-establishing violence, since the total absence of law in autotelic violence needs to be overwritten by a border of which the violence of this 'writing' is the enforcement. Autotelic violence neither seeks to inaugurate an era of justice. It does not care about law or justice, does not recognize the opposition justice–injustice, it does not worry, with Benjamin, about the mixture of justice and the law; it places itself beyond good and evil.

But how 'pure' can this violence really be? Is there not a paradox in the very notion of a 'pure violence'? Surely, the enlightened humanist will say, anything violent cannot be pure. But the paradox is not biaphobic in origin. For Benjamin, law-preserving violence is doubly violent. For it is a representation in a double sense: it represents a means–end category, a limit, a power; and it thereby represents law-establishing violence. Because, for Benjamin, the nature of representation is itself violent, law-preserving violence is perhaps 'more' violent than mythical violence itself. In fact, because of this double, law-preserving violence and law-establishing violence are impure categories. Purity, in Benjamin's sense, is reserved for immediacy. Autotelic violence is indeed immediate violence, a violence beyond the categories of means and ends. But beyond those categories, the 'purity' of violence necessarily gains a different meaning. Exactly how 'pure' can immediate violence be? A 'pure violence' would be a violence that is as violent as possible, in a qualitative, not necessarily a quantitative sense. That means it is a violence that stands out in its destructive aspect. Autotelic, immediate violence is a 'pure' violence in the sense that it too is doubly violent, since in autotelic violence, both the end and the means are violent. Empirically, autotelic violence is in that sense the most 'pure' form of violence. It does not seek to resurrect an order, to inaugurate a law or to punish according to a pre-existent law; it is *violence and nothing else*. But is such a thing empirically possible? Are there not, empirically, other aspects, even to autotelic violence? Perhaps a pure autotelic violence can best be seen as an ontological possibility, never realized but always possible, and as such the condition of possibility of the *autotelic aspect of all ontic violence*.

In its 'pure form', then, autotelic violence does not take place. For *any pure violence is a paradox*: 'pure' violence would violate itself. A violence that destroys indiscriminately would destroy itself to be, qualitatively, a 'pure' violence, that is, to be purely violence and nothing else. A pure violence would therefore annul itself (*sich ver-nicht-en*) and would not exist after all. Any ontic form of autotelic violence is therefore impure; it exists only by negating its potential purity. A 'pure autotelic violence' thereby becomes an ontic impossibility, but it can still be an ontological condition of possibility, or, perhaps more heuristically relevant, it can be a *model* for ontic forms of autotelic violence. More accurately, that means that the idea of a pure autotelic violence is a model for the autotelic aspect of all violence. All violence is characterized by the aspect of pure destruction for the sake of itself. The ontological limit of this is pure autotelic violence, which is a possible impossibility. This possible impossibility becomes apparent when gunmen killing people at random take their own lives. Such shoot-outs are characterized by an autotelic aspect, a wanting to wallow in violence, a *will to violence*, defiled by the impossibility of it being purely violent and nothing else. The suicide that ensues is both the result of the awareness of the impossibility of such a purity, and a last attempt to yet establish it. This example, it has to be stressed once more, needs to be seen in light of a fractured realism. One *aspect* of what takes place in shoot-outs such as those in Littleton is tentatively described with the help of the notion of autotelic violence and the possible impossibility of a pure autotelic violence. Any ontic autotelic violence is therefore the actualized possibility of the impossibility of a pure autotelic violence. The very fact that autotelic violence is also but one asect of ontic violence is what is at stake here. Even the one with the strongest will to violence, performing the greatest actualization of the autotelic aspect of violence, is operating with a false consciousness: he *cares* about more than pure violence, is only because he does not want to – or if he wants to, cannot – violate violence and still uphold it.

Pure autotelic violence is a limit which borders on ontic violence when the autotelic aspect of ontic violence is highlighted to an extreme extent. Yet as soon as ontic violence would become pure violence, it would cease to exist, since it would annihilate itself among everything else it meets. Therefore, however violent ontic violence may be, a 'pure violence' lies beyond the possible, as a possible impossibility. Pure violence is the limit that ontic violence is to a lesser or larger extent modelled by. Ontic violence always exists from an origin, it is executed through something which carries it. To turn against its carrier would be to achieve pure violence at the same time violence ceases to exist. It has run up against its limit, its model that it necessarily needs to fail to realize in order for it to be realized itself.

One can contemplate a pure violence, a violence beyond means and ends, but then one has to forego a political agenda such as Benjamin's. Divine violence is not a pure violence; it is not even immediate, autotelic, since divine violence is not a violence for the sake of itself (remember that Benjamin himself, in his philosophy of language, equates 'immediacy' to the auto-telic). Reason for Benjamin's somewhat uneasy construction is the political background of his writing. The double of *Gewalt* both as 'violence' and as 'power', in which, as Derrida stresses, even democracy is intertwined in *Zur Kritik der Gewalt*, indicates the historical materialist and critical background of Benjamin's text. Its Judaeo-messianic background is reason for its failure to contemplate a truly immediate violence, since its ultimate *goal* is justice, not violence. Indeed, 'if violence is wrong by definition, there is little point in talking about violence. What we should talk about instead are rights and justice' (Runkle, 1976: 368). This attitude leads Benjamin away from violence itself. Yet violence is the political aspect of the social, and when a pure vio-lence is concerned, one can think of politics only in terms of indiscriminate force and irrational will to power, turned into will to violence since no rela-tion of power is its goal, but violence alone suffices. Any political goal one wishes to establish will then be annulled by the radicalization of the political aspect itself. In the case of autotelic violence, politics is no longer a means to an end. Benjamin made the strange move to contemplate a pure violence out of a biaphobia towards all existing violence. He did, however, realize the problematic of this pure violence in the sense that, albeit for quite the wrong reasons, he saw a pure violence as unattainable, as undeclarable, unspeakable even, since not a part of nomenclaturist categories of language. The 'purest' existing violence lies in the autotelic aspect of violence, and in a far more banal way than Benjamin's biaphobic philosophy of history is able to high-light. It exists in all violence, more or less highlighted along a sliding scale such as that of the aspect of violence in a social situation. Sometimes hardly actualized, sometimes overwhelmingly present. Focusing on the aspect of violence, we do not learn from Benjamin's text what it promises to bring: we do not learn what the essence of violence is, or what a pure violence is. But what will here be maintained from this text, and highlighted in sub-sequent chapters, is most of all the possibility of autotelic violence, as an aspect of violence that entails the possible impossibility of a pure violence. With Benjamin, we have stumbled upon the ultimate paradox of violence in the ontological limit of autotelic violence. My thesis is that there is an autotelic aspect in all violence, and that, if there is one aspect of violence that could offer a possible legitimation of biaphobia, it is this aspect. More than anywhere, biaphobia reigns where the autotelic aspect of violence is actualized – reason, no doubt, for its oblivion, for blind spots causing texts supposedly about violence, even about 'pure violence', to contemplate law, and justice, both equal in their impurity of violence.

Part II Violence in Social Science

5
The Will to Violence

1.

In his *Confessions*, St Augustine states that he used to derive pleasure from crime for its own sake. He also asks whether it is possible that he used to derive pleasure from illegal activities because they were illegal. These are, however, two separate things: (1) to derive pleasure from crime for the sake of itself, and (2) to derive pleasure from crime because it is illegal. Augustine moreover continues to say that what he actually loved in the crime was the company of his fellows in crime, and that bad company leads to bad actions. Nevertheless when he discusses how his friend Alypius was fascinated by gladiator games (with an 'incomprehensible passion'), he describes how Alypius succumbed to the pleasure of the games and the lust for the spectacle of killing. Alypius was forced to attend the games by his friends, and closed his eyes, but not his ears. And thus, the *aisthesis*, the door through which evil enters the mind, was not properly closed, and Alypius was seduced by the lust for the bloody fight for its own sake.

2.

In 2004, a Dutch girl was murdered by a total of three boys, one of whom seemed to have taken the initiative and one of whom was a younger boy dragged along. The boys had taken the girl into the woods and had tried to strangle her. When they failed, they tied a rope around her neck, tied it to a car and drove for half an hour until the girl was dead. The two oldest boys were severely punished, especially the boy who had planned the whole thing. Some sociologically interesting points can be derived from his trial. One paradox is that the boy was sentenced to many years of prison, while at the same time being sentenced to treatment in a psychiatric hospital (TBS). The latter, however, seems to indicate that the boy was unaccountable for his acts and that he therefore could not be punished by means of a prison sentence. The most interesting thing from the point of view of the aspect highlighted in this chapter, though, was that he was punished as severely as he was because of the 'lack of reason' he had had to kill the girl. However, he himself had testified that he was fascinated by death and that he had always wanted to know what it would be like to kill a person. To the judges, however, this was still 'no reason'. What probably would have been a reason, was that he had been angry with her, that he was her lover but that she cheated on him, and so on. However, there remains a huge gap between having an argument with someone and killing her. In fact, when one has an argument with someone, there are many courses of action one might undertake, and killing that person is almost always the least likely option. Yet this was the sort of thing a judge could have accepted as a 'reason', as a reason for a less severe punishment too. A judge would happily pin a murder down on 'having had an argument', however blurred the causality between such a reason and the supposed effect, a murder, is. What the judges in this case did not accept as a reason *was in fact the best reason to kill a person*. For what could be a better reason to kill a person than wanting to know how it feels to kill a person? In fact, if one really wants to know what it feels like to kill a person, there is really only one thing one can do, and that is to kill a person. When, on the other had, one has an argument with someone, there are, as I said, many possible alternative courses of action. While the boy was so severely punished because he was said to have had 'no reason' for his actions, he in fact could not have had a better reason for them. A rare act such as his can probably only be reasonably understood when an equally rare reason is present. Yet in spite of his explicit confession to having wanted to know what is was like to kill a person, the judges decoded he in fact had no reason. Why was the best reason for murder not recognized as a reason for murder? Two things may be at stake here. (1) If the boy was in fact acting on the reason he gave, then he was acting, to a large extent, out of free will and rational calculation. And if someone acting out of free will and rational calculation could be capable of committing such an act, anyone could, in theory, be capable of doing so. In short, it is the *anthropology* that this boy betrays that is disliked by the judges and that is therefore disqualified and denied empirical validity. (2) If the boy did indeed want to know what it was like to kill a person, then he acted out of a love of violence for its own sake. This thought is unbearable in a culture frittered with that very same thought. Biaphobia is institutionalized in the legal system to such a degree that the idea that violence pulls, that it is perpetrated on grounds intrinsic to violence, cannot be accepted. What we want is less dangerous reasons, half-reasons, no reasons really. Violence cannot be a reason for violence itself, since violence has nothing to do with *Reason*.

In this chapter, I explore the possibility, unrecognized in biaphobic discourse, of private violence occurring for the sake of itself. What St Augustine calls 'incomprehensible' is the same thing a Dutch judge has a hard time coming to grips with. In fact, it is the same thing social scientists seem to be unable to grapple. The following would surely be an acceptable opening phrase for any social scientific paper on private violence: 'Interpersonal violence is a phenomenon that is of increasing concern, both to politicians and policy-makers as well as to social scientists.' In what would then probably follow, one would find data, either qualitative, or – more likely – quantitative. One would find analyses of either statistics or 'meanings'; there would be Chi-square's, Pearson's correlations, discourse analyses, followed by conclusions, discussions, policy recommendations and, to complete this picture of an eternal recurrence, there would probably be suggestions for further research. But there would be no violence. Or at least it would not be *about* violence. That is my claim: violence itself has been shied away from in the vast majority of social scientific enquiry concerning violence. What has been researched are certain patterns through which violence inscribes itself, and what has been understood are meanings given to particular occurrences, perhaps even particular kinds, of violence. But these are extrinsic to violence itself. They are added to it, they are facilitative for it, or they are the quantitative shape that violence assumes. But they are not violence itself. We have hardly begun to understand violence *itself*. That is, we have largely ignored the intrinsic aspects violence possesses. As Randall Collins has said: 'The prevailing reality of world history is violence [...] it is not merely the violence of a machine out of control; the disturbing thing is the viciousness, the vindictiveness, the deliberate torture in so much of it. Beneath the sociologist's patterns lies the personal dimension of evil' (Collins, 1974: 416). Now, violence has everything to do with force. It is usually seen as the carrier of a certain force, or as the exertion of force. But one might ask, apart from that, what the intrinsic *force* of violence could be. Violence can, after all, be regarded as a force itself, as the source of an *attraction*, a source that pulls an agent. In that sense, it is not violence that is the result of the exertion of force of a more or less autonomous agent, but it is the agent that is shaped in his or her agency by the force of violence, that may then be regarded as relatively autonomous itself. That is not to say an agent would 'fall prey to' the use of violence because of its intrinsic aspects, but rather that he or she *chooses* to engage in violent behaviour for the sake of that behaviour itself. It is precisely the paradox of most contemporary research that actors are at once regarded as autonomous agents making more or less rational means–end calculations, whereas at the same time their violent behaviour is *explained* by causes beyond their individual control. As such, the agent disappears along with the violence that is supposedly studied. For the agent, though thought of as the source of violent action, is reduced to his or her background characteristics, translated into variables. This leads to certain factors that are certainly not irrelevant to the understanding of the motives towards violence, but it draws the attention away from violence itself and from the agent, the 'I', whose signature leaves its trace upon the violent event. And something of that 'I' has to be retained in order not to lapse into an endless teleology without Telos of causes causing other causes serving other causes and so forth. As Merleau-Ponty has said: 'I am not the outcome or the meeting-point of numerous causal agencies which determine my bodily or psychological make-up' (Merleau-Ponty, 1962: viii).

I therefore first of all give attention to the supposed *causes* of violence. Then, I will indicate how there are two ways of thinking about and of observing violence. The first I will call *determinism*; the second *formalism*. I will clarify why I feel this distinction need be made, and what it amounts to in the study of violence. To conclude this chapter, I venture a more speculative analysis of the will to violence. I introduce the concept of *frictional violence*, a contemporary form of violence that resides in the friction between 'fictional' and 'real violence' – two opposites of which the relative inadequacy for an understanding of a morte general way of experiencing violence is captured by the concept of frictional violence.

Which 'why'-question?

When thinking about causality and violence, a lot comes down to the question with which research starts. Suppose I were to ask, in researching a particular outbreak of violence: 'why did this violence occur?'. That question brings with it all sorts of difficulties. For the question 'why did this violence occur?' may actually be understood in at least five distinct ways. It may, first of all, be taken to ask 'why did the violence start?', which would be a question seeking to find the direct occasion or immediate cause of the *outbreak* of violence.

Secondly, it may be understood as 'why did violent acts continue for the period of time in which they did, to follow each other?'. This possible way of understanding the question alerts us to the fact that it is often not 'violence' which is explained by sociologists, but rather a readiness to *use* violence. This is important, for 'violence' consists of violent acts. 'Violence', as a specific set of violent acts, can never be explained as a whole from the 'outside', since violent acts, once they appear, often cause other violent acts to follow them. 'Violence' is in that case either in part caused by itself, or it is an inappropriate name used to denote an aggregate of actions that has no empirical basis in itself. I will comment on this later on.

Thirdly, we may understand the question 'why did this violence occur?' as 'why did violence occur instead of something other than violence?'. The explanation that is thus sought, is intended to be linear and exclusive, in the same sense in which a prism is thought to break the light coming through it exactly the way it does, and in no other way. William James has said that the whole debate on 'determinism vs freedom' hinges on the idea of *possibility*. That is what this question implicitly pertains to. It asks: were there alternative courses of action? Was this course of action – the violent one – in the end, given the causes and conditions, the only possible course of action? This raises problems that are beyond this chapter, and they will be dealt with only in a rudimentary way.

Fourthly, it may be taken to ask 'what are the causes of this violence?' This is one of the most prevalent ways of questioning violence in the social sciences, and I will deal with it more extensively in this chapter. One problem it seems to raise *prima facie*, is that the distinction made between the first and second mentioned way of interpreting our question, comes back. The social sciences usually deal with concepts rather than processes, and thus there is a tendency to freeze reality. This is what Elias (1970) called *process-reduction*. In this case, this concerns the question whether we want to search for the *causes* of this outbreak of violence, which will, in some way, have to be located outside 'violence' itself, or whether we are interested in the actual process of violence, in which case one act of violence was, once violence was initiated, certainly one cause for its continuation through further acts of violence. This distinction is hardly ever made, since violence is either studied in an abstract sense, looking for governing laws at a macro-level, or in an all-too limited symbolic interactionist sense which entirely omits the possibility of such governing regularities that might be regarded as 'causes'.

A fifth way to interpret the question 'why did this violence occur?' is to see it as 'what were the reasons or motives for those involved to start it?'. Here, as well, the distinction I just mentioned remains unproblematized. A further problem here is that the question is raised – which, though it has often been discussed in philosophy, is not of a solely philosophical nature – whether or not the reasons for action can or should be seen as causes of action, and if so, in what sense they can be thus treated.

The above discussion is merely intended to show the ambiguities involved in a common social scientific questioning of violence; it is not intended to conclude with a 'best' or 'most scientific' way of interpreting research questions. This means researchers always have an implicit answer to the question how to interpret the question why violence occurred. I propose to first consider some of the most influential social scientific theories of violence with respect to the specific kind of question they are designed to answer. We can then see what kind of causality is presupposed. It will appear that all but one of them attempts to answer mainly the fourth question. Other ways of questioning violence are usually ignored. After this, I will discuss some general problems that these ideas on causality encompass. To conclude, I wish to offer a possible way out of these problems by distinguishing between a formalism and a determinism in the study of violence.

Social-scientific profiles of violence

For the sake of brevity, I will restrict myself here to instances of physical violence that do not fall under the heading of 'political violence'. It is the day-to-day interpersonal private violence, on a small scale, that I wish to focus on. That does include everything from bullying to murder, but not, for instance, the violence of war. Also, I would like to stress that I do not claim to give an exhaustive account of all theory on violence in the social sciences. Many will surely be undiscussed, as every distinction or classification has its blind spots. And I don't feel I need to have discussed all theories, if that were even possible. The aim is merely to confront certain familiar kinds of theory with an, admittedly, rather rigid criterion of causality.

A few features of social scientific research into violence are striking at the outset. (1) Research into violence is hardly ever concerned with violence itself. By that, I mean to say that many theories used to explain violence were designed to explain 'crime' more generally. I also mean to indicate that when violence is claimed to be the topic of investigation, it very rarely really is. That is to say, the violence itself is usually left out of focus. (2) Research is oriented heavily towards perpetrators and their backgrounds. In other words, instances of violence are the givens upon which research into determining factors of perpetrators is founded. There are five strands of social-scientific research of violence that I want to discuss here, at least three of which conform to this general picture of aetiological research, much like that which John Stuart Mill advocated. These five strands are made up of several theoretical perspectives on violence, that is, of several profiles of violence. As profiles of violence, they always already presuppose an ontology and epistemology of violence. Although there is no need to go into this further, their differences in explaining violence are to be situated on that level.

(1) A first strand of social scientific theory on violence of my admittedly somewhat crude distinction is anomie theory and the associated frustration–aggression theory. This theory is most often associated with Robert Merton, yet its originator is actually Durkheim. It immediately becomes apparent that this theory is not specifically a theory about violence but rather of crime in a general, unspecified sense. Anomie, for Durkheim, was a kind of shared mental state, of not feeling embedded in societal rules, that became increasingly frequent with the change from mechanic to organic solidarity. Anomic suicide actually sprung, as does the frustration among offenders in Merton's theory (1968), from a gap between wants and the possibility of their satisfaction. In that sense, anomie theory is an imminent critique of the culture of meritocracy and of society's class structure. Apart from the question whether or not that class structure can still be regarded to be so determining a factor, it can be said that the core of anomie and frustration–aggression theory is that people break rules, for instance in striking out

violently, out of frustration over certain unsatisfied wants. This theory might therefore be traced to Scheler's theory of 'resentment' [*Ressentiment*] (Scheler, 1992). The idea is that when people don't get what they want for a long period of time, and when what they want is societally desirable, then they may become violent offenders (cf. Agnew, 1997).

What kind of causal theory is presupposed here? The underlying assumption seems to be that there is a causal path from occurrences in the past, against a certain societal background, to a certain mental state. Then there is another causal path from that mental state to violent behaviour. The philosopher will immediately sense problems here. For these are not causes like the ones we see on a snooker table when one ball hits another. Moreover, it could be questioned that the answers these theories provide are causes at all, since not all people tend to get frustrated in certain instances and not all people break out in violence, not even all frustrated people. At best, we could say that these theories describe certain conditionals for violence to occur. But probably even that is too bold a statement, and we won't be able to make more of it than 'facilitating factors' which, in some cases, strengthen a causal chain.

(2) A second profile that explicitly seeks to 'explain' is Hirschi's social bond or control theory (Hirschi, 1969). Again, it is not specifically violence the theory wants to explain but rather delinquent behaviour per se. But it has been much used to explain violence (for instance, Weerman, 1998). The core of this theory is that people have several 'bonds' to 'society' and that, when these bonds are somehow broken, people stand a greater chance of engaging in non-conventional, that is, delinquent behaviour. Therefore, the theory assumes, like the later self-control theory (Gottfredson and Hirschi, 1990), that people are initially prone to be delinquent, or in our case, violent. There are, however, in the 'normal' situation, certain controls in place that prevent people from following their primary evil instincts. As long as people are strongly tied to conventional society, they won't engage in non-conventional behaviour, such as violence. Elsewhere, I have elaborately criticized this tautological theory, but I wish to restrict myself to the assumed causality here. The theory suggests that there is a causal path leading from the bond to conventional society to behaviour. Where the bond is strong, conventional behaviour will probably occur; where it is weak(ened), non-conventional behaviour is the likely result. Now, this bond consists of several elements. They are attachment to others, commitment to the rules of conventional society, involvement in conventional institutions and a belief in the legitimacy of conventional society's rules. These four, entirely diverse, elements are supposed to cause behaviour. Since they 'explain' that behaviour, according to the author. But again, it is highly unlikely that the claim that these are really *causes* can be successfully defended.

(3) A third kind of profile is actually not so much *a* theory as it is a collection of theories that share a common feature and that I therefore group

together as though it concerns a single profile. Their common feature is that they highlight certain aspects of the violent offender's personal background, and claim, for example on the basis of percentages of explained variance, that these background factors are causes of violent behaviour. I subsume many theories under this general aetiological heading, such as Sutherland's differential association theory (Sutherland and Cressey, 1978), Akers' differential reinforcement theory (Akers, 1985), theories concerning the role of 'masculinity' in violence (for example, Jefferson, 1994; Gadd, 2000), but I also include in this group of approaches to violence the random bits of empirical research that get reported in articles we all know where one or two factors are stressed as important (one of the most interesting I recently came across concerns the relationship between loss of hearing and violent behaviour). If we were to combine all these factors we would probably find a huge causal construction in which there would be well over a 100 per cent variation to be explained. These theories are conveniently grouped together here, because they miss an emphasis on the opposition between delinquent and society at large, like Hirschi's theory has, while they can also not be said to be such coherent theoretical bodies as anomie and frustration–aggression theory are. Yet this group of theories is on the other hand much like these other two, for they are all aetiological in the sense that they exemplify what the *Oxford Handbook of Criminology* calls 'the criminologist's whatsortofpersondunnit' question (Maguire et al., 1997). In searching for causes of violent behaviour, what are highlighted are personal characteristics that needn't even be part of a personality, although that is what various socialization theories assume. And so, with regard to causality, the same goes here as in the two previous cases. I will elaborate on what kind of problem I have here, after I have discussed a fourth kind of social scientific theorizing about violence.

(4) As a fourth characteristic strand in the study of violence, rational choice theory should be mentioned. Its focus is the actor as an individual, rationally calculating the source of action. The actor's 'free choice' is a central feature, and in general terms, it is possible to say that rational choice theory assumes that an individual will undertake violent action if he or she thinks, on the basis of a rational calculation, that such action will be most rewarding – in the sense of maximizing wealth or 'utility' in general – in a given situation (see, for example, Sullivan, 1973; Heineke, 1978). This theory has the advantage of having a relatively close focus. It tends to blot out general determining factors and sticks to the situation of an agent acting on the basis of a calculation of pros and cons, of profits and losses. This ignorance of a larger social context has often been what rational choice theory has been criticized for (see, for example, Bourdieu, 2000). This critique is directed towards the idea of the individual as a *homo œconomicus*, and though I believe this is a legitimate critique of the theory, I shall for now strictly focus on the causal links that the theory assumes. But also the situational aspect tends yet to be ignored. For rational choice theory cannot

account for triggering causes in situations. It starts from the moment an actor makes a rational calculation, and a violent situation may then already have emerged. The only role of any importance the situation really plays in this theory is that of 'situational possibilities', which, in itself, does not explain anything. The general causal chain that is assumed in rational choice theory, then, seems to be that of an individual making a rational calculation which leads to a more or less predetermined outcome (since the calculation is 'rational'). This outcome exists as a perception of rewards on the part of the actor, which leads to the actor's choice to use violence, which then leads, in case of a positive outcome of both calculation of rewards and of choice, to violent behaviour. Because of its limited scope in the pretended explanation – rational choice theory restricts itself to the level of the 'individual'; it is a so-called 'micro-theory' – this theory does not involve causal constructs that are at first sight counter-intuitive. Although the precise link between the factors in the causal chain is somewhat fuzzy – it is especially not clear how a 'choice', which has the character of a volition, can 'cause' actions, which have a physical character – the problem is rather, even if there is such a causal chain as the one described above, why exactly do some people resort to violence more frequently than others? In other words, what have we explained with rational choice theory alone?

(5) Conflict theories offer a fifth way of dealing scientifically with violence. They are really the only kind of theory that is not so much interested in the background characteristics of the single perpetrator, but rather in the contextual features that make for the setting of violence. And therefore, they are not restricted to a single way of taking the 'why'-question. That is, they don't necessarily restrict themselves to the question of the causes of violence. Literature on collective violence is a good example here. In the study of collective violence, it is proper to ask why a particular outbreak of violence developed the way it did; why, for instance, does collective violence become 'collective' (cf. Senechal de la Roche, 2001)? Or why did violence occur instead of peaceful congregation (Sherman Grant and Wallace, 1991)?

Yet most conflict theories are 'macro-theories', like that of Dahrendorf (1990), Coser (1956) and Collins (1993). Indeed, Collins' recent theory of violence, which is a micro-theory, does not advocate itself as a conflict theory (although Collins does appear to see 'violence' as necessarily involving a conflict of some sort) (Collins, 2008), which leads to a problem similar to the one other kinds of theories pose: there is an avoidance of violence itself. Moreover, conflict theories only deal with violence in the case of a conflict. Violence is thus said to be caused by the strained relationship between actants; it is at the same time the culmination of conflict and its temporary settlement. In many conflict theories, violence is thus seen either as a dialectical or as a functional–structural effect of the broader social context in which it is situated. In terms of causality, again, the precise link between cause and effect is blurred. For exactly how does the causal path from strained macro-relations to the use of violent force by individuals run? Most functionalist theories avoid this problem by weakening, at the outset, the notion of 'function'. While a more harsh criterion of 'function' would involve both a causality in the usual sense and a teleology, the notion is most often reduced to something which relates two or more phenomena to each other on the basis of a problem and its possible solutions. But then the causal path becomes obscured, which is indeed what a functionalist thinker might claim (cf. Luhmann, 1991: 49). I propose to now discuss some general problems concerning causality in the social study of violence.

General problems concerning causality

The vast majority of social scientific studies of violence is directed towards the causes of violence. Consider, as an illustration, the introductory Internet page of the five-million-pound violence programme of the UK Economic and Social Science Research Council. It reads: 'The overall aim of the programme is to expand and enhance understanding of the various forms of violence to the person, in order to increase our knowledge about their causes and how they might be prevented, reduced or eliminated.'[1] Another example, taken from Messerschmidt (1999: 197–8): 'In June 1993, the American Sociological Association (ASA) convened an intensive workshop of leading sociologists working on violence. The goals of the workshop were to examine existing research directions, and address policy issues. Three years later the ASA published the workshop report, *Social Causes of Violence: Crafting a Science Agenda*, highlighting the nature of research conducted thus far on violence and identifying priority areas for future study.' Accordingly, research usually takes the question 'why did this violence occur?' to be 'what are the causes of this violence?'. It is therefore appropriate to consider some of the problems inherent in such a focus on causality.

In the philosophy of causality there exists a wide array of criteria on which to decide whether or not one may speak of a 'cause'. One criterion that seems to be recurring in some form or another is the argument from necessity. It holds that for A to be a cause of B, B must occur when A occurs. Added to this is the counterfactual conditional that, all other things being equal, had A not occurred, B would not have occurred. This is, however, seen as a strong criterion, and it is beyond doubt that the social scientific theories I have discussed cannot live up to it with the 'causes' they claim to identify.

The biggest problem for criminology and sociology is not that they cannot investigate the patterned occurrence of certain events, but rather that they cannot include the counterfactual situation into its research, for in social life, all things are never equal to what they were. And so, each time we attribute the label 'cause' to some phenomenon, we are far from the obviousness of billiard ball A being the cause of ball B. In social science, the causal path remains in the dark. Statistical significance is very often taken to signify active causality, without any actual evidence.

There is, in the philosophy of causality, a distinction between an epistemological tradition and an ontological tradition. Broadly speaking, it can be said that Hume's regularity-theory of causality is an exemplar of the first tradition. Here, a cause is merely the name we give to the coinciding of the phenomena where, because they always coincide in such a way that the 'cause' precedes the 'consequence' in time, a *belief* exists that there is a cause (Hume, 1984 [1739]). In this epistemological tradition, the social scientific study of violence is soon without a cause, for its 'causes' do not always coincide with their assumed consequences. Sometimes the cause occurs, but not the consequence. In the alternative ontological tradition, of which I take Mario Bunge to be a representative, causality is regarded as something actually happening in reality. Bunge speaks of the productive element in causation, and warns against an epistemologizing of the concept of a cause (Bunge, 1959). Here too, social scientific causes seem to fall short, for precisely that production cannot be accounted for. The causal path, as I said, remains vague. How exactly are 'bonds to society' or 'frustration' a cause of a particular violent event?

Another general problem here is that the social study of violence rarely, if ever, treats individual occurrences of violence. That means that the 'causes' it identifies, are never the active triggering causes in a particular situation, but at most predisposing causes or conditionals. A common claim in the philosophy of causality is that both cause and effect are *actual* (Sosa, 1975). But in what respect is frustration or a 'bond to society' actual? On these terms, this is a rather meagre result of efforts that aim and claim to *explain* violence.

A third general problem concerns precisely this will to *explain* violence. I will make a distinction between 'classical' and 'relationist social science' here. This distinction comes from Bruno Latour (Latour, 1996a). 'Classical sociology', Latour contends, 'knows more than the "actors"; it sees right through them to the social structure or the destiny of which they are the patients' (Latour, 1996a: 199). He continues: 'For classical sociology, there are classes, socioprofessional categories, fields, roles, cultures, structures, interests, consensus's, and goals.' Clearly this 'classical social science' is what the theories of violence I have discussed amount to. Now, leaving Latour's 'relationist' perspective aside, what classical social science is prone to do is to explain phenomena by pointing out underlying causes, that is, it directs attention to other phenomena that are themselves not a part of the phenomenon of violence, but that are thought to be causally related to it. This kind of social science, as Latour says in *We have never been modern*, doesn't want to take anything as 'natural', for fear of 'naturalization'. Here Latour's critique joins a phenomenological tradition that wants to leave the object it studies 'in tact'. To Latour, sociology doesn't even *have* an object

(1996b). If we try to *explain* violence, the argument goes, we trace it back to *something else*, and in doing so, any intrinsic aspects it may have are lost, denounced as a mere social construction that can be unmasked by a sociology such as persistent from Durkheim to Bourdieu. Especially Bourdieu has warned against ascribing intrinsic aspects to social phenomena, since that would amount to a naturalization of what is socially constructed (see, for instance, Bourdieu, 1994).

I admit that this has been the main issue for me in discussing violence and its causes. I do not intend to develop a kind of harsh criterion of causality in order to then debunk many social scientific theories. Nor do I wish to develop what has been rather strangely named a kind of 'postmodernist' idea of causality (see Henry and Milovanovic, 1996: 152–84). Though it is no doubt true that the social sciences have often been too easily persuaded to speak of the causes of violence where these are in fact far from obvious, the main point I want to make here is that the exclusive focus on causes per se leaves something important unsaid. Perhaps it is time to end the exclusivity of the 'why-question' altogether. For in the case of violence we may ask not only what its 'meanings' are, but also what its intrinsic attractiveness might be. This would mean to ask for the aesthetics of violence. The observant reader will have noticed that the tension I describe here is an old one; it is the quarrel between those that want to explain, *Erklären*, as Max Weber said, and those that wish to understand a phenomenon from the inside out, those that want to strive towards a *Verstehen*. Now, it was always Max Weber's goal to come to a sociology of an *erklärendes Verstehen*, a combination of both, which would offer explanations that would be at once 'kausal adequat' and 'sinnhaft adequat'. This, I think, is a realistic balance between two extremes, no one of which can make a claim for comprehensiveness. In the case of violence, it is clear that the theories I mentioned are on to *something*. Socio-economical status, to name one, has something to do with the chance of someone being violent. Or conflict on a macro-scale certainly will have its effects in terms of interpersonal violence. Yet on the other hand, the assumed causality in such theories is far from convincing. And it omits a close analysis of actual violence from its research. Nor can general problems concerning causality and explanation be ignored. So we need, I think, to compensate for this long-standing one-sidedness of the social science of violence. When *Erklären* has been the prime focus, it is time to add a dimension aimed at *Verstehen*, without granting universal validity to any one of these two. I now want to propose a possible way of expanding the study of violence to include that dimension.

Determinism and formalism in the study of violence

In accordance with the *Erklären–Verstehen* dichotomy, I wish to make a distinction in the social scientific study of violence between what I will call a *determinist* attitude and a *formalist* one. Under the heading of determinism, I place the most common ways of researching violence, which are ways of *explaining* violence. As a parallel, let's consider violence to be like a sign, the meaning of which social scientists intend to uncover. A sign may have at least two ways of referring. If it is taken to refer to something in the outside world, that is, in the case of external reference, we are dealing with a determinist account of violence. If, however, the sign is thought to refer to no more than itself, the case of self-reference, then a formalism of violence is unfolded. The difference between determinism and formalism boils down to a distinction between an external referent or a supposed meaning and a 'pure' *form* in the sense that the form takes priority regardless of extrinsic motivations. In a sense, this may be compared to the disinterestedness that Kant ascribes to the aesthetic judgement (Kant, 1957: 116). This is where a search for external causes halts, and attention is being directed towards what Collins has called 'the personal dimension of evil'. Yet recall Collins' statement on that dimension, lying 'beneath the sociologist's patterns'. It would appear he is adopting what I have called a formalist attitude here. However, the opposite is true. The following statement in his essay shows the tenacity of a solely determinist analysis of violence. For he immediately adds that 'the problem is not to justify evil, but how to explain it. Is there a pattern, a meaning to the cruelty itself?' (Collins, 1974: 416). And he continues to say sociology should be concerned with 'isolating a causal theory' (Collins, 1974: 416). Yet 'to explain' is not to find a pattern. A pattern explains nothing, it is rather, one might say, what needs to be explained. It is a regularity beneath which one suspects – whether justified or not – a (regulative) rule. Furthermore, finding a pattern is not finding a meaning. Collins speaks of 'a pattern, a meaning' as though these are synonymous, which they are not. And finally, his attempt to explain is indeed in line with 'isolating a causal theory' (at least, if by that he means 'a theory which allows one to isolate causes'), but 'to explain' is not to find a meaning. So in the case of Collins, it is precisely the 'cruelty itself' that remains out of sight. But such confusion is, I believe, symptomatic for the study of violence (though it is probably not limited to the study of violence alone).

As soon as there is a need to state explicitly what one wants to do, all comes down to an effort to explain violence, which is indeed a search for causes. Yet thereby two things are lost. The first is a real focus on the meaning of violence. This has been indicated by more phenomenologically oriented researchers, and an example of a study that does focus on the (moral) meanings of violence is Jack Katz's *Seductions of Crime* (1988). But still, there too, these 'meanings' are located outside violence itself in the sense that violence is studied not because of its intrinsic 'meaning', but rather as something referring to a meaning outside itself. So the second thing that is lost in contemporary research – and this is the thing that I believe is really 'lost' with very few exceptions in social science – is the violence itself, since it is not being studied in a formalist way. The main problem with rational choice theory, for example, is that it reduces actions to simple means–end relations (and, at that, the actor to a rationally calculating agent). This is one way in which the researcher is totally blind for the action itself. The violence 'itself': that which remains when all causes are revealed, when external connections are uncovered, such as means–end relations, or meaning-facilitating constructions. What then remains is surely what one might consider as the most 'disturbing' of all: a violence for the sake of itself, without morality, extrinsic meaning, but purely destructive. Evil, we might call it. Perhaps that is why this aspect to violence has been carefully avoided in the social sciences. We are afraid of it. We desperately try to explain all there is to violence, to come to a maximum of explained variance, but we know it won't happen for a 100 per cent, we know it won't ever be enough. And when it comes to violence, that residue scares the hell out of us.

Determinism and its limits

Let me clarify a bit further what the determinism–formalism dichotomy amounts to. The attention for the external *meaning* of violence, that is, that of which it is a symptom, to which it refers, is a determinist account of violence. Structural causes are thought to be the underlying meanings here, to which violence, as an outcome or a symptom of these causes, is thought to refer. In this sense, violence 'means' a certain background of the violent person. From another determinist perspective, violence fulfils certain 'functions' within society at large. Here too, violence is not taken to be intrinsically meaningful as such, but rather as being indicative of larger structures. It is a vehicle of social cohesion, nothing else. Quite often, determinist accounts of violence make the assumption that violent behaviour is irrational behaviour. This assumption is determinist in that it, again, looks away from violence itself, towards some cause, paying no attention to possible intrinsic characteristics violence may possess. Another common deterministic assumption with the same effect is the idea that violence is a *means* to a certain desired *end*. That end is a goal that is *extrinsic* to violence itself, and so, again, violence is reduced to some underlying feature, be it social or personal in nature. In short, in *explaining* violence, all these deterministic accounts have in common that they reduce violence to something other than it. Violence is *caused* by something else, and this explanation in effect *explains violence away*. There is no need to take a closer look at violence itself, for it is a mere symptom of structural causes that the social sciences are capable of uncovering. Determinism is in that sense a kind of *semiotics of violence*: it sees violence as referring to underlying, extrinsic factors and searches for that reference, thereby ignoring that very violence itself. What is in that semiotic approach in fact ignored, is the *aesthetics of violence*. That is exactly the focus of a formalism of violence, which I believe to be a necessary addition to the 'semiotically' interested determinstic account.

Determinism has been avoiding its object. It has explained it away, traced it back to deeper sources, but it has never really faced violence itself. It takes a different attitude to look violence in the face. That is what a formalism of violence does. A formalism starts with the idea that violence may be self-referential. Apart from everything it may tell us about deeper causes there is something to be said about the *nature* of violence. An aesthetic approach of violence seeks to uncover such intrinsic features of violence. What does that mean? It means that apart from possible structural causes of violence, violence may occur *for the sake of itself*. There may be intrinsic features of violence that appeal to a *will to violence*. If we do not deterministically wish to explain violence away, we will have to acknowledge that violence may be an end in itself, for itself. Like there is sex for the sex itself, which is to me the most important element there is to sex, apart from all sorts of biological, psychological and whatever other causes, there is violence for violence's sake.

To summarize, we may say that determinism has a kind of structure of tracing reference that is external to the object of enquiry (violence) itself. It seeks to explain that object without dealing with anything essential to that object; it therefore pays exclusive attention to factors that are contingent and external to the object. By contrast, a formalism has the structure of an aesthetics of its researched object. It places the form as intrinsically meaningful in the first place, and therefore, it deals with any essential characteristics of that object. And of course, determinism stands on the side of *Erklären*, while formalism is a way of *Verstehen* of the object. Before I try to integrate both approaches as supplementary to each other in a realistic social science of violence that does not shy away from its object of enquiry, I wish to elaborate on the formalist side of this dichotomy, since this is the side that has, up to now, been much neglected. However, I want to stress right here that my attention for a formalist study of violence does by no means imply a dismissal of what I have labelled 'determinism'. The concepts of 'determinism' and 'formalism' are used in a non-normative sense. And neither do I wish to claim the study of violence should abstain itself from searching for 'causes'. There is no *Kausalitätsfurcht* here, as Lorenz signalled in his ground-breaking study of aggression (Lorenz, 1963: 219). There is no need to fear, in any sense, a causal explanation. But there is reason to fear that the exclusive attention to (external) causes of violence leaves something essential to violence itself unsaid.

Formalism: The possibility of an autotelic violence

The above-quoted Merleau-Ponty has stressed that the sphere of meaning escapes, in a fundamental sense, the realm of causes. One might generalize this towards the idea that intrinsic characteristics of phenomena are facilitated by, yet essentially independent of, external constraints. They are relatively autonomous, like the way in which a social system is relatively autonomous in Luhmann's sociology: a system is open towards its environment with which it upholds functional relations, but it is (autopoietically) closed with respect to its operations, that is, the reproduction of its basic elements. In a similar sense, there remains an intrinsic, relatively autonomous force within violence, even after – if such a thing were possible – all its causes have been laid bare. In *Thinking Sociologically*, Zygmunt Bauman refers to the sociologists' "habit of explaining events by pointing out that they are *effects* of a *cause*" (Bauman, 1990: 107). He then continues to say that "when applied to human conduct, however, this habitual explanation leaves something important unsaid. What it leaves out is the fact that the event we wish to explain was someone's action, and the person whose action it was had a choice" (Bauman, 1990: 108). Now, without venturing into a debate on free will, I would say that this perfectly highlights the place of a possible will to violence. Whatever causes may be present, and whatever external goal violence may be a means to, we have to admit that it can be a forceful attraction by itself. We don't rationally calculate which means to use in order to achieve our goals, we rather feel comfortable about some means and less inclined to the use of others that might be more efficient means to our desired ends. One point is that we don't just desire ends and rationally calculate means, but we also desire some means more than others. And so, many people feel drawn towards violence because violence itself can give pleasure. Means and ends then become fluid concepts that are inseparable. Form and meaning become one and the same. It is my hypothesis, therefore, that we may speak of *autotelic violence*, a violence that is its own goal, in which means and end are melted together.

I want to maintain that in any instance of violence, autotelic aspects are present. The main reason for this is that means are never chosen purely because they promote a certain end; they are rather also selected on the basis of an intrinsic attractiveness. In the case of violence, therefore, even if we wish to speak in terms of means and ends, there will still be an autotelic aspect to those violent means. For means and ends are analytical categories that cannot be surgically separated in reality without a residue that escapes this dichotomous categorization. In the social sciences there has been, up to now, very little attention for autotelic aspects of violence. The types of violence that are discerned never include an autotelic violence that is willed for the sake of itself by the actor. To take one classic example that is in my view symptomatic of this void in the bulk of studies of violence, consider the distinction Wolfgang and Ferracuti made in their classic work *The Subculture of Violence*: 'There are basically two kinds of criminal homicide: (1) premeditated, felonious, intentional murder; (2) slaying in the heat of passion, or killing as a result of intent to do harm but without intent to kill' (Wolfgang and Ferracuti, 1967: 140). What is therefore unconsidered, or what falls out of this distinction, is autotelic murder. In fact, the recognition of autotelic aspects to murder would destroy the very distinction. For we would have to take into account a premeditated and felonious yet at the same time passionate murder, or a 'slaying in the heat of passion' *with* intent to kill. I believe that the distinction between certain *types* of violence never relates to actual occasions as violence. There may be ideal types, for in Weber's description these are indeed never actually found in reality. But it might be preferable to not speak of types at all, and instead focus on *aspects* to violence. Where we are used to saying that a murder at a robbery is a specific type of violence – say something like criminal intentional murder motivated by financial profit – we might be more accurate if we were to describe it as a kind of violence *in which that particular aspect was predominantly present.* For we cannot know for sure that it was or was not an intentional murder – the actor might even have doubts about this! A robbery is in most cases a rather amateuristic rush that is characterized by very little possible planning, therefore very little rational choice and very much fuzziness, spur of the moment actions, of which the actor might think back with a sense of incomprehensiveness at what were, at the time, his choices. The actor might be aware of his choices, but still wonder whether or not – and if yes, how – he chose his choices. In such a situation it does violence to the reality of violence to want to maintain more or less clear-cut types of violence. There may be a dominant aspect to a particular case of violent behaviour, but there are always other aspects as well. One of them will be the autotelic aspect of violence that we cannot rule out to be present in the moment the most intended or the most unintended murder takes place. Perhaps it coincides with that strange rush of adrenaline the actor feels the moment he empties his gun; a feeling that may surprise the actor, but which he won't be able to deny, certainly not the next time he finds himself in a similar situation.

Formalism in culture

There is much evidence for the idea that violence is willed by people. Popular culture is full of violence that serves no other purpose than to please. From the early sixties on, researchers have written about the effects of violence in films. Whatever these effects may be, the sheer demand for violence is indicative of the pleasure people derive form it. When he or she is 15, the average American kid has seen over 10,000 people being killed on television. An American TV programme called 'Battle-bots' – it's about fighting robots – tells the viewer: 'We're here to restore your faith in senseless acts of extreme violence.' It looks like a topsy-turvy world, but that changes once the infinite violent possibilities of the Internet are explored. On sites like 'Gore.com' or 'Filth.com' one can witness the most gruesome acts of violence. 'Faces of death' also has an Internet site, and there is a wide variety of violence to accommodate varying preferences. If one wishes to see people being hanged, choking on a rope, one can find them. Again, these appear in two varieties: one with actors, and one with real-life photos and videos. Computer games become increasingly 'realistically' violent as well, and that 'realism' is precisely what reviews of those games in computer magazines cheer at.

But it's not only in popular culture that this love of violence can be found. Art, and especially (post)modernist art has been preoccupied with violence as well. The autotelic aspect of violence can be said to be a recurring theme in contemporary art. From the many centuries of literature and the manifold presence of autotelic violence or autotelic evil in general, De Sade is especially telling. Take his description of the Duke of Blangis in his *120 Days of Sodom*: 'From necessary murders he soon went on to murders out of lust. He discovered that one can take pleasure in the pain of others; he felt how a shock, no matter who it is inflicted upon, generates in our nervous system a vibration that has the consequence that the animalistic instincts, hidden in the hollows of our nerves, generate an erection that, in the end, leads to a lustful feeling.' Or take the following excerpts from Baudelaire's poem *The sweetness of evil*:

> *Among the vermin, jackals, panthers, bitches,*
> *Monkeys, scorpions, vultures, serpents*
> *The monsters squeeling, yelling, grunting, crawling*
> *in the infamous menagerie of our vices*
>
> *There is one uglier, more wicked and foul than all!*
> *Although he does not make great gestures or great cries,*
> *He would gladly make the earth a shambles*
> *And swallow the world in a yawn;*
>
> *It is boredom! His eyes weeping an involuntary tear,*
> *He dreams of gibbets as he smokes his hookah.*
> *You know him, reader, this delicate monster,*
> *– Hypocrite reader – my twin – my brother!*

> From Charles Baudelaire, *The Flowers of Evil*
> (translated by Wallace Fowlie)

It is a confrontation within the reader himself that Baudelaire is after. And he says:

> *If rape, poison, the knife and arson*
> *Have not yet woven with their pleasing pattern*
> *The banal canvas of our pitiful fate*
> *It is because our soul, alas, is not bold enough*

Translated into my terms, one could say Baudelaire alerts us to that hidden motive that everyone possesses: the will to autotelic violence, the attraction, the pull, or quite simply the love of violence for its own sake. This autotelic aspect to violence that resides in every mind and in every violent act is surely no more than one aspect of a multifaceted phenomenon, yet it *is* an essential feature of that mind, of violence, or in short, of sociality. Dostojevski hints at it in *Crime and Punishment* when he says: 'the tenants walked back to the door close to each other, with that strange feeling of satisfaction, that one can always observe when a man is suddenly struck by misfortune, even in those that are the closest to him, a feeling no man can escape from and that even the deepest feeling of pity and sympathy does not preclude'. Dostojevski elsewhere describes how soldiers take 'pleasure in torturing children, too; cutting the unborn child from the mother's womb, and tossing babies up in the air, and catching them on the points of their bayonets before their mother's eyes. Doing it before the mother's eyes was what gave zest to the amusement.' Modern literature has continually given contemporary expressions to the autotelic aspects of violence and of evil and human suffering in general. Literature in the last century has gone, to name but a few, from Kafka (is there autotelic state-violence?) via Kosinsky to the cool descriptions of extremely violent occurrences by Hubert Selby and Brett Easton Ellis. To move on to other art forms, a recent Dutch 'high culture' Opera-performance of Verdi's *Rigoletto* advertised with the words 'Lust, Love, Violence in the Rotterdam Harbor'. In film, also the 'serious' filmmakers, which, in an age of 'intermediality', have come to be regarded as artists, have filmed increasingly violent scenes. That excludes many violent blockbuster movies. One might perhaps say that these are indeed more adapted to aesthetic standards of displaying violence. A relatively young audience would probably not prefer movies like *Assassins* or *Baise Moi*, precisely because the autotelic aspect of violence is being shown in a very explicit way in such movies. The average violent film that is directed towards a large audience allows the viewer to enjoy autotelic violence, but in an acceptable and non-explicit way. Therefore, the violent main character in such films is a *hero* (and as such, he is not a tragic hero). *The Terminator* only 'terminates' in the name of the Good. But certainly *A Clockwork Orange* should be mentioned here as a film that shocked its audiences in the seventies precisely because of its *Leitmotiv* of violence for the sake of itself. But the film probably wouldn't shock a contemporary audience. A whole movement called 'nouvelle violence', like a new 'nouvelle vague' saw the light in the nineties, and, to name the extreme that I feel is hard to top, we may now enjoy Marquis de Sade's *120 Days of Sodom* in the cinema as well. Does this mean autotelic violence is progressing rapidly in popular culture? And if so, does that mean it increases in reality too?

Formalism and philosophy

There also exists a widespread tradition in philosophy and sociology that, though often only sideways, recognizes the need for violence for the sake of itself that people have. Though these ideas have often been ignored, they are highly relevant today. Collingwood, for instance, speaks of 'malice, the desire that others [...] should suffer', as 'a perpetual source of pleasure to man' (Collingwood, 1958: 87). This need of man for (autotelic) violence, his will to violence, has been given many names. William James has written about 'man's fighting disposition' (James, 1953), and Simmel spoke of a 'need for hostility' and a 'fighting instinct' (Simmel, 1993), Jaspers of a 'will to war' (Jaspers, 1953), and Benjamin of a 'destructive character' (Benjamin, 1996), but Homer already noticed how the iron of a weapon pulls a man towards violence. And then there is – as there has always been – De Sade, of whom Safranski has said he marks a kind of 'inverted Platonism' (Safranski, 1998: 165–6). One could just as easily say De Sade's philosophy is a complete reversal of Kantian ethics. And the troublesome thing for many is that, in his reversal, he is just as rigorous and consistent as Kant is in his ethics. Consider again what he says in *120 Days of Sodom* about the Duke of Blangis: 'People often heard him say that to be really happy here on earth, one would not only have to commit oneself to all sins, but one should also never practice a virtue; that it was not sufficient to just do evil things, but that one should never do something good' (De Sade, 1992: 10). Kant's *duty* towards the good has here been turned into its complete opposite. When searching for clues of autotelic evil in philosophy, one cannot ignore Nietzsche's plea for a 'vivisection of the good man', as he says in *Jenseits von Gut und Böse*. As he says there, 'at times something higher and more sublime is done: we learn *to despise* when we love, and precisely when we love best' (Nietzsche, 1979: III: 682). Nietzsche elsewhere states that pain and lust are not opposites (Nietzsche, 1964: 470), and though his polemics against Christian morality certainly should not be taken to be a plea for what I have called autotelic violence or autotelic evil (though it can be seen as a kind of autotelic immorality), he does hint at its existence, even at its essential presence in what he calls the 'general economy of life'. And he often speaks of the aesthetic beauty of crime (Nietzsche, 1979: III: 631) or of the desire for pain and suffering, and its 'normal' repression (Nietzsche, 1979: I: 714). I believe it is warranted to say that in western philosophy (apart from De Sade), Nietzsche has most explicitly recognized the fact that violence, as its opposite (if such a thing exists), can be willed, or in his terms, that it has a value of its own.

Is the will to violence a western thing and does autotelic violence, or the autotelic aspect to violence, not exist outside western civilization? I believe not. For although my examples from art, philosophy and literature are western, many anthropological findings point in the same direction. One example is the lust for fighting for the sake of itself that is found among the Kwakiutl Indians, or the Ganda (see Fromm, 1973). Another example would be the attitude of the Japanese to depictions of violence in cinema and *manga*, that often amount to cold representations of violence with no other aim than itself. I believe there are aspects to violence that are universal because of their essential role in our being as being-together. The will to violence goes from the Kwakiutl Indians to the National Geographic camera-man who, after weeks of waiting in the heat and dust, speaks of that 'rush of adrenaline' he feels when he finally witnesses a crocodile jumping its prey. I believe there are aspects to violence that are culturally universal because of their essential role in human being as being-together. Violence is such an aspect. It is then not unlikely to conclude that a will to violence is equally universal, as an aspect of the aspect of social life that violence is.

Frictional violence and the hate of the victim

In criminology and especially in the newly emerging 'cultural criminology' (see Ferell et al., 2004; Ferell et al., 2008), the phenomenon of autotelic violence finds some recognition. Mike Presdee, for instance, comments that 'the fascination with violence and crime clearly experienced in the final two weeks of April 1999 [...] shows that there is also potential entertain-ment value to be realised from such acts' (Presdee, 2000: 4). Presdee hence focuses on the important role of *emotions* in dealing with crime in general and violence in particular. At the same time he regards the performance of crime as at times characterized by ecstasy and irrationality (Presdee, 2000: 7). Emotions are, in a time of mass medially produced excitement, not spontaneous responses to external occurrences. They are rather, as the recent sociology of emotions argues, constructed, and they are given shape through mass medial polishing. With respect to the mass media, such as television, and violence, the question should not be whether television vio-lence has an effect on actual violence. The answer to that question would be: probably not, and one can rest the case concerning the relation between violence and the mass media (cf. Gorman and McLean, 2003: 148). The relation between the mass media and behaviour is, however, not one of one-sided determination. The media do not, as various members of the Frankfurt School held, directly determine what we think. Rather, as Niklas Luhmann had argued, the media determine our freedom. This means that the media offer a pre-selection from which we then further select opinions, feelings and ideas (Luhmann, 2000).

In this last section I therefore wish to further explore the will to violence by discussing the fascination for violence not of the individual perpetrator of private violence but of the general public in its guise of a mass medial audi-ence. For what is probably the majority of the public, a form of schizophre-nia exists: it is able to condemn the acts of violence reported on the news and to then switch to the latest movie in which violence is the prime sales mechanism. What is operative here is a distinction between the real and the fictional. Fictional violence is unreal, real violence is not fictional. But of course that distinction is broken once we realize that the real/fictional distinc-tion can be doubled upon itself: the fictional *is real as well*. The many media reports on actual private acts of violence mesh with the fictional violence on the other net. And they fascinate at least as much. It is *real fiction* that is loved in the mass medial portrayal of violence. Yet if that is the case, then is not the moral denouncement of violence hypocritical in a sense? The love of fictional violence may be a love of *fictional* violence; it is also a *love of violence*. The real and the fictional coincide and it is the space of their friction, the merging of real violence and fictional violence into what I will call *frictional violence* that now deserves the attention of disciplines such as the newly developing 'cultural criminology'.

What we find in frictional violence is clearly a victimless violence. If actual violence is abhorred by most people, is it not because of the fact that it has precisely that: victims? In all the worries about the victims of violence that have in the last few decades come up (cf. Garland, 2001; Greer, 2004), is it not precisely the victim that is hated at least as much as the perpetrator of the violent act? For the victim, especially in acts of 'random violence', is indicative of the *possibility* of being the *object* of violence in the sense of being *subjected to* violence, of being reduced to an object. Could not the hate of the victim of violence then be interpreted as the transposed fear of violence of the subject itself? Rather than arguing, with Garland (2001: 11) that 'the victim is now, in a certain sense, a much more representative character, whose experience is taken to be common and collective, rather than individual and atypical', I would venture that the attention given to the victim is much more a way of containing the victim, of constructing the victim as anything but a morally violated singular being. In the fascination for violence, it is the victim that signals the breach of the experience economy. The victim is a potential crack in the autotelic economy of desire. A fissure in the friction between the real and the fictional. It is the victim that threatens to break through the facade of fascination and to infuse the will to violence with its uttermost consequence: the morality of a singular human being. Not the autotelic aspect of violence, but the aspect of its fundamental process: its reduction *qua* reduction. The attention given to the victim can thus be interpreted as a way of sublimating the dark side of the fascination for violence. Analogous to the way 'zero tolerance' 'cleans up' the streets and allows the urban to be experienced without the nuisance it would necessarily mean for the middle class, the victim is overcoded as a symbolic victim and thereby neutralized. This is comparable to what Kathleen Barry, speaking of violence against women, problematized as 'victimism': 'victimism denies the woman the integrity of her humanity though the whole experience, and it creates a framework for others to know her not as a person but as a victim, someone to whom violence was done' (Barry, 1979: 45). But this pinning down of the victim is of more general relevance. The construction of the victim in an overzealous work of care, often initiated by the state, allows a blotting out of those aspects of the victim that would be potentially arresting. It is precisely the *attention* for the victim that *neutralizes* the victim and allows for the unbridled experiential engagement with what *happened to* the victim.

In the attention for the victim, it is the perspective of the perpetrator the public is interested in. Hence the pornographic detail – photo's included – in an Oprah Winfrey show on paedophiles ('predators'), where a police officer is asked 'what's the worst thing you've seen?' so that all of America is allowed to see.

We love the perpetrator and cannot get enough of him (indeed, usually 'him') on TV – we want to *see* the face of evil, as in the case of Josef Fritzl (at last, a glimpse of his face!). The victim we feel no desire towards, except in the case of sexual violence, when best-selling books are available describing something along the lines of 'my years in hell'. But there, is it really the victim that is cherished, or the sexually molested woman that is desired – the legitimate indignation of her fate the moral cloak of a voyeurism that retraces the perpetrator's steps? The victim is to be morally neutralized, in science by analysis, in media and politics by collective emotion and symbolic construction, in law by construction as prime witness, and in the process the victim is reduced to a non-moral character who no longer offers a see-through to the morally unsettling act that violence was for instance for Durkheim.

So if it is the perpetrator that is wanted on TV, how does the real/fictional distinction hold? Clearly, what Mike Presdee (2000) calls the 'carnival of crime' is a mass medial carnival. The idea that fictional violence is unreal and that real violence is not fictional loses credibility once the mass media are the main machine of agitation concerning forms of violence. For then, it is the paradox of 'real violence on tv' that produces outcries of indignity. What is more, the *reactions* to violence can, in a sense ex post facto, *construct* violence. This happened for instance when 'senseless violence' was born as a concept in the Netherlands. It did so as a consequence of a deadly beating followed by a 'silent march', but this allowed for the construction of a similar beating a year before as 'senseless violence' as well. And so this later construction of violence gave rise to an ex–post facto reaction, and a year after the case now recoded into 'senseless violence', another silent march was organized (Schinkel, 2008). 'Real violence' and 'fictional violence' mesh in unpredictable ways. It is rather the *friction between* these two forms that opens up a space of political constructions, of collective emotions and of shared fascination. The desire for autotelic violence is neither a recognition of real violence nor of fictional violence. Rather, this desire forms the gridlines of a space of friction between the real and the fictional, which one could call the *frictional*. It is *frictional violence* that is the supreme object of mass-mediated late capitalist longing.

This is an admittedly radical reversal of the idea that the victim is missing in analyses of violence (but see for an experimental test of the rejection of the victim: Lerner and Simmons, 1966). But even when the victim is supposedly at the centre of analysis, (s)he is not the victim of *violence*. It is not the meaning of violence to the victim or the construction of violence by the victim that is of interest in analyses of victims. It is rather the effects of violence on the victim, or 'victimization' is researched in order to assess the occurrence of violent crime. Again, the formalist approach takes a back seat relative to a determinist analysis. In other areas, such as domestic violence, a move away from victim's wishes towards acting in their interests by the state has been noted (Hoyle, 1998). And when the effects of violence on the victim take precedence, is that not because the only fascination we can muster for the victim is a fascination for the victim *as a potential perpetrator*? For that is what various analyses show: the susceptibility to violence by victims of violence is greater than that by 'normal subjects'. Without wishing to sound inexcusably dismissive of victims of (autotelic) violence then, and without wishing to aim at a cheap shock effect, I would suggest the thesis that the insistence on the perspective of the victim is in fact hypocritical. We need an analysis of the construction of violence by the victim, yes, but we need a *critical* analysis instead of a *hypocritical* one.

Two perspectives on the will to violence

Ok. Let's change the aspect. Let's tentatively venture the question from whence the fascination for violence of the general public stems? I should like to offer two general perspectives here. The first is that in the pleasure derived from autotelic violence we see the reflection of a much more general fascination with safety and violence. In a sense, it is the mirror image of the frantic search for safety, of the frenzy of identifying the morally depraved in society and the ritualized indignity with which instances of violence are clothed. If some people perpetrate acts of autotelic violence, then, these are only in a sense circumstantially contingent and contracted forms of a more general anxiety concerning violence. In other words, the perpetrator of autotelic violence is not to be seen as the instigator, but rather as the contracted consequence of a more general fascination with violence. He or she is not what gives rise to mass indignity, but what *legitimates* it – and there is a significant difference between these two processes. To say that the perpetrator gives rise to indignity is to follow the linear model that wholly attributes violence and the fascination for autotelic violence to a perpetrator as an individual subject, and according to which the ensuing indignity and moral condemnation are caused by the acts of that individual subject. That model thus constructs the perpetrator as an individual subject, as a self-emanating source of violence, cut from all social bonds. And that is precisely what legitimates the idea that the perpetrator of autotelic violence is in a sense an extra-social being, who has no real bonds with 'society' (cf. Hirschi, 1969; for a critique, see, Schinkel, 2002). A non-linear model allows for the social interchangeability of cause and effect and describes the acts of the perpetrator as fully social, as fully normal, in fact as *more normal than normal* in the sense that they embody the contracted or instantaneously intensified form of the normal fascination with violence. That fascination, in turn, is once more apparent in the condemnation of the perpetrator that can always be coded as 'the normal moral response'. The study of violence must crack open the linear model, it must open Pandora's Box in order to fully face the complexities of violence in everyday life. It will not do to analyse violence solely in terms of its perpetrators, for contemporary violence is always already a hybrid of the real and the fictional. It is always already a frictional violence that is situated in the frictional space *between* the real and the fictional, spun in a web of threads of desire. It does not 'give rise to' or much less 'cause' a response of an otherwise passive audience. We are not dealing with billiard ball type causality here. Rather, as Bateson has emphasized, we are dealing with communication systems, with cybernetic feedback loops in which the energy of a response is delivered by the respondent him- or herself (Bateson, 1972: 409). The audience or the public is constitutive of a frictional violence that promulgates on the threads of the public's desire for violence.

A second perspective that does that is more strongly focused on what one might call the 'function' of mass indignation over autotelic violence. In the fascination for fictional transgression, the norm is strengthened. It is precisely the real transgression that is needed to give the norm its ultimate plausibility. But today, in a post-ideological and post-political age, the norm no longer derives its credibility from anything other than its transgression. And the transgression is no longer desired to be understood. What is desired is the transgression pur sang, the 'senseless transgression' of 'senseless violence'. For it is the most meaningless, most 'pure' and autotelic transgression that most distinctly demarcates the norm, that sets it apart by dividing the land of the normal from the land of the abnormal, by identifying those who venture beyond the norm without maintaining any ties with the normal, with the sensible. So the perpetrator is in a sense celebrated in the form of a moral critique. But he is celebrated, and this celebration, which strengthens recognition of the 'normal' and all the while allows for the celebration of the 'abnormal', becomes nowhere more apparent than in the indulgence in fascination for the fictional perpetrator, for what Walter Benjamin called the figure of the 'grossen Verbrecher'.

Here, the fascination for violence is matched by another problematization of violence. I am referring to the relatively recent problematization of 'Muslims' and their supposed 'culturally determined' violations of women and women's rights in Western European discourse. All of a sudden, second wave feminists and conservative politicians find common ground (van den Berg and Schinkel, 2009) in what Judith Butler has called an abuse of women's rights in the construction of Muslims as an 'other' (Butler, 2007). Here, the fascination for violence is much less autotelic and pertains directly to the definition of the 'well integrated' citizen, the true 'member of society'. 'Muslims', so the popular discourse goes, are too 'culturally incompatible' to be genuinely seen as 'members of society'. Hence the frequent and highly stereotypical problematizing associations between 'Muslims' and 'respect for women'. Here, the state actively engages in a cultural construction of the victim. Women are construed as passive victims of their Muslim men (van den Berg and Schinkel, 2009). Recently, Dutch populist politician Geert Wilders for instance critiqued a Dutch journalist who had been raped by members of the Taliban because she was 'politically correct' in also having words of sympathy for her treatment at other moments by Taliban members. Politics here means the active effort to control the experience of the victim in order to be able to clearly demarcate a superior 'Enlightened, western, secular' but nonetheless 'Judeo-Christian' civilization from its 'Muslim' other. This is a wholly different construction of the victim, one that does not predominantly entail a will to violence per se, but one that likewise has the consequence of demarcating the normal and the abnormal.

Constructions of victims, therefore, are never without a politics of violence. The same goes for the victim in autotelic violence. In that case, the victim is to be construed as an object, not as a moral subject. The 'abyss' of subjectivity (Žižek, 1999) all too soon threatens to invade the experience economy that runs on frictional violence. In order to secure the recognition of the normal by means of the fascination for its transgression, the victim is sacrificed in the space of friction between real and fictional violence. In the very attention devoted to the victim, the victim is neutralized. For the true recognition of the victim – whatever that would be – would be a far too unsettling affirmation of the normal order. The indulgence of desire for violence and the fascination for its perpetrator offers, paradoxically, a much safer way of demarcating the realm of the morally permissive, of the true 'society', and the trauma of its transgression.

At least two perspectives are thus possible, or rather plausible, in shedding light on the phenomena of a will to violence and of an indulgence in frictional violence. The first is that the fascination for autotelic violence is the concentrated form of a general fascination with violence and safety. The second is that the norm is nowhere more clearly demarcated than in the case of autotelic violence. Both these perspectives open up an ontological field. The space of friction between the real and the fictional is the site of desire of transgression. That desire may, in the final instance, be interpreted as the necessary flipside of the foundational energy that ensures any kind of sociality. Any order sets itself off against a lack of order, any order is an achievement out of chaos (Luhmann, 1984) and the transgression of its boundaries therefore promises the creative enjoyment of the new and the as yet unexperienced. In a late capitalist experience economy, nothing could be more tempting. But of course this desire for transgression is immediately sublimated and acted out in a safe manner. It is contained in the friction between the real and the fictional, such that it can always at the same time be *enjoyed* as if it were real and *legitimated* as if it were fictional. But is not the reduction of being in general a process of subjectification taking place in that between? Is it not part of an *inter-esse*, a being in-between? 'We' are formed in the fissures of friction.

To conclude

Most that has been said about a will to violence won't surprise anyone who's ever witnessed football hooliganism. Yet if there is a will to autotelic violence, that has to be faced in its formal aesthetic aspect. Social scientific accounts of football hooliganism, or 'disorder', rather focus on the 'rules of disorder' (cf. Marsh et al., 1978) or on the ways group solidarity is fostered by means of hooligan violence (King, 2001). That is legitimate, but it omits the autotelic aspect to violence itself. It has been my contention that one reason why this aspect has been neglected is that there has been a fear of facing violence in its purest form. That is why we either cling to a wholly irrational hope of one day explain the phenomenon in all of its aspects, or we maintain the metaphysical stance that there are no such things as intrinsic aspects to a social phenomenon, that to say that is a metaphysical stance that fails to recognize that the social is socially constructed. I believe those lines of thought that are clung to with great tenacity are due to the fact that autotelic violence has to it what the Greeks called *to deinon*, the unsettling, the appalling, the outside which, because of its 'out' in relation to the inside, is yet so familiar. It is repressed, negated. Biaphobia causes an evident cause of violent behaviour to be forgotten by a social science that shies away from violence itself by seeing 'causes' of *violent behaviour* as factors having nothing to do with *violence*.

I claim that there is autotelic violence, and this kind of violence, or at least this aspect of violence, needs to be taken into account in social scientific research of violence. The way to do that is to set apart, yet not to separate, a determinist analysis from a formalist analysis. The latter will be more equipped to study the autotelic aspect of violence. From this perspective, the interesting task for criminology and sociology is to explain how and why some people seem to have a stronger will to violence than others. This would be to combine determinism and formalism in the study of violence, and that is what would lead to a realization of Weber's *erklärendes Verstehen*. So I am certainly not suggesting the social sciences should abandon their determinist research, but rather that they should add something to it. An aesthetics of violence can no longer shy away from violence itself, and the addition a formalism would bring, consists of, for the first time, really dealing with *violence* in the study of violence. I want to express the hope that such an analysis would give us better clues as to what violence *is*, that is, how it could be sensibly defined. But perhaps the greatest challenge lies in combining all this in an account of predisposing factors, like a *diathesis*, which lead to a will to violence in some people, which others, without these predisposing factors, do not have, and which combines with (other) triggering causes into an eruption of violence. Is boredom, for example, a factor that is related, as Baudelaire suggested, to the seemingly most senseless outbursts of violence? Are such conditions that can be found in 'sleeping' suburban areas like Columbine, as Michael Moore seems to suggest in his film *Bowling for Columbine*, facilitative for the autotelic violence that some are already more disposed to than others? How is the everyday experience of frictional violence related to both a fascination and a condemnation of auto-telic violence – a violence that perhaps does no more than to render a more generally shared experience visible and to expose its moral hypocrisy? These things deserve serious attention, rather than a biaphobic blind eye for aspects of violence that run counter to commonsensical notions of violence.

One last comment is in place to conclude this chapter. From a norma-tive perspective, autotelic violence clashes with Kantian ethics. For while Safranski has called De Sade a kind of 'inverted Platonism', one could also say that De Sade's philosophy is a complete reversal of Kantian ethics. And the troublesome thing for many is that, in his reversal, he is just as rigorous and consistent as Kant is in his ethics. Consider again what he says in *120 Days of Sodom* about the Duke of Blangis: 'People often heard him say that to be really happy here on earth, one would not only have to commit oneself to all sins, but one should also never practice a virtue; that it was not sufficient to just do evil things, but that one should never do something good' (De Sade, 1992: 10). Kant's *duty* towards the good has here been turned into its complete opposite. The 'positive feeling' that Kant (1961: 120) describes as inherent to the moral imperative is thus preserved, since its 'intellectual basis' is preserved. While Kant says he takes this feeling as the only *a priori* knowable, it may also function as a solid basis of an imperative of evil. The *form* of practical reason is thereby preserved, but the *content* has been radically changed. But the problem with Kant's ethics is often said to be that it is a form without content. From a biaphobic perspective, autotelic violence is evil for evil's sake. But this is an impossibility in Kant's ethics. For while there is such a thing as radical evil (which is 'radical' because it is willed), Kant in the end denies the possibility of evil for evil's sake. A propensity to evil means a propensity to develop maxims that are exclusively directed towards self-love (cf. Allison, 2002). Even the propensity to evil does not entail evil for the sake of evil. Moreover, Kant denies the possibility of pure practical reason in the morally bad (Kant, 1974: 42). The impossibil-ity in Kant's moral theory of wanting evil for the sake of itself is in fact already a consequence of his *Kritik der praktischen Vernunft*, which is of a *descriptive* character, and which does not intend to prescribe rules for cor-rect moral behaviour. The notion of always also treating the other as an end in itself is thus, according to Kant, innate to man as a moral being. While this duty may be sinned against in practice, it can never be absent. Yet the notion of autotelic violence sheds doubt on this. While it does not refute Kantian ethical theory, it does suggest that this theory may be up for reconsideration with respect to its *empirical* conditions of responsibility, similar to the way Durkheim amended pure theoretical reason and to the way Bourdieu set social limits to the judgement of taste.

6
The Continuation of Violence by Other Means: Terrorism

Political aspects of the work of definition

That the conceptualization of violence is often highly political and strongly related to the state's definition of violence nowhere becomes clearer than in the case of 'terrorism'. However, there is no lack of definitions of terrorism, albeit that these often forego explicit conceptualization. It is perhaps best to say there are a lot of working definitions of terrorism. Many, however, tend to have a highly restricted focus in identifying 'terrorism' with an intitial violent event. And while in the case of autotelic violence, social scientists often focus too little on the violence itself, in the case of terrorism, the violent aspect of what is in essence a *political process* is usually overstated or even the exclusive focus of analyses. Many contemporary conceptualizations thereby inadvertently reify political conceptions of terrorism. Mainly because they in the end rely on the intentions of terrorists in defining 'terrorism', the *process* of terrorism, which involves an unfolding dialectic of actions and reactions, is omitted from researchers' focus. Thus, terrorism becomes simplified to intentional actions by terrorists, and this short-cutting of the causal chain of the process of terrorism facilitates both a political 'negation of history' and a 'rhetoric of response' (compare, Nuzzo, 2004). I believe a more comprehensive conceptualization of terrorism is both more realistic and runs less risk of reifying political definitions of terrorism (compare Tilly, 2004), and I argue that terrorism is a political process that is always a part of a larger political process.

In this chapter, I therefore put forward a conceptualization of terrorism that encompasses many aspects of terrorism contained in currently existing definitions and conceptualizations, but that transcends them by conceptualizing terrorism as a paradox: what terrorism is, is inextricably bound to the reaction to 'terrorism' which makes for terrorism as a political process instead of a singular event. It is, I will argue, in fact the reaction of some state to terrorism that, in a sense *ex post facto*, constitutes an act as 'terrorism' by 'refolding' actions that unfolded subsequent to an event into that event as the root cause of the entire chain of events.

The main problem in defining or conceptualizing terrorism is political in nature. That is to say that what counts as terrorism and what does not fall under its heading is subject to political pressure and consequence. Such a political import of conceptualizations of terrorism can take different forms. After the experience of the 1878–1914 'wave' of terrorism, for instance, the *Convention for the Prevention and Punishment of Terrorism* (1937) laid much emphasis on terrorism as *anarchism*, and hence as a form of violence directed mainly towards heads of state. Reason for such emphasis lay in the murders of Alexander I of Yugoslavia and the president of the Council of the French Republic (Louis Barthou) in 1934. Such a conceptualization of terrorism neglects the 'positive' political substance of terrorism, that is, its revolutionary aspect. It does so precisely as a political negation of the threat of revolution (the murders were committed by the Macedonian nationalist-revolutionary VMRO and the Croatian fascist-nationalist Ustasa). Another kind of political import in the definition of terrorism becomes apparent in the statement of the *Organization of American States*, in 1970, that 'the political and ideological pretexts utilized as justification for these crimes [acts of terrorism, WS] in no way mitigate their cruelty and irrationality or the ignoble nature of the means employed, and in no way remove their character as acts of violation of essential human rights' (quoted in Dugard, 1974: 72). Thus, the political character of terrorism is, in what is itself a thoroughly political move, declared as violating 'human rights', the conceptualization of which is, again highly politically, framed as 'essential' and 'universal'. This is replicated in the May 2002 statement on human rights (in 2001) of the US *State Department*, in which countries depicted as 'human rights violators' are equalled to 'governments that promote international terror' (see Tilly, 2004: 6).

The greatest political problem in the definition of terrorism surely lies in the decision when to discern 'terrorist' from 'freedom fighter' (Hess, 2003; Hoffman, 1998; Jenkins, 1982) or when to differentiate between 'terrorism' and 'war of liberation' (Dugard, 1974: 75–7). Freedom fighters fall under *jus ad bellum*, while terrorists do not. A historical case is that of the 'Islamic terrorism' of Mohammed Ahmed (self-proclaimed Mahdi) in Sudan in the 1890s, who initially succeeded in driving the British out of Sudan (Bergesen and Lizardo, 2004). Another is the aforementioned case of the Yugoslavian killings in 1934, in which the Macedonians were explicitly not portrayed as 'freedom fighters' during the International Conference on the Repression of Terrorism which led to the Convention. A case more relevant today has been the US response to supposed terrorists held in Guantanamo Bay. The detainees of Guantanamo Bay did not fall under *jus ad bellum*, and they were not seen as prisoners of war (POWs). They were labelled by the US as 'unlawful combatants' (former US Secretary of Defence Donald H. Rumsfeld) or 'enemy fighters'. As such the Geneva Conventions were deemed not to apply to them (as, according to the US, both Taliban and Al Qaeda are not parties to those Conventions) (White House, 2003), although in July 2006, after a 5–3 Supreme Court ruling against military tribunals proposed by the Bush administration, Common Article 3 of those Conventions became applicable to all detainees. In 2009, the dismantling of the entire facility has been announced by president Obama.

The political substance of the definition of terrorism has not become an issue only recently. The US State Department stated on the concept of 'global terrorism' in 1992 that 'the term does not have unanimous definition because the United Nations has been incapable of agreeing on its definition [...]. No definition has been unanimously accepted' (quoted in Nuzzo, 2004: 335). Yet in 1987, only the US and Israel opposed a UN definition of 'global terrorism', because the definition on vote separated the right to self-determination from terrorist activity. It did so mainly with a view to the then pertinent situation in South Africa, but the consequence of such a definition would have been that Palestinian 'terrorists' could no longer be regarded as such. Likewise, after 9/11, the Organization of the Islamic Conference (encompassing 56 states) blocked a UN counterterrorism proposal on the grounds that it should exclude national liberation fighters, including anti-Israeli groups, from its provisions. In September 2005, mainly Arab nations opposed a UN definition of terrorism (designed to become a world-wide standard) which amounted to equalling terrorism to all military violence against civilians. The issue whether to speak of freedom fighters or terrorists is in fact age-old. St Augustine's questioning of the difference between Alexander the Great and a pirate already illustrates the value judgment inherent in the use of the term 'terrorism'.

Characteristic of the political substance of the concept of 'terrorism' is, furthermore, the isolation of events. In 'the war on terrorism', the US slogan is 'America Responds'.[1] Thereby, the flow of geopolitical events is frozen at a certain point in time – 'terrorism' – which serves as an index and anchor point for subsequent actions now termed as 'responses' – even when much that the US has done under that heading perhaps hardly qualifies as a 'response' to 'terrorism' (Bobrow, 2004; Schwartz, 2004), at least when *prima facie* notions thereof are considered. As Nuzzo says, '9/11 is presented as the Nietzschean "monument" that has lost any connection with causal explanation – a monument placed outside any causal chain of explanation, a hypostatized event placed outside history' (Nuzzo, 2004: 337). Indeed, the *negation of history* in labelling certain acts as 'terrorist' is part and parcel of the *political* act of definition. The identification rests on a particular balance of remembrance/forgetting. A *rhetoric of response* is often in place, which identifies state action as response subsequent to an initial terrorist act. Such a rhetoric of response that enables a negation of history – and is still active also in scholarly circles – was evident in US involvement in the Second World War as a 'response' to the 'unprovoked' Japanese attack on Pearl Harbour, which, from a Japanese point of view, has been seen by some as a 'response' to Commodore Perry's opening up of Japan in 1853 (which led to the subsequent Meiji revolution of 1868). A similar logic of 'response' led the US into Vietnam. Freezing the flow of global events is often accompanied by a kind of *argumentum ad hominem* of what motivates 'the' terrorist, thereby psychologizing what is essentially a political process. It leads for instance to the conducting of brain tests on Ulrike Meinhoff (Hess, 2003), or to accounts of the vindictiveness of mythicized figures such as Osama Bin Laden, in whom the whole issue of terrorism is condensed in a simplifying move that fits the routine of scoop-searching media.

Definitions and conceptualizations of terrorism

As Walter Laqueur said in 1996, terrorism has many faces, and there are 'many terrorisms' (Laqueur, 1996: 25). Today that may be even more true. Yet the fact that a phenomenon is manifold in appearance does not preclude its being defined. In order to take steps in the direction of a definition of terrorism, it is useful to review currently existing definitions. A round-up of some authoritative 'official' as well as scholarly definitions can serve to indicate the notions common to most definitions. According to United States Federal Law,

> The term 'terrorism' means premeditated, politically motivated violence perpetrated against non-combatant targets by subnational groups or clandestine agents, usually intended to influence an audience. [...] The term 'international terrorism' means terrorism involving citizens or the territory of more than one country. [...] The term 'terrorist group' means any group practicing, or that has significant subgroups that practice, international terrorism
>
> (US Code, Title 22, § 2656f(d))

Such definitions leave a considerable degree of latitude for discussion on terms such as 'subnational groups or clandestine agents' and 'politically motivated violence'. However, within the US, different definitions are deployed. For the FBI, terrorism amounts to 'the unlawful use of force or violence against persons or property to intimidate or coerce a government, the civilian population, or any segment thereof, in furtherance of political or social objectives' (FBI, 2006). These definitions entail various elements also present in academic conceptualizations of terrorism. There are a great deal of scholarly definitions and conceptualizations of terrorism (in 1983, Schmid and Jongman (1988) counted 109), and I shall review some of them in order to single out the recurring aspects. Hardman described terrorism in 1948 as 'a term used to describe the method or the theory behind the method whereby an organized group or party seeks to achieve its avowed aims chiefly through the systematic use of violence' (Hardman, 1948: 575).

The *International Encyclopedia of the Social & Behavioral Sciences* describes it as referring to the 'systematic use or threat of violence to communicate a political message rather than defeat an opponent's military forces' (Crenshaw, 2001: 15604). This definition describes as further characteristics of terrorism the fact that symbolic targets are often chosen, that a wider audience is victim of terrorism, and that it is a means of fighting deployed by persons deprived of conventional means of fighting. The last point refers to what James Scott (1985) has called 'weapons of the weak': terrorists are lacking in real power, and hence they resort to alternative ways of 'warfare'. Paradoxically, perhaps, this often involves severe forms of violence. Many conceptualizations of terrorism hold that it involves extreme violence: '[terrorism, WS] lies beyond the norms of violent political agitation that are accepted by a given society' (Thornton, 1964: 76). Terrorists are often forced to deploy forms of violence that, according to Tilly, 'fall outside the forms of political struggle operating within some current regime' (Tilly, 2004: 5). This is precisely what gives terrorism, in contradistinction to other forms of (political violence), its 'war-like character' (Black, 2004: 17). The extreme violence that is involved in terrorism is a violence that violates norms of violence. The extreme violence of 9/11 may also be recalled, or the cutting off of the noses of victims in Algeria during its war of independence. In general, the use of violence against persons not representative of the state's monopoly of legitimate violence is a violation of norms of violence, and is hence in a specific sense more violent than the same force exerted against combatants (e.g., Crenshaw Hutchinson, 1972; Drake, 1998; Hoffman, 1998; Laqueur, 1987), extreme violence (e.g., Crenshaw, 2001; Tilly, 2004; Thornton, 1964), against civilians (e.g., Black, 2004; Rodin, 2004; Stern, 2003) or symbolic targets (e.g., Crenshaw, 2001) by some organization that seeks to influence some state by means of intimidation of an audience (e.g., Crenshaw, 2001; Gibbs, 1989; Primoratz, 2004; Stern, 2003). These characteristics are well summarized in, to take one example, Enders and Sandler's definition of terrorism:

> Terrorism is the premeditated use or threat of use of extranormal violence or brutality by subnational groups to obtain a political, religious, or ideological objective through intimidation of a huge audience, usually not directly involved with the policy making that the terrorists seek to influence

> (Enders and Sandler, 2002: 145–6)

The indirect instrumentality of terrorism

In the remainder of this chapter I will expand on such a definition, in part by tacking onto some of its aspects and by introducing another, borrowing from Raymond Aron's definition of terrorism. What can be first of all distilled from current conceptualizations is that terrorism works by way of an *indirect instrumentalism*. That is to say that terrorists lack the power to directly influence the actors (states, mostly) whose behaviour they wish to change, and therefore they target third parties. Thus, Stern defines terrorism as 'an act or threat of violence against non-combatants, with the objective of intimidating or otherwise influencing an audience or audiences' (Stern, 1999: 30; 2003). By targeting a few non-combatants directly, terrorism targets an entire 'audience' indirectly (compare Crenshaw, 2001; Enders and Sandler, 2002; Gibbs, 1989; Primoratz, 2004). The same is captured in Wardlaw's definition of terrorism as 'the use, or threat of use, of violence by an individual or group, whether acting for or in opposition to established authority, when such action is designed to create extreme anxiety and/or fear-inducing effects in a target group larger than the immediate victims with the purpose of coercing that group into acceding to the political demands of the perpetrators' (Wardlaw, 1982: 16; compare Primoratz, 2004: 24). But the indirect instrumentalism by means of which terrorism takes place is in fact a double one. For as the persons directly hit in a terrorist attack are not the ultimate focus of terrorism, neither is the wider audience in which terrorism raises fear. Schematically, one might say that A (terrorists) influence B (an enemy political entity) by means of an attack or the threat thereof on C (random civilians or symbolic targets) which is hoped by A, through the spread of fear among D (larger populace), to result a political pressure exerted on B by D and possibly E (foreign political entities). Since fear is an instrument in terrorism, terrorism is most effective when C and D are interchangeable. That is to say, it is most effective when its direct targets are civilians, not material symbolic targets, and it is furthermore most effective when its direct targets can be anyone of the larger audience in which terrorism raises fear. The interchangeability of the direct victims and members of the audience of terrorism most effectively raises fear. For this reason, Michael Walzer holds that 'randomness is the crucial feature of terrorist activity' (Walzer, 1977: 197). Hence, I would claim that the above description refers to terrorism in an ideal–typical sense (see Weber, 1988), which is more readily embodied by Al Qaeda than by the Baader-Meinhoff group or the Red Brigades. In Al Qaeda's 9/11 attacks, the randomness of the direct victims of terrorism was evident; in Rote Armee Fraktion actions, such was usually not the case. The latter group for instance kidnapped and killed bankers and businessmen, and its goal was not the spread of fear, but rather of class consciousness, as it was a communist terrorist organization. In that sense, therefore, Al Qaeda qualifies as a more ideal–typical terrorist organization than the Rote Armee Fraktion. Likewise, the IRA is a more ideal–typical terrorist organization than the ETA. Such ideal–typical classification of terrorism can encompass definitions of terrorism that negate the necessity for randomness (e.g., Laqueur, 1987), but it holds that randomness of immediate or direct targets is a feature of the most ideal–typical forms of terrorism.

Terrorism and terror

Scholarly definitions of terrorism usually differentiate between state- and non-state-perpetrated violence. In that case, 'terrorism' is often explicitly regarded as a type of violence perpetrated by non-state actors (e.g., Black, 2004; Enders and Sandler, 2002; Gibbs, 1989; Hess, 2003; Laqueur, 1996). In many cases, the same is implicit in the conceptualization of terrorism (e.g., Alexander, 2004; Hardman, 1948). On the other hand, many conceptualizations do not differentiate between state- and non-state-perpetrated violence at all (see Schmid and Jongman, 1988; Wardlaw, 1982; Wellman, 1979). In that case, 'terrorism' is something states as well as non-state actors may engage in. Again, this may be explicit, and then terms like 'terrorist states' (e.g., Chomsky, 2001) or 'state terrorism' (*le terrorisme d'état*) (Camus, 1951: 214ff.) are being used. In another sense, Lefebvre called the most repressive society a 'société terroriste' (Lefebvre, 1968: 273ff.). In yet other cases, terrorism is said to possibly occur in the service of states. In a famous article on the 'causes of terrorism', Martha Crenshaw (1981: 379; 2001) states that terrorism takes place both in the service of state interests and against states. From an ethical point of view, David Rodin (2004) has argued that the concept of terrorism can at times apply to state violence when that violence is directed towards noncombatants. In many social scientific analyses, acknowledgment of the possibility of state-perpetrated terrorism is given, and either explicit (e.g., Bergesen and Lizardo 2004: 38; Bergesen and Han, 2005: 134–5) or implicit (e.g., Wilkinson, 1997) mention is made of a deliberate neglect thereof, and of focusing instead on non-state perpetrated terrorism. According to Charles Tilly (2004: 12), the definition of 'terrorism' and 'terrorist' cannot be laid down unequivocally. He regards 'terror' as a strategy used by widely differing actors that cannot be properly discerned as belonging to a single category, partly because 'most groups and networks that engage in terror overlap extensively with government-employed and government-backed specialists in coercion – armies, police, militias, paramilitaries, and the like' (Tilly, 2004: 6). Thus, although he intends to counter the conflation of 'terror, terrorism, and terrorists', Tilly does not properly discern 'terror' from 'terrorism'. While his concern is that sociologists might reify such concepts (Tilly, 2004), he evades the problem by dealing with 'terror' as a strategy that he conceptualizes in terms corresponding 'approximately to what many people mean by terror' (Tilly, 2004: 9). Yet the lack of distance vis-à-vis commonsensical understanding leads all the more to the risk of reification. I believe it is necessary to untangle 'terror' and 'terrorism'.

An important indication of the difference between the two is gained from the etymology of the word 'terror', to which the affix 'ism' has been attached. The concept of 'terror' – etymologically rooted in Greek and Sanskrit words for 'fear' – was first used in a political context by Edmund Burke, who spoke of Robespierre's revolutionary government (from September 1793 to July 1794) as a 'Reign of Terror'. Robespierre himself regarded 'terror' as a form of justice. Hence, 'terrorism' has been defined as 'the attempt to govern or to oppose government by intimidation' (Pye, 1956: 102). Likewise, the *Oxford English Dictionary* entry on 'terrorism' speaks of 'government by intimidation'. Yet since the original formulation used the word 'terror', I believe here lies a highly useful way of distinguishing between 'terror' and 'terrorism'. Terror refers to actions designed to spread fear by states, and hence it works 'top down'. It is not a state that needs to be influenced, but the people. By means of terror a state causes a shock though its own institutions, inducing fear in order to remain control. As Lefort (2000: 201) has said: 'terror works in the service of foundation'. The Machiavellist idea that the prince or ruler is better off feared than loved is expressed *par excellence* in the idea of terror. The state of terror – one might think of Stalin's USSR or Saddam Hussein's Iraq – therefore runs directly counter to the state Hobbes finds preferable. Terrorism, by contrast, is perpetrated by non-state actors, works 'bottom up' to create, from the outside, a shock in institutions that induces fear. Both in terror and in terrorism, therefore, an indirect instrumentality is at work, but only in the case of terrorism is this a doubly indirect instrumentality. Only terrorism targets a state via fear of an audience induced through direct targets. Terror is a 'domestic' affair, and induces fear among the public through randomly targeted acts of (threat of) violence upon its direct targets. What it seeks is no more than compliance. Typically, dictators use terror to remain in power. Some might say, however, that a democracy such as the US is at times also characterized by aspects of terror, for instance when terrorism alerts are raised during election times or when troops are deployed overseas. To regard terror as a domestic affair is to regard state action against other states or against foreign civilians not as terror, nor as terrorism. In such cases, I believe such labels are better unused, and 'political violence' or 'war' (legitimate or not) are more appropriate.

The paradox of terrorism

Having conceptually separated 'terror' from 'terrorism' leaves us with the notion of terrorism as a form of violence or threat thereof deployed by non-state actors against random or symbolic targets to induce fear among a wider audience, in order to influence some state. This is a conceptualization taking various clues from existing definitions, which differentiate 'terrorism' from 'terror'. So far, however, a 'naïve realist' ontological perspective has been adopted, according to which what 'terrorism' is can be defined without taking stock of the political process of which it is part. The account given thus far, while certainly relevant for instance in the legal context, still fails to encompass a crucial aspect of terrorism, which has to do with the political entity (usually an enemy state) which terrorism aims at by means of this doubly indirect instrumentalism. We shall have to leave the 'realist ontology' of terrorism here, according to which a definition of terrorism encompassing primary and secondary qualities, or the essence, or the prime connotations, of terrorism are thought to cover actually existing 'terrorism' in a way separable from a larger political process. The need for another conceptualization can be illustrated by taking up the problematic of the question of intentionality in terrorism. From there, a problematization of the relation between terrorism and its (indirect) target will provide further clues in the direction of terrorism as a dialectical process that cannot be 'realistically' pinpointed but for which a fractured realist perspective proves most suitable.

Beyond intentionality

However many aspects or characteristics of terrorism are discerned, there are basically only two aspects of current conceptualizations of terrorism which make up its core. All definitions or conceptualizations assume that terrorism concerns (1) a certain form of violence (or possibly a threat thereof), and (2) a specific kind of intentionality. My preliminary definition of terrorism as 'a form of violence deployed against arbitrary or symbolic targets to induce fear in a wider audience, in order to influence some state', consists of two parts. It starts from 'a form of violence' and moves on to a 'deployed ... to', with appending specifications concerning the doubly indirect instrumentality of the phenomenon. Yet however specific the qualifications, what is at stake is retraceable to some kind of intention – a violence deployed to ... Something similar is at stake in the US Federal Law definition of 'terrorism' as 'premeditated, politically motivated violence perpetrated against non-combatant targets by subnational groups or clandestine agents, usually intended to influence an audience' (US Code, Title 22, § 2656f(d)). Here, what is at stake is a form of violence that is 'premeditated', and 'usually intended to'. The same holds in case of Hardman's definition: 'a term used to describe the method or the theory behind the method whereby an organized group or party seeks to achieve its avowed aims chiefly through the systematic use of violence' (Hardman, 1948: 575), or in that of Crenshaw: 'systematic use or threat of violence *to communicate* a political message rather than defeat an opponent's military forces' (Crenshaw, 2001: 15604). This list can go on, I believe, for several pages. There is a definite problem to the intrinsic reduction of definitions and conceptualizations of terrorism to the aspects of (1) violence and (2) intentionality.

For since the violence of terrorism is manifold and is, rightly therefore, in the great majority of definitions, not further specified, what differentiates terrorism from other forms of violence according to these definitions is, in the final instance, a specific form of intentionality. Terrorism is thus usually defined, in the end, in terms *solely* of *intentions of terrorists*. Consider, once more, a definition that encompasses many aspects of terrorism, defining it as 'the premeditated use or threat of use of extranormal violence or brutality by subnational groups to obtain a political, religious, or ideological objective through intimidation of a huge audience, usually not directly involved with the policy making that the terrorists seek to influence' (Enders and Sandler, 2002: 145–6). This definition falls into four parts, namely first, 'the use or threat of use of extranormal violence or brutality by subnational groups' (P1). Second, the qualification P2 which specifies that what is described in P1 is 'premeditated [...] to obtain' what is described, thirdly, in P2a as 'a political, religious, or ideological objective', through, fourthly, P2b: 'intimidation of a huge audience, usually not directly involved with the policy making that the terrorists seek to influence'. The authors speak of the 'premeditated use' of violence (or threat thereof). Hence it becomes clear that the definition entails, next to violence, the aspect of intentionality, and two auxiliary specifications of the content of that intentionality which is at the same time believed to be the way 'terrorism' works. The means used in terrorism are the means intended by terrorists. These specifications (P2a and P2b) can in fact be seen as elaborations of P2, in which the aspect of intentionality is highlighted. They are indeed a specification thereof, leaving the definition as consisting of two basic parts with further specifications. The aspect of intentionality is present in many if not all discussions of terrorism (e.g., Crenshaw, 2001; FBI, 2006; Laqueur, 1999; Scheffler, 2006; Wardlaw, 1982), although at times somewhat covertly, as for instance in Chomsky's definition of terrorism as 'the use of coercive means aimed at populations in an effort to achieve political, religious, or other aims' (Chomsky, 2001: 19). In the 'aimed at' and the 'effort to' lies the intentionality of the terrorist. Similarly, in Wellman's definition of terrorism as 'the use or attempted use of terror as a means of coercion' (Wellman, 1979: 250), the means (terror)–end (coercion) rationality at the core of the definition betrays the intentionality which forms the actual basis of the definition. Even in an 'object-centred' definition such as Coady's (2004: 5) definition of terrorism as 'the organized use of violence to attack non-combatants ('innocents' in a special sense) or their property for political purposes', the intentionality is imminent in the choice of object (and in the political purposes).

Now, there is certainly no doubt about the existence of some form of intentionality in case of acts deemed 'terrorist' – for instance, a great deal of planning usually precedes such an act (e.g., Gurr, 1979). Conceptual problems arise, however, when intentionality becomes the crucial element in the conceptualization of terrorism. I argue that terrorists' intentions are not enough to produce 'terrorism'. The silent assumption in many conceptualizations of terrorism is that terrorists are in principle able to produce intimidation or terrorization by means of a terrorist attack, whether they do so in a particular instance or not. Although intentionality is but one aspect of definitions of terrorism, this involves the idea that terrorism *begins* with some intentional act of terrorism. This is a view which is highly relevant in certain contexts, for one in the legal context. It plays a significant role in the political context as well. That is precisely why I feel a political philosophical account should change the aspect here. From that point of view, one might say that, in fact, terrorists are quite aware that they themselves are incapable of producing 'terrorization'. Besides intentions, something else is therefore needed for 'terrorism' to occur. In the focus on their intentions, something escapes us which indicates the 'extension' of terrorism to not just an intention or an occurrence of violence deemed 'act of terrorism'. When what 'terrorism' is, is in the end defined in terms of terrorists' intentions, a reduction to intentionality takes place that is part of a simplification and a reification of 'terrorism'. Such simplification enables the *negation of history* and the *rhetoric of response*. In order for conceptualizations of terrorism not specifically geared towards legal or political contexts to move beyond reifying terrorism, rendering lip service to politicians keen on isolating 'terrorism' in a rhetoric of response, a conceptualization that encompasses more of the complexity of the political process of terrorism, is needed.

Terrorism and the strength of the other

The point made in the last paragraph can be further developed by first invoking a somewhat forgotten definition of terrorism by Raymond Aron, according to whom 'an action is labeled "terrorist" when its psychological effects are out of proportion to its purely physical result' (Aron, 2003: 170). Aron here draws attention to a significant characteristic of terrorism which I have left as yet not discussed. What his definition – which falls short on many counts but nonetheless forcefully grasps a highly important aspect – comes down to is that the 'weapons of the weak' are forceful only when they are backed by *the strength of the other*, which is in most cases a state. Terrorism, because of its lack of resources and its unconventional ways of fighting, is in fact characterized by *a triply indirect instrumentality*. It is the *overreaction of the other (the enemy state)* which is crucial in terrorism. It is that overreaction which is able to produce sympathy for the terrorists' cause by third parties such as populations hostile to the attacked and over-reacting state, and other states. Recent history offers a prime example of this dialectic. After 9/11, the US response consisted of the declaration of a 'war on terrorism'. Yet since a 'war' can only be waged against states and not against 'terrorism' in the abstract nor 'terrorists' in a more specified sense, the US response was redirected towards a more traditional geopolitical form of conflict. Thus, the sovereign states of Afghanistan and Iraq were attacked as part of the 'war on terrorism'. The war against two such states may be said to have been an overreaction to terrorism that in a sense *constituted* the 'terrorist' acts as terrorism. What ensued was widespread support for Al Qaeda in the Islamic world (e.g., Haddad and Khashan, 2002), and the most serious post–Cold War rift between continental Europe and the US. Yale sociologist

Jeffrey Alexander therefore completely misses the point when he says that 9/11 in the end led to 'exactly the opposite performance results from those the Al-Qaeda terrorists had intended' (Alexander, 2004: 88). According to Alexander, Bin Laden must have been 'deeply disappointed' (Alexander, 2004: 103). He misses the point in a way similar to George W. Bush, who said that

> The pictures of airplanes flying into buildings, fires burning, huge structures collapsing, have filled us with disbelief, terrible sadness, and a quiet, unyielding anger. These acts of mass murder were intended to frighten our nation into chaos and retreat. But they have failed; our country is strong.[2]

The fact that the US is strong is precisely what Al Qaeda had anticipated; terrorism works via the strength of the enemy. Having thus added a crucial characteristic to the conceptualization of terrorism, have we not reverted to the kind of intentionality critiqued above? I would say we have not. For, although we acknowledge the aspect of intentionality in terrorism, the characteristics we have discerned in terrorism in the above, constituting a triply indirect instrumentality, tip the scales and render a 'realistic' account of terrorism, relying wholly on the terrorist intentionality of terrorists, useless as such an approach falls short in grasping the paradoxical character of terrorism. Crucial in a definition of terrorism is the *dialectical aspect* of an overreaction in the process of terrorism. We come, then, to the paradox that it does not make a whole lot of sense to speak of terrorism where an overreaction to it is absent. The paralogical character of terrorism may be one reason why the aspect of overreaction to which Aron's definition points, is usually not mentioned in conceptualizations of terrorism. But reality does not always follow the logic of conceptualizations. The paradoxical character of terrorism consists of the fact that *'terrorism' is constituted by the (over)reaction to it*. The 'reaction' to it is therefore as much 'action' as it is 'reaction'. What the realist account of terrorism cannot encompass is the *temporalized dialectic* of terrorism. Paradoxes can be 'deparadoxized' through temporalization. 'Contradictions' following one another in time can exist in the same causal nexus without being contradictory. The nexus of events itself has a definite paradoxical character of apparent contradiction. In such a conceptualization of terrorism, the question of intentionality – while there *is* no doubt intentionality – simply becomes less relevant, since what in the end defines terrorism is not the intentionality of terrorists. Reason for the lack of relevance of intentionality in the conceptualization of terrorism is not that, as Rodin has argued, 'negligent and reckless' use of violence can also amount to terrorism (Rodin, 2004); it is irrelevant when seeking to conceptualize terrorism since it is not part of the core of what that concept entails. This is the crucial point I wish to make, and the following paragraph is devoted to developing it further.

Terrorism as a dialectical process of unfolding refolding

Terrorism as a process

Terrorism, as it is a temporalized or dialectical phenomenon, should be seen not as a determinate or fixed action, but as a process. Charles Tilly holds a similar position. In critiquing the 'naïve realism' of Stern's (2003) explanation of religious terrorism, he reacts to her comparison between terrorism and a virus: 'Beware of virus analogies when it comes to human affairs! Viruses exist; we can see them under a microscope [...]. To use the virus analogy for a social process, one must make sure one pins down the agent, the mechanism, and the consequences and make sure the agent produces its effects in essentially the same way every time' (Tilly, 2005: 20). The trouble, according to Tilly, lies in the homogenization of terrorism and terrorists that often occurs. His problem is, furthermore, that 'dispositional' analyses 'explain the actions of [coherent entities] by means of their orientations just before the point of action' (Tilly, 2005: 19). In other words, he critiques the intentionalist stance, which for instance seeks out the individual motives (Tilly, 2005: 19) underlying terrorism. Tilly, instead, opts for the analysis of what he calls the 'strategy of terror' (compare Tilly, 2004) 'as part of a political process' (Tilly, 2005: 21). This involves a relational perspective in which events prior to the violence in question are taken into consideration, and in which what Tilly calls 'terror' (which differs quite a bit from my conception of terror as rendered above) is seen as part of a political struggle. A perspective in some ways similar to Tilly's is that of Walter, who in 1964 wrote an article entitled 'Violence and the Process of Terror', in which he states that the ambiguity of the concept of terrorism leads him to speak of the more 'precise concept' of 'the process of terror' (Walter, 1964). The process of terror involves three elements, namely an act or threat of violence, an emotional reaction and the social effects thereof (Walter, 1964: 248). While, like in Tilly's case, I do not agree with the use of the term 'terror' here, the paradoxical character of terrorism discussed in the previous paragraph does seem to necessitate its conceptualization in terms of such a process, in which terrorism does not exist (as does 'terror' for Walter) independently of reactions and effects. Such are conclusions not easily drawn in analyses of terrorism that claim to pay attention to 'process' or that move beyond intentionality. Randall Collins has for instance said that 'sociological theory does not pay enough attention to the dynamics of processes over time' (Collins, 2004: 53). He continues, however, to discuss the process of US reactions to 9/11 while unproblematically assuming 'terrorism' to have already occurred. In other words, terrorism was, in his analysis, not part of the process. Such omissions need to be amended in a social theory or philosophy of terrorism. Likewise, I agree with Alexander that 'we need to theorize terrorism differently, thinking of its violence less in physical and instrumental terms than as a particularly gruesome kind of symbolic action in a complex performative field' (Alexander, 2004: 88). Attention to the complexity of the 'performative field' of terrorism, as he calls it, is crucial in moving beyond the circularity of intentionalist conceptualizations of terrorism.

Of course, the idea of a process in which events unfold does not preclude the delineation and designation of events within that process. One might argue, then, that 'terrorism' is one such event that can, in principle, be regarded as isolable from history and subsequent events. Such is the 'naïve realistic' perspective on terrorism. However, precisely because terrorism is a temporalized event itself, a meta-event, one might say, consisting of several events, such a perspective misses the fundamental point in conceptualizing terrorism. Terrorism cannot be regarded without the temporalized aspects of terrorization and the dialectic of (over)reaction. Moreover, the political reality of terrorism precludes isolating an event and labelling it 'terrorism'. Such a conceptualization would be lacking in distance from competing political perspectives. Speaking in either politicians' or terrorists' terms will not provide insights fundamental enough to capture the dialectical process in which both politicians and terrorists are involved, and from which they necessarily make abstractions, freezing process, isolating events for political reasons. Since we are dealing with a political process, the only 'realistic' and non-reifying way of conceptualizing terrorism is to indeed regard it as a specific type of political process.

The unfolding refolding of terrorism

I will hence regard terrorism as a process in which events unfold that, only when taken together, constitute terrorism. One such unfolding event is usually a *refolding* of events into a designated starting point of terrorism, which is a specific instance of violence. The point to which events are refolded is where current definitions usually locate 'terrorism'. Yet the point of a processual approach is to see the continuous political act of the defining of terrorism as part of an unfolding process. It is that part of the process which continually ensures consistency of that process by refolding all events unfolding in time into the one event that, according to the rhetoric of response espoused, set it all in motion. This refolding is vital in the negation of history that is part of the process of terrorism, since events are refolded into one neatly distinguishable point in time that is recognizable from a 'naïve realist' perspective, and they are not refolded to a time before that point. In other words, events prior to the event in which the sequence is refolded, are not observed as part of terrorism. Yet precisely because they are not observed as such, their exclusion is a defining part of the process of terrorism. It is, thus, a defining characteristic of that process that its processual character is negated. This is achieved by the continuous refolding of those events through which the process unfolds itself. Two approaches can further elucidate this perspective. The first is the Hegelian dialectic perspective, as deployed in analysing terrorism by Angelica Nuzzo. The second is the communicative approach of Niklas Luhmann.

Nuzzo offers a Hegelian approach to the 'causes' of war, and applies this to 'terrorism' as the 'cause' of war in Iraq. Her approach allows a dialectics to be seen in which the 'effect' precedes the 'cause'. For, as she says, 'it is the effect that first constitutes the cause' (Nuzzo, 2004: 333). This dialectical approach breaks with the metaphysics of cause and that of intentionality, and it at once breaks down the concept of terrorism. Reasons, according to Nuzzo, are never 'just there, simply to be "found" and brought to light' (Nuzzo, 2004: 332). Her Hegelian-dialectical approach starts from the intrinsic historical nature of reality and departs from the linear logic of history and causality. She is thus able to unravel what I have called the rhetoric of response, by turning the 'official' perspective topsy-turvy in claiming that terrorism is the 'true effect' or 'real consequence' of the 'war on terrorism'. Along these lines, I maintain that 'terrorism' is a temporalized process consisting of an *unfolding refolding* of events. An act setting off a causal chain is transformed in that causal chain, and as events unfold, a refolding takes place that pins the process of unfolding down on an initial act that is only observed as 'terrorism' because subsequent unfolding events allowed being refolded or retraced, and as such re-moulded, into the act. Another way to frame this view is to invoke Niklas Luhmann's perspective on communication. I leave aside the main body of his social theory here and focus only on his conceptualization of communication. Luhmann moves beyond the outdated model of communication as a three-tier system of sender–message–receiver. This view is quite similar to the intentional view of terrorism, since what is received at the end of the communicative loop is quite simply what was put into it by the sender. To replace this view, Luhmann speaks of the 'self-referential retroactivity of communication' (Luhmann, 1984). He sees a communication as occurring the moment another communication follows it – communication, in other words, is only retroactively identified. What a 'communication' is, is socially speaking only relevant from the perspective of what it is thought to be by the 'receiver', and hence 'communication' is formed at the 'receiving' end. Communication only exists, paradoxically, when a recursive communication follows it. In a similar way, 'terrorism' is constituted in the process of (over)reactions to it. It is seen to unfold events that come to be taken as reactions to the initial terrorist act the moment what is unfolded can be refolded into that act. Such refolding takes place, in practice, with the help of several discourses that supply the process of terrorism with new impetus by allowing new events to unfold or, in short, by supplying the process with time. To conclude, I shall briefly discuss these discourses.

Discourses of refolding

What is needed in support of the refolding of events into 'terrorism' is first of all a consistent twofold *discourse of identification*. This entails first of all an identification of the terrorist act by neatly tracing events to the event labelled 'terrorist'. That event is thereby construed as an 'action' in which responsibility can be allocated solely to its 'actor(s)'. Furthermore, events prior to that event can be construed as 'causes', and events subsequent to it can be coded as either 'responses' or as 'repetitions'. Secondly, a discourse of identification identifies the initial event as an act not against the randomly targeted citizens in case, nor as an attack against the state, but as an attack on the collective body of the *nation*. The state is the mere embodied representation of the presence of the people. It is significant here that terrorism indeed utilizes the figure of representation, since it randomly targets civilians *because the random citizen is most representative of the people as a whole*. The greatest dispersal of fear among the collective is reached by targeting someone who could be anyone. The message 'you may be next' is conveyed during the unfolding of the process of terrorism (Price, 1977; compare, Walzer, 1977). That is to say that neither 'terrorists' nor the state actually 'convey' that message, but that the dialectic between terrorist action and state action brings with it the fear of 'being next', even though the odds of being killed in a terrorist attack are far smaller than the chance of being killed in a traffic accident. Part of the discourse of identification are the *rhetoric of response* and the *negation of history* discussed in paragraph '**Definitions and conceptualizations of terrorism**'. The idea of (over)reacting to terrorism or of 'response' presupposes a refolding of events to a starting point in which response anchors, and refolding enables a further unfolding through responsive action. A particularly pertinent rhetorical device of identification that allows for an anchoring in a 'starting point' of 'terrorism' is the capturing of terrorism in symbolized images, such as 'axis of evil' or 'evil' in general. Another form of symbolized identification consists of reference to acts of terrorism through date or place of attack, such as 9/11, 11/4, or 'Madrid', 'London', 'Casablanca'. In particular '9/11' has become a signifier with a 'supplement' (Derrida, 1974).

Secondly, a *discourse of denunciation* needs to be in place. The initial event – which is only turned into the 'initial act' of an identifiable sequence of events through a discourse of identification – needs to be constantly condemned and the public needs to be reminded that that which constitutes terrorism is the provocation which instigated subsequent state-action – with all its discomforting but necessary consequences for the public. This discourse of denunciation assures the image of an almost automatic mechanism between terrorism and retaliation or prevention of future terrorism, similar to the way Foucault describes the 'automatic' link between crime and punishment which appeared in the nineteenth century (Foucault, 1975). An often-used tactic of denunciation is the establishment of an opposition between human rights and terrorism, as has for instance been done by former UN Secretary General Annan, who stated that 'by its very nature, terrorism is an assault on the fundamental principles of law, order, human rights [...]' (UN, 2005). Such oppositions at the same time strengthen the discourse of identification, since where universal human rights exist, the random citizen is most representative.

Thirdly, then, a *discourse of endurance and victory* is required. Endurance is required for the dialectics of action–reaction to unfold. The rhetoric of victory is required in order to envisage an end to the unfolding of events, a final wrapping up of the whole process by means of a total annihilation of terrorism. History learns that terrorist organizations don't often end by means of 'victory', and hence the most severe forms of terrorism are most effectively sustained by means of a bellicose counter-rhetoric drawing parallels between the struggle against terrorism and a war, as in the current 'war against terrorism'. The discourse of endurance ensures a necessary stability to the process of terrorism, which gains its legitimacy from the prospect of a future victory. That prospect gives the dialectic of events the promise of an ultimate *Aufhebung*, a utopian image of unification, of the suspending of oppositions.

Conclusion: Politics in the process of terrorism

The account I have given here is counter-intuitive and breaks with everyday conceptions of both violence in general and terrorism in specific. One might respond to it by arguing that it is nonsensical to assume that responses to 'terrorism' are part of 'terrorism'. But such can really only be argued while clinging to a notion of terrorism as a priori consisting of a single event, not a process. I would claim that from the perspective of political philosophy, it is more heuristically relevant to consider terrorism as a political process or in fact as a process that is itself part of a larger political process involving international relations between states. It is significant from such a perspective that the *process* of the 'unfolding refolding' of events is regarded as 'terrorism'. In the process, the ideology of events allots to the initial event the signifier of 'terrorism'. As such, only the event in which all unfolded events are refolded is regarded as terrorism. But from our perspective, 'terrorism' is a designation arising from the whole process of an unfolding refolding of events. Moreover, the *refolding* of events into an initial event *is part of the unfolding* that characterizes the entire process. This process of terrorism itself is, given the interwovenness of the world in an age of globalization, always a sub-process of a larger political process. One might say a political problem of this conceptualization of terrorism is that the state becomes an accomplice in the process of terrorism. After all, there is no real 'terrorism' without the overreaction on the part of the state which acts upon the *representation of terrorism* and *constitutes its presence* by means of a violent performativity. One might claim that this turns the facts topsy-turvy, or that it amounts to 'blaming the victim' since states, in the realist rhetoric, merely respond to clearly recognizable acts of terrorism. What the rhetoric of response does is, as we have seen, forget history. It freezes the flow of events and conceives as a terrorist attack as something occurring out of the blue, without incorporating either the dialectic of events leading up to the attack, nor the dialectic of events that stabilize, through a refolding of events into a singularity, the image of 'terrorism' and the 'terrorist attack'. Yet as the conceptualization of terrorism is a non-pejorative one, saying that events involving state action constitute a process of terrorism, is not much different from saying that a 'political process' is not constituted by the actions of only one party. Camus quotes Kaliayev, who asks the pertinent question 'can one talk of terrorist action without taking part in it?' (quoted in Camus, 1962: 311). In the conceptualization of terrorism I propose, at least when state 'response' to 'terrorism' is concerned, the answer is 'no'. Invoking the image of terrorism as an unfolding refolding of events with the help of the discourses of identification, denunciation and victory, and of the rhetoric of response rules out the realist image of 'terrorism', which nonetheless functions as the ideological basis on which terrorism operates. What 'terrorism' is, is not up to terrorists to decide. That is why Sheldon Wolin is able to call terrorism a 'formless form' (Wolin, 2004: 559). The formation of terrorism, then, is a political process of continuous folding.

There is, then, a reduction of being present in terrorism. It is beyond doubt that the attacks of 9/11 were extremely violent. In fact, extreme violence is an integral part of the process of terrorism. Which reduction of being actually 'is' the core event of the terrorist process is, however, another question altogether. The political process of terrorism involves at many points in time severe forms of violence, each of which can be coded as a 'response' by the various parties involved. The process as a whole, however, while consisting of severe violent events as well as ongoing forms of violence, is best understood not in the first instance as 'violence', but as a political process in which the aspect of violence plays an important role both in the reality and in the rhetoric of politics. So while autotelic violence is one form of violence that is shied away from and in a sense negated for political reasons – reasons related to the undesirability of the anthropology that it appears to underscore – terrorist violence is a form of violence that is too much focused on for political reasons. Again, the identification of violence is highly political. But that does not mean social science is unable to offer a description of violence from a second-order perspective that highlights the aspects of violence present in political processes such as terrorism. In this case, such a perspective leads us to abandon the commonsensical notion of terrorism. But such a break with common sense, as I have argued throughout this book, is one necessary requirement a sociological theory of violence must fulfil.

7

A Note on Causes of High School Violence

We cannot get away from reasons, motives and causes. Even if we could, the question would be raised: 'why?', and then we couldn't after all.

Of all violence in the Western world, youth violence stands out in public and academic attention, and in the degree of moral indignation and the repertoire of normalization rituals that follow cases of juvenile violence. Why? Maybe because youth turning violent disturbs dreams and hopes for the future; youth should be innocent, how much worse is then a guilty youth compared to us adults, fallen anyway. And of all juvenile violence surely none sends greater shockwaves through nations than extreme cases of high school violence. Why? Maybe because violence in school is more violent than violence on 'the streets', since the streets are violent, whereas schools are sites of moral education. Violence in high school not only violates victims, but also violates expectations of behaviour to be found at school. Street violence much sooner confirms expectations, since in the public realism of public space violence is thought of as, 'sad but true', a part of 'the street'. Of course violence in high school needs to be 'extreme' in order to be televised and publicly probed, but the same extremities of the street stand much less chance of collective appal. Cases of high school violence, more than anything, lead to 'why-questions' that tend to take on a 'what'-form, indicating the answer is to be some identifiable unit, preferably object-like. First of all: 'what were the motives or reasons?'. But whatever the answer to this question, if there is an answer to it, it is discarded and forgotten. It gets completely snowed under by another 'why'-question, the question 'what are the causes?'. Everyone has an opinion regarding this issue, and experts excel in distinctive strategies of finding new formulations of worn out causes. Politicians feel intellectually educated enough to speak of the 'causes' of high school violence; scholars feel the need to publicly declare the need for a no-longer-politically-correct Realpolitik of scientific reason in search for causes. When scientific reason flourishes, scholars try to find novel and erudite ways to express the 'multi-facetedness' of the problem. No doubt with a keen eye for the direction of funds for 'further research' (which is always more of the same – in scientific terms: research among a 'new popu-lation', 'replication-research', 'larger scale research' – or more of similar one-sidedness – in scientific terms: 'longitudinal research', 'time-series analysis'), statements such as the following are made: 'in reality it concerns a complex form of behaviour which is influenced by very diverse causes, processes and circumstances' (van den Brink, 2001: 17), 'It is equally known [...] that serious and violent delinquency is a resultant of a multitude of factors in society, in the broader and the close environment of the juvenile, as well as in the juvenile himself. The large variety of causes makes an early recogni-tion of juveniles that run the risk of developing seriously violent behaviour very difficult' (Junger-Tas and Slot, 2001: 265), or to take some serious advice from a long-standing international classic: 'To establish the existence of a sub-culture of violence does not require that the actors sharing in this basic value element express violence in all situations' (Wolfgang and Ferracuti, 1967: 314). Experts are everywhere in the social scientific study of juvenile violence. And so are the complexities and ambiguities they see, yet these are not placed within the scheme of a fractured realism.

Reasons and motives are forgotten when causes are demanded. Some clever social scientist who has read Davidson might subsume 'reasons and motives' under 'causes', but the focus stays on causes that move away from boys in schools. When causes of high school violence become a market commodity, these persons are forgotten and replaced by their 'background characteristics' or by characteristics of their schools, neighbourhoods, cities, societies, ethnic groups just so long as these characteristics can in their turn be replaced by 'variables' that are identifiable through data reduction methods. It is telling that the public reports of social scientific inquiries regarding the causes of juvenile violence are, without social scientific indignation or resistance, most of the time published not in the science sections of news-papers, but on the 'opinion' pages. In all this, the relations between boys in schools and all kinds of aggregate social levels are ignored. The causal *paths* are blurred, the question *why* a cause causes is not raised. And there is really no need to do so, since a homology exists between the academic habitus and the political, and maybe also the various forms of 'public' habitus, in the sense that all are inscribed to produce satisfaction with the answers to the question of causes as long as the question is 'seriously addressed'. That is, as long as the question is moved away from it is presumed that all is being done to find the answers, since answers are found away from the questions – answers cannot lie before questions, causes cannot be effects.

I propose a change of aspect, which intends to introduce the relational aspect of an issue that is an issue by means of a negation of that relational aspect – a negation made possible only within a misrecognized constellation of relations. I propose the following hypothesis: *the responses to 'high school violence' are part of the 'causes' of high school violence*. Of course there is no such thing as 'high school violence'. That is, the term does not refer to phenomena bearing more than a remote family resemblance to each other. This misrecognition of cases of violence dubbed 'high school violence' is, as I will argue, one way in which 'responses' are 'causes' of 'cases'.

To illustrate what is *seen* when high school violence is considered in light of this hypothesis, consider two cases of high school shootings, and consider them in the light of the law of the conservation of violence. The first is the shooting of a teacher in The Hague, the Netherlands, in January 2004; the second is the case known as the Columbine high school shootings in the American town of Littleton, Colorado, in April 1999. A distinction is in order between the two cases; they are substantially different in the kind of violence they embody. That also means there is a difference between these two cases in the degree of violence. The Hague was a vengeance, out of a kind of *Ressentiment*, a *ressentimental murder* one might call it. The perpetrator was frustrated in being suspended, perhaps – this is uncertain given the information available – offended in his honour. Frustrated, in any case, in achieving certain goals. It has been reported that he felt frustrated solely by one person, the man he shot (Volkskrant, 2004: 1). Columbine might instead be called a case of *anomic murder* (With the terminology of 'ressentimental murder' and 'anomic murder' I simply intend to distinguish between these two cases, and I do not claim to develop a rudimentary taxonomy with the help of which to classify all cases of 'high school violence', nor do I wish to make the juridical claim that 'murder' was the case in The Hague, instead of manslaughter). In the Columbine case, there were no 'goals' to be achieved, except for 'having fun' while executing a plan.

One student present in the building at the time of the shootings reported: 'You could hear them laughing and running upstairs.'[2] Randall Collins hence

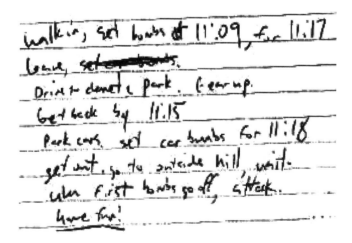

Figure 7.1 Dylan Klebold's last notebook entry

describes the Columbine shooting as a case of 'forward panic'. Forward panic denotes a highly sudden falling out of the 'tension zone' in a case of conflict, not away from but towards the enemy. It takes off when tension and fear in a conflict situation are high (Collins, 2008: 82, 85, 132). Forward panic is triggered by some enemy move and it involves a being entrained in violent frenzy that is strongly related to bodily and emotional factors. Some cases of forward panic Collins describes are atrocities during the Vietnam War, the beating of Rodney King and the Columbine high school shooting. These are very different cases, but Collins sees similarities. Although he generally finds it a myth (Collins, 2008: 19), he is right in claiming that laughter, and sometimes hysterical laughter, can be characteristic of situations of uncontrolled violence (Collins, 2008: 92). But what sets the Columbine case apart from both Vietnam atrocities and the Rodney King beating is that whereas the latter two cases indeed involve an uncontrolled frenzy of violence, the former case was well planned. The actual shooting of course was contingent upon the situation, but there was a plan. And the plan involved 'having fun'. There was indeed not only laughter during the violent situation or process, but *before* its take-off. While Collins is certainly right in stating that searches for motives all too often simplify situations of violence (Collins, 2008: 20–1), the record left behind by the Columbine shooters hardly justifies an exclusive focus on the foreground of the violent situation.

Probably the day before the killings, Dylan Klebold wrote in his notebook: 'About 26.5 hours from now the judgement will begin. Difficult but not impossible, necessary, nervewracking & fun. What fun is life without a little death?'[3] While there was an element of revenge in the Columbine shootings, the plan's execution did not serve the furtherance of a goal the two boys wished to accomplish. They did not relish a future accomplishment. There is an essential difference here with the case in The Hague, where the shooter first fled the scene, and then went to the police himself. A message posted by Eric Harris in an America Online chat room at 8:41 am the day of the shootings read: 'Member name: Eric Harris. Hobbies: today is my last day on earth.'[4]

The plan's execution was at the same time the execution of the plan. That *was* the plan. It was a total negation of juridical or moral authority. A payback, for sure, but a *dernier effort* in the literal sense, a goal in itself, not a payback the fruits of which would be harvested. It was to be enjoyed with an apocalyptic kind of pleasure, as the second version of the plan, reprinted above, indicates. This is the plan for an anomic payback, for its own sake, annulling its economic rationale of a payback, since no future gains were to be expected. The day of payback was the day to die for the executors as well. A day beyond *nomos*.

Another aspect of the difference between The Hague and Columbine: Columbine was an *impersonal affair*; The Hague a *personal matter*. In The Hague, the shooter did not even dare to look at the victim, nor did he intend

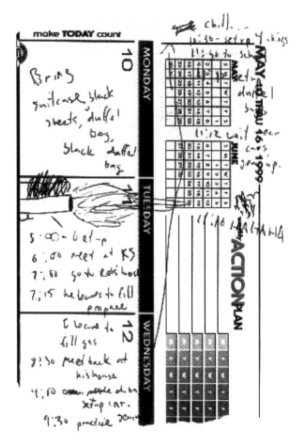

Figure 7.2   Eric Harris' itinerary, written on a page in his daily planner

or wish to shoot anyone else. In Columbine, the shooters did not even *see* 'victims', they simply wanted to *make* as many as possible. As one student reported: 'They didn't care who it was and it was all at close range.'[5] On a Denver television station, another student said: 'They were just shooting. They didn't care who they shot at. They just kept shooting. Then they threw a grenade.'[6] Eric Harris said on the web site that he himself, Klebold and a supposedly third person made:

> I will rig up explosives all over a town and detonate each one of them at will after I mow down a whole fucking area full of you snotty ass rich mother fucking high strung godlike attitude having worthless pieces of shit whores. I don't care if I live or die in the shootout, all I want to do is kill and injure as many of you pricks as I can.

Next, characteristic of the anomic murder is the 'whiteness' of the perpetrator: he is autochthonous and not from the big city or broken family. Ressentimental murder more often involves people of foreign origin [what is the meaning of 'foreign' here? How 'foreign' has the anomic killer grown?], boys from 'ethnic minorities', broken homes.

The law of the conservation of violence entails the identification of violence exerted upon the violators. Speaking in terms of violence on both the side of the perpetrators and on the side of the causes of what they did, balances the scale in the sense that an analysis is possible that speaks in a uniform terminology. The problem of *translation*, of having to account for the *generatio spontanea* of violence, where non-violent causes by some as yet unknown process are transformed into violent effects, is overcome. The law of the conservation of violence sees violence in light of the aspect that only violence 'causes' violence.

The case of ressentimental murder may well be related to the micro-effects of structural violence originating from a 'macro' field of relations: the Turkish-Dutch boy whose father is in jail, the 'humanistic' educational policies insisting on educating all children the intellectual way, through books, since all are equal in equality. An education, nonetheless, hierarchically organized, which means there necessarily are 'losers', especially considering the 'societal weight' that is attached to education in general and to higher education in specific.

Anomic murder, such as that of the Columbine shootings, springs from another kind of structural violence, and from a complex dialectic between structural violence and individual response to it. This is the reason anomic murder embodies a 'higher' degree of violence. First there is the structural violence of a web of commodities: the violence of laptops, guitars, suburban calm with trees and cars and houses. Added to this is the violence of empty time, of nothing to do because everything to do, for the everything has sucked the meaning out of every anything that is necessarily contingent if anything else could be done as well. Then there is the violence of well-meaning but hypocritical grown-ups, of boobjobs, make-up, weapons and sports. This becomes apparent for instance in the following remarks Eric Harris placed on a web site that he initiated together with Dylan Klebold and a third person:

> JO mamma wears so many sunglasses so much of the time that everything seems bright when she takes em off … JJJJEEEEEEEAAAAAAA!
>
> JO momma has so many keys on her key rings that people say 'Gosh, you must be a janitor or something', but she isn't … she just has a lot of keys! JEEEEYAAAA!!
>
> Jo mamma uses Vidal Sasson so often, that she has really good hair … its not damaged … or dry … or oily!! JEEEYAAAA!!![7]

There is a violence in the organization of social life around all of this and the utter *lack of sense* that screams from all of it. But in Columbine, a second level of structural violence was the precondition for this meaninglessness. A school is a relatively autonomous field of relations, as is a class within a school, and it is characterized by its own structural violence, which casts out the 'losers', the ones that don't fit. This cleansing process, existing in any school, defines the necessary 'normality' and 'pathology' of everyday high school life: the 'cool' and the 'uncool'. René Girard's analyses of the violence of the mimetic and the resulting scapegoating practises are nowhere more applicable than in a high school environment (Girard, 1982). These processes have already been documented in basic group-psychology. And this violence, which takes the shape of private violence and emanates from the structure of a group of students under external educational performance pressure is justified by its own truth. It is a self-fulfilling prophecy: whoever gets bullied because he is 'weird', starts acting accordingly, whether he wants to or not. The language of the body betrays the bullied boy. He is introvert, which can be interpreted as secretive. He is shy, that means he's boring. He does not dare to look people in the eye, which means he's sneaky. He sits alone, which means he is poor company. He looks sad, so he must be the antithesis of a good time. [...] That is why Dylan Klebold wrote in his journal: 'The lonely man strikes with absolute rage.' And in similar vein, Harris wrote: 'I hate you people for leaving me out of so many fun things.'[8] In a home video the two boys made, they play scenes in which they avenge bullied kids, even offering to 'take care of them' (the bullies) for $1000 or $2000. The two shooters in Columbine were 'marginalized', bullied and came to look upon the everyday order as a contingent one, one they could no longer be easily and willingly sucked into without at the same time reflecting on the meaning and value of it. They had cast off bad faith. As Eric Harris wrote in his journal: 'I am higher than you people.'[9] Another note reads:

> I hate this fucking world ... You may be saying, 'Well, what makes you so different?' Because I have something only me and V have, SELF AWARENESS .... We know what we are to this world and what everyone else is .... We know what you think and how you act .... This isn't a world any more, it's H.O.E. 'Hell on Earth'.[10]

This was their response to a structural violence they could see through, the violence of the structure some report their 'cool memories' about. The dialectic between that violence and their partial recognition of it, which showed itself in the lack of *sense* of a commodified world, led to their 'sticking out' in school, their 'weirdness'. And vice versa, their being bullied placed them in a position diametrically opposed to everyday social order, which to them therefore seemed to be a contingent one. While most people, confronted with a lack of sense or meaning, seek new meaning in the same commodities that caused the lack of sense in the first place, the

Columbine shooters saw through such paradoxes of a contingent social order. As Eric Harris says in a statement written on the web site mentioned above:

> No I am not crazy, crazy is just a word, to me it has no meaning, everyone is different, but most of you fuckheads out there in society, going to your everyday fucking jobs and doing your everyday routine shitty things, I say fuck you and die.

The phenomenological 'natural attitude' no longer existed with respect to everyday sociality, perhaps as a consequence of 'societal alienation', which is strongly related to private forms of violence (cf. Sankey and Huon, 1999). A hermeneutics of extreme suspicion took its place. Klebold spoke of 'a weird time, weird life, weird existence' in his journal. Staples has argued that alienation is the key factor in much of what is called school violence. For him, such violence is 'an act of despair, powerlessness, and hopelessness' and an 'unfulfilled call for meaning' (Staples, 2000: 40). Violence can, according to him, be an epiphany, an awakening, a highlighted moment emerging from everyday concerns, seeking significance. It is plausible that a lack of such significance in everyday life and too-lazy-to-be-decadent feeling of feeling nothing occupied the two soon-to-be shooters. They were born without being asked to be, and were then bullied and humiliated as if ordained by a higher power. It is here that they might have found a justification. What could happen to them, could happen to anyone. They decided to bestow the contingency of fate on the others. There wasn't even the *possibility* of moral condemnation of their plan, since any moral condemnation, they knew, was hypocritical, since it arbitrarily judged in some cases and remained silent in other instances. There was no *nomos*, for there was no sociodicy. Their being expunged from the cave had given them the knowledge of the cynic: a knowledge through *Weltschmerz*, a knowledge that others, immersed in the social order, could never gain, except maybe in the final moments that were given to them: 'Do you believe in God?!' [...] 'Yes'; 'Then go be with him' [...].

Social order needs structural violence to maintain its systemic integration. But it can be at risk by the very same process. It can create its own antithesis. Columbine High School was known for a competitive atmosphere when it came to athletics (which was one point on which the two shooters did not score well), and the American high school system in general can be characterized as highly competitive, which becomes apparent in bullying-practices (cf. Brezina et al., 2001). Yet it was part of a wider competitiveness that becomes apparent everywhere and that has already been highlighted in Merton's anomie theory, which can be read as a critique of meritocracy. Thus, Merton stated: 'a cardinal American virtue, ambition, promotes a cardinal American vice, deviant behaviour' (Merton, 1968: 137). Durkheim explicitly relates this to the sphere of the economy in social life, which leads to an insufficient regulation of the individual by society, thereby causing the individual to be ill with the 'malady of infinite aspiration' (quoted in Lukes, 1967: 139). A 'meritocratic' adage becomes apparent in an influential U.S. residential programme designed to change the behaviour of juvenile offenders, entitled 'Achievement Place' (Braukmann and Wolf, 1987). In a highly competitive environment outcasts are necessarily created, since if everyone could make it to the top, it wouldn't be a 'top' anymore. And whoever loses his sense of *sense* in the competition might turn against it. The dialectic of *suburban structural senselessness* and a highly competitive high school system, which provides home for a multitude of in-group–out-group processes, can lead to a complete experience of the contingency of the ontological horizon of any other. Only a multi-layered structural violence such as this pushes down the spring as far as was the case in Columbine. Until it releases, and the violence that was conserved breaks free. Here, violence only negates the violent world of its origin. It only wishes to destroy, and wants the destruction badly, like a long sought-after release. It negates a world of multi-layered structural violence, a world that is always negated, forgotten, not mentioned. But it negates it more *fundamentally*. Here, violence negates its origin by returning to it. A violence that erases itself. A release, relief. A friend of the shooters said he remembered thinking: 'Eric and Dylan, why'd you do this?', and at the same time: 'You guys finally did it. You did something.'[11]

Perhaps anomic murder is so exciting – there is no doubt that it is often deemed exciting – because it disturbs the pattern of which it is a perverse effect, a pattern that is more or less familiar to all of us. Just like Benjamin's 'great criminal' excites, somewhere, pushed away to the depths of the brain. But, as Wittgenstein said, there is nothing to be found in the 'depths' of the brain, there are only resultants of practices, *relations*. Cases of 'high school violence' are isolated, cut loose from their relational settings and de-historicized. The very notion of 'high school violence' is indicative of this, since it assumes an essential similarity between vastly different phenomena. To return to my hypothesis in this chapter, it is this individuation of perpetrators of what becomes known as 'high school violence' that is part of a situation that breeds violence because it fails to fully recognize it in a multitude of aspects. This collective misrecognition can be said to be a 'cause' of violence in a sense as much philosophically justified as the notion of 'causes' is used in the discourse of social science when perpetrators are probed for 'background-characteristics' are said to have caused them to do what *they* did.

Why are the structural settings, the parameters of all social action, always omitted when 'risk factors' for juvenile violence are searched for? One answer would be that the exposure of the violence of a social order is considered to be a destructive effort most social scientists do not feel obliged to engage in.

Another would be that most social scientists are far too immersed in the social order they supposedly analyse to even see the at-the-same-time productive and destructive connections immanent to that order. In any case, the question of the causes of high school violence springs from an *a priori* neglect of structural violence. Quite paradoxically, it both individualizes violence to, and de-individualizes it from its perpetrator. This becomes apparent in answers to the why-question and in solutions to the problem underlying it. In the case of The Hague, on the one hand, the perpetrator's honour has been invoked as a crucial factor in the incident. But this honour is not only the perpetrator's honour; it is a 'Turkish' honour. Likewise, the perpetrator's apparent lack of 'integration' is a lack of integration of ethnic minorities in general.

What is forgotten here is that a cultural construct such as 'honour' fulfils a valuable function for any individual. A kind of honour that is often regarded as 'primitive' has to be seen in light of its being an alternative practice of reputation that fulfils an integrative function for the personality system of any person excluded from the dominant social means of gaining reputation. In debunking 'honour' as primitive, what is forgotten is that reputation is an integral aspect of modern Western life. It is honour unrecognized as such, a kind of symbolic capital all the more effective due to its misrecognition, as Bourdieu might say. In fact, 'honour' is strongly connected to the modern humanist category of 'dignity'. It is likewise forgotten that 'integration' is not a concept that can be individualized, as if attributing 'guilt' to an individual. Integration necessarily concerns multiple parties. Like there is no social 'disintegration' of the individual, there can be no social 'integration' of an individual; 'integration' always necessarily refers to a social system as a whole. The violent misuse of the concept of social or societal integration is at this point but one symptom of a complex of responses that are part of the cause of high school violence. The points 'was this boy integrated enough?', and 'what consequences does this murder have for the integration of foreigners in general?' were part of a counterviolence that was launched in the media nation-wide the same day the incident in The Hague took place. With respect to Columbine, a guilt that conservative America could live with was not the availability of arms, but the availability of computer games and video games. The real problem much sooner resides in the lack of *sense* that these games are intended to compensate for. A creeping nihilism in a commodified world will not go away by taking one or two commodities away, or by possibly replacing them with a few others. A conservative appeal to morality sounds hollow when it emanates from a culture that is instrumentalized through and through, in which a final or universal morality becomes a fiction and any kind of morality is at best a means, never an end. Any response to high school violence, therefore, which does not recognize the aspect of the prior structural violence that emanates from the social order as a necessary and constant dehumanization of an 'optimal minority' – as economists speak of an economic 'optimum' of unemployment – misses an important aspect of the point. This aspect is missing both in the strategies of individualization and in the strategies of de-individualization of perpetrators. It is missing in all the ways one can battle the symptoms of a problem, as is done in the pleas for metal detectors in schools (which are supposed to make someone entering the school intent on inferno hand over his or her gun?). This aspect, which becomes visible from the point of view of the law of the conservation of violence, can never be all there is to say about singular cases of high school violence. It is, after all, but one aspect of that violence. But precisely because it *is* such an aspect, it should not be ignored. This not only has epistemological reasons. For the negation of the aspect of structural violence (and its dialectic on different levels) in public and academic responses to cases of high school violence in fact perpetuates the existence of preconditions to, and perhaps even 'causes' of that violence, precisely in the effort of seeking those causes and preconditions elsewhere. We are always much *closer* to violence than we might think.

8
The Trias Violentiae

Introduction

Three main ideal-typical forms or types of violence have throughout this book been discerned: private violence, state violence and structural violence. The term 'private violence' has been meant to denote both individual and collective forms of personal violence. This category is called 'private', especially with reference to its opposition to state violence. In this chapter, these three forms of violence are discussed in their varying empirical forms of appearance, their self-reproducing powers, and their mutual influences. In each of these aspects, comprehensiveness cannot be claimed, but the relations between the three types need to be highlighted, albeit only in a preliminary sense. Next to reviewing existing knowledge concerning the three main forms of violence, it is now crucial to see how these are linked together – it is crucial to unravel the web of connections that exist between them. For the exclusive focus on private or personal violence so often entails a blindness for the workings of state violence and structural violence. And the theory of the state usually loses sight of structural violence and of the active side (other than the mere reactive side) of the state in its violence – political theory here in fact reveals its own political being. In the trias violentiae, the state plays a key role, and ample attention will therefore be devoted to it. For the state is the mediator between private violence and structural violence. At the same time, however, it may be the medium of private violence set off as a result of structural violence, and of structural violence directed against the private sphere. This central place of the state will be further discussed in the following paragraphs.

With each form of violence, it is relevant to see what kinds of agency are concerned with the execution of violence. Who or what can it be attributed to? Who or what *is* it usually attributed to? Each type of violence comes in subtypes that vary in their degree of subjective agency on the active side of violence. In the case of state violence, and even more so when structural violence is concerned, looking for such subjective or personal agency would be to chase ghosts. Therefore, various subtypes of violence will first be discussed, but the relations to the two other main types of violence will be an equally important focus. This will bring some clarity in the relations between these main types, since they do not stand isolated, and yet with the exception of relatively few isolated texts or even only remarks, their interrelations are ignored by researchers of violence. This chapter has two main goals: (1) to gain a view as comprehensive as possible of what the three ideal-typical forms of violence amount to and (2) to gain a view of their interrelations and of the mixes that exist between them. The four parts this chapter is divided into are (1) State violence, (2) Private violence, (3) Structural violence and (4) The *trias violentiae*.

It will seem, again, that to focus on private forms of violence leads to a blind eye for the connections between these and both state violence and structural violence. Thereby, a social science exclusively focusing on private violence runs the risk of becoming a political instrument of social technology, since it ignores the whole of the politics of violence and thereby *functions* as an instrument of legitimization of that politics. So it is the entire web of violence spun throughout the social that occupies me now. I take that cut-out of social reality, that *aspect*, called 'violence', and I try to grasp it in a universal description of the violent triad of violences that I will call the *trias violentiae*. Is it then causality between the main types of violence that is searched for? Possibly, but more likely: influence, association, dissociation, or: affinity, negative or positive. The trias violentiae is the web of different types of violence that influence each other, that pull, associate, dissociate, in the end all in accordance with Cicero's clue: 'Quid enim est, quod contra vim sine vi fieri possit?' – 'For what could be done against violence, without violence?'.

8.1   State violence: Active and reactive

The violence of the state consists not merely of police violence, but also of the force of law in general, and of the procedural violence that is inherent to the proper functioning of the state. Moreover, state violence entails the crucial possibility of defining what Carl Schmitt (1996) has called the 'state of exception' (*Ausnahmezustand*). The ultimate consequence of this is war. Here, however, I focus only on the monopoly of the legitimate use of force that characterizes the modern western state. The state primarily directs the explicit use of its monopoly of violence towards its own subjects, more specifically towards those subjects not satisfyingly subjectified, or, as is common language in sociology and intercultural psychology, those subjects not properly 'socialized', 'adapted' or 'integrated'. The state demands subjection of its subjects only to the degree to which the variation of being-subject – that is, all the ways of being a subject of the state – does not exceed the limits of legitimate being as defined by that state. Physical state violence is mostly directed against the agency of subjects exceeding those parameters. Most prevalently, therefore, physical forms of state-violence are used internally as a counter-violence against private forms of violence. Social and political theory often suggests that the violence of the state in general is therefore an exclusively reactive kind of violence, that is, a violence that is set into motion by the occurrence and the appearance of non-legitimate private violence. Illustrative here is the criminologist Bonger's classic definition of crime: 'crime is a serious anti-social action to which the State re-acts consciously, by inflicting pain (either punishment or correctional measures)' (Bonger, 1936: 5). This is in line with the view that the state is a guardian or 'trustee' of the common good (cf. Barry, 1965: 226–36). It is also a consequence of consensual theories of the state and of theories on deliberative democracy (cf. Bohman, 1996). The mechanisms of social control possessed by the state are, according to modern criminology, part of the 'organized social *responses* to deviance' (italics added) (Blomberg and Cohen, 1995: 5; compare Melossi, 1990).

But this view offers a one-sided sketch of the violence of the state. For since the state defines the borders of the legitimate, it is imprecise to conclude that internal state violence is merely reactive. The view of the violence of the state as being only reactive in fact legitimates the active forms of violence by the state by taking them to be induced by illegitimate forms of private violence. And, in this sense, a more neutral and realistic view on the violence of the state underlies Max Weber's definition of the state as defined by the power of men over men on the basis of the legitimate use of violence (a use that, he adds, is *seen* as legitimate) (Weber, 1972: 257). In order to progress beyond this view, the 'reactive-violence view' thereof has to be *liquidated*, that is, it is to be exposed as being the *productive negation* of the opposition of both the reactive and the active violence of the state. State violence always functions in a double sense; it is, as Benjamin (1965a) says, both *rechtserhaltend* (law enforcing) and *rechtssetzend* (law establishing). Luhmann notes that the deciding difference between the modern system of law and that of older societies, resides in the abandonment of ad hoc and ad hominem reasoning in the juridical process. In modern law, a *norm* becomes a rule of decision concerning justice. But this means that the juridical system is able to recognize norms and to devise concepts that allow for a generalization of justice to similar cases on the basis of such norms (Luhmann, 1993: 262–3).

Here, however, lies a performative act on behalf of the juridical system, since it needs to decide what the deciding norms actually are. This too has an aspect of active state violence, since that act, on the basis of egalitarian principles, tends to erase existing differences. It is thus more realistic to state that the state exists as the *negation of the difference between its active and its reactive violence*. For the *activity* of the state installs the juridical limits of the legitimate, only *after* which the state is able to pose as being merely re-active against private forms of violence. The difference between illegitimate private violence and legitimate state violence is an activity of the state itself, rooted in the exceptional state of *superanitas*; it is, so to speak, its inaugural difference, enabling it to exist, from then on, as the legitimately reactive force. This inaugural moment of the state has, from its existence onward, to be negated. The coding of the legal and the illegal in law can only operate effectively for as long as the binary opposition itself that grounds it remains unreflected upon (Luhmann, 1993). In coding both the legal and the illegal, the legitimate and the illegitimate, the differences between these terms – as the *differential unity* of the concepts – are what are negated. This negation, which is a *self-negation* of the state, is in turn facilitated by the social production of what Durkheim calls the 'normal situation' of a society, in which the *conscience collective* at any time draws boundaries through the array of ways of being and acting, as a societal reproductive mechanism in which the 'normal' is separated from the 'pathological'. The state is to be seen as the autonomous sphere of this function of self-maintenance of the social system as a whole. It is the state which ultimately holds the power to define the legitimate and the illegitimate. But it can only do so with the help of the ideological negation of its active role. In order to be what it is, the state has to negate a part of itself, and, moreover, it needs to negate the difference which enables that negation to negate. It not only needs to negate its active side, but it needs to negate the difference between active state violence and reactive state violence altogether.

Theories of the state of nature appear to be attempts at justifying the opposition between illegitimate private violence and legitimate state violence. That is why such theories, as Nozick (1974) has said (although he said it in a different vein), try to 'back into a state without really trying'. Hobbes' 'natural laws', based on which a society of men in the end decide upon their reason that a covenant be effectuated through which they express their will to obey a sovereign power, offer such a justification as a solution to the problem of legitimization of the state's legitimate monopoly of violence. For, in this theory, 'the people' want the state – since to want otherwise would not be rational – and the state's violence can hence not be seen as an intrusion the people would condemn as violating them from an autonomous position not perceived as legitimate by them. But in reality, the state is what it is only by reflexively denying itself its active role in the application of its monopoly of violence. It would therefore be one-sided to say that the source of state violence lies solely in the private violence of the state's subjects (or of foreigners), as a result of which a counter-violence is reactively executed.

However, it would be quite as unrealistic to maintain that the source of the violence of the state, active or reactive, is to be found in the individuals that make up the body of the state. The main weakness of Weber's definition of the state is that the formulation of 'the rule of men over men' in part denies the autonomous social sphere of the state that cannot be entirely reduced to the rule of *men*. In Hobbes' view, to give but one example, a radical distinction is in place between the sovereign and his subjects (Hobbes, 1969: 177). But the Western democratic state now highlights what is in fact the case in any type of state: that sovereignty is the power – the force, *potestas* – immanent to the state as a whole, which, *pace* Hobbes, cannot be attributed to the individual, whether he be at the head of a state or at a lower intermediate position. The decisions of a state, and, therefore, also the decision to deploy violence, are not rooted in individuals that are in the service of the state. State decisions are processes that can only be attributed to the state as such – to attribute them to individuals within the state would be a fallacy of mixing up levels of analysis. Rather, the ritualized ratifications by individuals of the state's decisions are the end results of processes that are relatively autonomous with respect to those individuals. The state's decision to use violence is made by the *state*, just as the unplanned violence immanent to the functioning, the being, of the state is not attributable to particular individuals in the state-body. A sociological 'decomposition' of the state into individuals would lead to what Whitehead called the 'fallacy of misplaced concreteness'. It would be similar to ultimately decomposing a human being into cells and to then claim to have found the proper origin of human agency in them. Somewhere along the way, the agency that resides in the autonomy of the person as a whole, and, in our case, in the state as a whole, is lost. It would not simply pop up again in a scientific reconstruction of the decomposed components. From the perspective of the autonomous executive agency of violence, therefore, the situation of state violence is radically different from that of prevalent forms of private violence, at least where the paradigmatic situation thereof, in which two individuals fight one another, is considered.

To conclude, the violence of the state cannot be seen solely as counter-violence vis-à-vis private forms of violence, as a violence that operates only re-actively, but the violence of the state is always also instigated on the state's active initiative without prior provocation. This can manifest itself in the primary means of the state to counter private forms of violence, the police, of whom Walter Benjamin has said that 'its violence is formless as is its elusive, ubiquitous ghost-like appearance in the life of the civilized states' (Benjamin, 1965: 45). But it can also be the other way round: the state's actions – in the form of, for instance, legislation – can define actions as being provocations upon which the state is in turn to act. From the point of view of the origin of violence, then, the provocation cannot be attributed to the private action that is yet *defined* as provoking, as if by means of a rational calculus, a proper state-response. The state is not only a guardian of the land of the legitimate; it also continuously reshapes that land's borders. It does so through semi-autonomous procedures, through system-reproducing mechanisms such as budgetary rewards for police-efficiency and prioritization-plans, and it does so by defining what will be thought of as legitimate at a certain time. The standard example here is of course the strike, to which the subjects of the state have a right, except when a general strike is at stake, in which case the state will define, by way of state of exception, the strike as a form of private violence (compare Benjamin, 1965a). Apart from this, the active side of the state's violence lies in the continuous threat, the immanent possibility, of a burst in the enormous bubble of violence that the state's monopoly of violence constitutes.

State violence and the modern subject

Now, one might say that such a big bubble of potential violence as resides in the state's monopoly of violence cannot remain closed and has to lead to actual use of violence, but a more appropriate description is that, since the autonomy of the state is largely dependent on the legitimate use of violence, the self-reproduction of the state entails a self-reproduction of state violence. It may be recalled that, as explicated in Chapter 3, the threat of violence, or 'potential violence', is in this case also to be regarded as a form of violence, since it constitutes a reduction of being. It is for this reason that the threat of violence by the state is productive.

> Violence and the threat of violence, far from being meaningful only in international politics, is an underlying, tacit, recognized, and omnipresent fact of domestic life, of which democratic politics is sometimes only the shadow-play. It is the fact that instills the dynamism to the structure and growth of the law, the settlement of disputes, and that induces general respect for the verdict in the polls. [...] The dimensions of commitment and potential violence constitute the real substratum which give (sic) the myths of consensus reality
>
> Nieburg (1963: 43, 45)

And so, as Benjamin has said, the state does not discard its violence after the inauguration of the law. One might say that is only the beginning of the continuing presence of a violence that is inaugural always anew.

Violence is at thus the core of the state's origin and this is expressed in theories of the origin of the state, whether in a positive or negative sense (cf. Albrow, 1996: 62). Machiavelli praises Romulus for killing his brother, which enabled Rome to be founded and become a great state. Bodin, Hobbes, Kant and the English empiricists in the end see the state as the way out of the violent situation of the natural state. Other historically minded political theorists such as Voegelin stress the fact that centralized states often appear as a consequence of war, which forces feudal fiefs to combine. The Marxian theory of the state sees in the state a perpetual violence in the form of a legitimization and juridification of bourgeois interests. Either way, violence is of foundational relevance for the state. Looking at the state in light of the aspect of violence, then, one has to say that the state always has the character of a Leviathan, a monstrous entity spreading its arms wider with each new regulation and procedure, and with each regulation providing for the exceptions to each regulation. The modern Western state has an immanent tendency to become an autonomous force directed towards self-preservation. Wolfgang Sofsky sees in this development a final act in the history of violence, wherein the people find a common ground in their absolute equality before the autonomous law (Sofsky, 1996: 25). After the inaugural violence of the state, the state has become a usurper of violence over people whose power has been diffused in an ever expanding network of representation. For Sofsky, the inaugural violence of the state withers on in the present as an undefinable threat (Sofsky, 1996: 13).

A similar analysis can be found in the work of Michel Foucault, who relates the state's 'institutions of subjugation' to a subjectification of the people to the smallest detail, from the measurement of holiday time to the measurement of the normal body and mind. In a totalizing movement of inclusion, the prison, the school, hospital and workshop all take on their role in the atonement of the subject in accordance with juridical and anthropological forms, which became entirely appropriated by state power during the Middle Ages, according to Foucault (1994). His study on the prison shows how the disciplinary apparatus moulds the criminal into the desired shape – that of the epitome of the socialized subject, the *homme aimable* – by meticulously parcelling both space and time in prison (Foucault, 1975). With Foucault, one could say that the violence of the state can be experienced everywhere as the fabrication of *subjects* according to a juridico-anthropological form (which, is seen in a Marxian-influenced perspective of discipline of the worker in the workshop, according to capitalist logic). An alternative perspective is that of Elias, who emphasizes an all-pervasive movement of civilization and a progressive disappearance of violence from society. With Elias, one reads history in light of another aspect. The disappearance of corporal punishment in the eighteenth and nineteenth centuries, in Elias' perspective, does not point towards a more refined violent movement of a large degree of external subjectification of the subject, but rather indicates a near disappearance of physical forms of violence altogether, and a substitution of *Fremdzwange* by *Selbstzwange* (Elias, 1980). This seems to bear resemblance to Hobbes' idea that the obligation *in foro interno*, the compliance with the natural laws 'to a desire they should take place' is stronger than the obligation *in foro externo* (Hobbes, 1969: 166). Elias' *Selbstzwange* could be seen as the empirical realization of Hobbes' idea of the obligation *in foro interno*.

But the reverse can also be claimed: that Hobbes' theory of such an internal obligation to compliance with those (internal) natural laws is a consequence, or a symptom, of a historical development towards *Selbstzwange*. And then, Foucault's analyses seem to have the advantage of indeed also positing a *Selbstzwange*, but while at the same time explaining that will of the prudent as being a result of a historical creation of subjects that are, as subjects, subjected to a certain *episteme*, a 'dispositive' and a discourse in which they can be what they are: subjected beings – with the possibility of being within epistemico-ontological parameters, and at the same time, in that possibility, being subjected to the power of discourse, itself a product of a historical interplay of forces that arbitrarily combine to the configuration in which the modern subject could appear. Foucault is able to show how *Selbstzwange* and a theory such as Hobbes' are the products of the onto-logical embeddedness of the 'empirico-transcendental subject' in power-knowledge structures (Foucault, 1966: 329), in which *Selbstzwange* is the mere product of a quite literal incorporation of anthropological forms that are meticulously adjusted to juridical forms. With respect to the biopower inherent in the sexual dispositive, Foucault notes that the irony of this dis-positive is that it makes us believe it concerns our liberation (Foucault, 1976: 211). But, as explicated in Chapter 3, the irony is rather in the paradox: for as Foucault stresses the productive force of power, so too must the subject of this dispositive be seen as the product of a certain violence in the sense of a reduction of being, which at the same time constitutes the ontological facilitation of enabling the subject to be.

Foucault's work is convincing enough to reject the counterfactual notion of the state arising out of a 'natural state' by covenant or contract. Rather, a centralization of violence was at stake – a redistribution of violence, accord-ing to Zygmunt Bauman (1995: 141) – together with a widening of control that was not without a certain initial violence. But one may wonder whether the subjects of the state and the sovereign state itself were therein only opposing parties in a violent inauguration of the state, since as Voegelin (1951: 146) notes, both England and France, the two pivotal nations in late medieval Europe, only really became governed by sovereign monarchs dur-ing, and as a result of, their 100-year war, which, so to say, drove the internal factions in these nations to some form of nation-state under external pres-sure. Machiavelli's plea for citizen armies as an alternative to the mercenary army can equally be seen as giving expression to a violent external demand for state-formation (Machiavelli, 1997: ch. 12–13). In such cases, the inau-gural violence of the state is merely a reaction to a bilateral violent conflict. But then, once sovereign states exist, the violence of the state cannot be seen as merely reactive towards morally corrupt forms of private violence. Since the very presence of the state's juridical apparatus implies a legitimi-zation of some actions versus a condemnation of others. Here always lies a certain degree of historical contingency.

The violent tautology of state and society

The inaugural violence of the state and its continuous reproduction are immanent to the state and cannot, therefore, be said to be based on the state's guardian-like function of merely reacting against private forms of transgression of the order the state is said to preserve. It is crucial for the preservation of the legitimate, or, as Weber says, allegedly legitimate basis of its violence, that the state is able to suppress the visibility of its initiative in the execution of violence. The situation in which the state derives its self-observation from the difference between its active and reactive forms of violence can exist as a consequence of the state's ability to keep that difference itself undisputed. A paradox is at work in the definition of the state and its monopoly of legitimate violence. The state survives only by overcoming the paradox of acting violently upon violence. In other words, this situation can exist because of the political semantics whereby the state's violence is actually 'the people's' reactive violence against not properly subjectified subjects. From this point of view, state violence is, in the end, a reduction of such subjects to legitimate subjects. The *paradox of state violence* as *legitimate* because it is *opposed to something illegitimate which is nonetheless violence* as well is resolved by *turning the paradox into a tautology*, which then in turn needs to be detautologized. The apparatus of state control functions under the sole premise that the self-image of the state is functionally adjusted to the self-image of the society from which the state differentiates itself by claiming a central position in the *communis civilis* – as opposed to peripheral parts thereof – or by claiming a position at its 'head' – in the language of the hierarchy of the body (from *logos* to 'lower parts') that, since Plato, has been an exemplary model of the state and the 'body-politic' (Schinkel, 2009a). Only this 'ideological' self-image of state and society facilitates the overt subjection of people acting in violation of the legitimate order. But it also facilitates the subjectification of 'normal' subjects within the social system, since only by virtue of the differentiation of 'state' and 'society' is it possible to speak of 'subjects of the state'. With respect to the violation of persons violating the legitimate order, the most obvious example is the reduction of being of the inmate, who is subjected to fit the wall and bars of the institution, and also to fit the parameters of the larger legitimate order within what is legitimately called 'society' by means of programmes of 'resocialization' or 'reintegration' (Schinkel, 2003b).

The very separation of the society of 'integrated' subjects and an 'outside' of maladjusted is indicative of the difference that is constitutive of the self-definition of state and society. Functionally, these self-observations are mechanisms of social control. The self-observation of the social system as a whole is facilitated, first of all, by a differentiation of state and society, wherein the state is observed as the means that society deploys in order to secure itself against threats. Such threats may be internal or external, but the concern is here mainly with internal threats to the unity of the self-defining distinction between state and society. The definition and subsequently the existence of crime in general and more specifically of private violence makes the existence of the state as a societal subsystem functionally plausible. So next to the state-society differentiation, a second differentiation exists between 'society' and a general category that is placed outside it, as a hostile environment. Mead, for instance, defines the criminal as a person living in a small community outside the larger community, who then makes depredations against that larger community (Mead, 1962: 265).

But the performative speech-acts in which society is separated from an illegitimate outside are pervasive throughout social science and popular discourse (Schinkel, 2007). In the popular media, such statements can be heard each day, realizing what they supposedly depict. To this 'outside' realm, crime and private violence (sometimes structural violence as well) are attributed. The discursive exorcism of the criminal from society cleanses society itself from illegitimate elements – a secularized form of 'deliverance from evil' – and of blame for the illegitimacy of the criminal, thus ensuring that a society of properly subjectified subjects remains a *communitas perfecta*. As soon as subversive elements appear, these are ex-communicated as existing 'outside society' (Schinkel, 2002). Society itself, in this common discourse, *has* no problems and no violence. This leads to a tautological self-definition of the social system by means of a state–society differentiation: it is what it is, because it is not what it is not. Precisely the tautological nature of this self-definition needs to be negated. It is an *a priori* of the self-observation of society that persons that resort to violence thereby actually betray the fact that they really *are not a part of that society*, since society consists solely of socialized subjects that do not resort to violence. Here, society's self-observation clearly takes on a tautological form (compare Luhmann, 1988). Yet the ideological and moral legitimization that facilitates this is a necessary de-tautologization. The exorcism of the violent person is therefore a *functional a priori* of the undisputed functioning of the *differential* unity that underlies the self-definitions of state and society. State violence then becomes an integrative tool to 'get the violent person back into society', to 'reintegrate' him. It is not surprising that Kant condemned resocialization efforts as violating a subject's autonomy. But it needs to be said that the autonomy of law-abiding subjects is facilitated by a form of state violence as well. In society, autonomy presupposes heteronomy. This sociological adagio, which exists at least since Durkheim, has hardly ever been regarded in light of the aspect of violence. When this is done, it appears that even the quiet state at the head of utopia itself functions on the basis of an ever present differentiation of active and reactive violence. Crucial for the future existence of this 'contract' is the negation of its violent origin – the negation of the inaugural violence of the state: 'we must forget the beginning' (Pascal, 1976: 64). For in the beginning, there is violence. This is the *secret* (Foucault) that the state rests upon. Where reactive violence is absent – where, in other words, the subjects of the state are perfectly 'integrated', having abandoned the resort to physical forms of private violence – there still remains on behalf of the state an active reduction of being of those subjects *to* sub-jects. This violence is indeed a functional prerequisite of the distinction that facilitates it.

In functionalist terms, the violent subsystems within the state have an 'integrative primacy' within the social system, since they facilitate the reproduction of the social system as a whole. In the same sense in which the tautology is always true, the tautological process by which the social system defines itself through a state–society differentiation as opposed to an environment, an 'outside', if undisputed – that is, if ideologically legitimized and thereby de-tautologized – always works.

8.2 Private violence

Private violence is a form of violence the executive agency of which can be located at the level of one or more individual agents. Individual persons may be such agents, but organizations can as well, which is why 'personal violence' is not equal to 'private violence'. Typically, the performance of private violence is not legitimized, that is, it is not based on the authority of the state. That several forms of state violence are nonetheless characterized by an aspect of private violence will be discussed in the concluding paragraph of this chapter. For now, the ideal-typical *form* of violence designated as 'private violence' will be characterized as a form of violence not deployed by the state, but as to a large extent reducible, qua execution, to one or more individuals. This last characteristic is what distinguishes private violence from structural violence. Private physical violence is the form of violence that comes to mind for most people as the prototypical form of violence. Of course there are other forms of violence, and there are also other forms of private violence. One crude distinction that needs to be made here is between *physical* and *psychic* violence. Yet the archetypical form of private violence has reference to a situation where ego and alter are involved in a physical fight. However reductive that situation is as a representation of private violence in general, it does provide a simplified model to elaborate on some aspects of private violence that may be characteristic of many different kinds of private violence.

While state violence concerns a self-maintenance of the state by means of a negation of the difference between active and reactive state violence, private violence concerns the self-maintenance of an individual (or a group or organization) over against one or more other individuals by means of the negation of the being of the other. While a state primarily subsists by means of a negation of the difference between two of its forms of violence, private violence is one way in which individuals subsist, yet not by negating this violence, but by negating the violated, that is, by violence itself. State violence, like private violence, concerns the negation of an other, a reduction of being. The fundamental difference between the role of violence in the self-maintenance of state and individual is that the state only achieves self-maintenance through violence if it manages to negate part of its violence, whereas an individual resorting to private violence may, if executed properly, achieve self-maintenance by virtue of that violence as it is. Only afterwards, when the individual is confronted with the reactive violence of the state, does the negation of private violence serve the self-maintenance of the individual in question. In the following, it is to be remembered that private violence, whichever form it assumes, is *a reduction of being that is attributed to an agency outside the state.* Private violence often raises questions concerning *why* it takes place. Depending on their paradigmatic alliance, social scientists usually interpret such questions in two general ways. One is to research the 'causes' of private violence. Another, less frequently chosen path, is to research the 'meaning' of private violence.

The 'meaning' of private violence

Does (private) violence make sense? The 'meaning' of this kind of violence is subject to social scientific debate. While this debate, as will be shown in the next chapter, is not free of pollution by public discourse, the question whether or not one can say that private violence has a meaning or makes sense, is best analysed by means of particular cases of violence designated as 'senseless violence'. This label is indicative of an apparent lack of sense that can otherwise be recognized. And the will to understand private violence is extremely strong – even those cases that cannot be understood because they appear 'senseless' are categorized and thereby somehow neutralized, understood, grappled (compare Levi, 1965: 395). A murder for apparently 'no reason' often gives rise to calls for high punishment. The reason for this is that, apparently, a reason for homicide has to be able to be understood. If it is not, the murder is deemed more severe, so strong is the will to under-stand even in the juridical system. But what could be the 'meaning' of the 'meaning of senseless violence' anyway?

Cases of 'senseless violence' (Schinkel, 2008) are usually understood as cases in which physical violence occurs in public space where there is no clear immediate cause. The Dutch WODC (the research institute associated with the justice-department) defines senseless violence as 'physical violence on the public road, in which perpetrator and victim do not know each other' (WODC, 1999). But this definition is not in line with the use of the term senseless violence. That is to say that, as a definition of what the public understands by 'senseless violence', it is imprecise. It is equally imprecise when it is meant as a scientific definition, since it restricts a certain type of violence to the public road – this would rather be 'street violence' – or to people that do not know each other – 'stranger violence'? And anyway, this definition is inconsistent with the findings in the same report that the public street is only the second most frequent site of senseless violence, while even the direct living environment – which the definition of 'sense-less violence' seems to rule out as a possible location – is included in that list. When media coverage of 'senseless violence' is considered, it is seen to include a case of revenge of Turkish honour, physical violence in traffic and public transport, and a schizophrenic vagabond stabbing a man to death in a library 'just like that'. While there are those that state that violence is always and by definition devoid of 'sense', social scientists usually take issue with the predicate 'senseless' to the subject 'violence' (Katz, 1988; Best, 1999; Schröder and Schmidt, 2001). Anton Blok states it like this:

> It is more plausible to consider violence as a form of interaction and communication – as *meaningful* action, and to not take it to be senseless or irrational to begin with [...]. Without a *thick description* of those cases they can not appear as anything but incomprehensible and senseless [...]. Research into violent actions must begin with questions concerning their meaning
>
> Blok (1991: 190)

This claim is prevalent among social scientists. It is in line with a tradition based on Weber's theory of action. Weber (1988: 429) defines 'action' in terms of an understandable relation to objects specified by a subjective meaning follows (*subjektiven Sinn*). In combination with Weber's definition of sociology as the *deutendes Verstehen* of social action (Weber, 1988: 542), this leaves the sociologist with the claim that any action regarded as object of research is meaningful. The question is what it means to say that (all) social action is meaningful, and does it make sense to always allot to violence a 'sense' of some sort? One problem with the statement that violence is always meaningful is that it might block access to the meaning of violence. For it might be said that as soon as we are dealing with a category of sense, we leave the field of user-independent statements. But this is not necessarily the case in Weber's opinion. If this were true, according to Weber, all history would be senseless. We don't have to be Caesar to understand Caesar. That is why Weber's definition of action allows for a subjective sense that may be *more* or *less* experienced. Of course the question is then what it means to say that a *subjective* meaning is sometimes not subjectively felt to exist. Weber clearly places the ultimate grounds to decide upon the meaning of action in social science.

But the notion of 'subjective sense' or 'subjective meaning' runs into difficulties the moment one asks *for whom* a meaning is legitimately regarded as such. Why is the meaning of the social scientist more valid than another meaning? In the case of private violence between ego and alter, both may or may not allot to violence a subjective meaning, and if they do, these are likely to differ. Moreover, one might speak of a 'meaning' in situations of violence the moment it becomes clear to those involved in it that the aspect 'violence' is highlighted in interaction, that is, that the situation they are in is a relatively violent one. The 'meaning' of the situation is then 'violence'. As soon as this is understood, one might say that a 'meaning' of the situation is seen, like Wittgenstein says that to understand a sentence we first have to recognize it as a sentence, which means that, one way or another, we already understand it (Wittgenstein, 1969: 39). When social scientists speak of the 'meaning' of violence, they often do not specify exactly which meaning, they are concerned with, and for whom this is a meaning. Roughly speaking, there are three ways to speak of a 'meaning' of violence. One is that violence 'says' something about the violent person. First of all, this can be taken to mean that the fact that the person is prepared to use violence is meaningful in itself, which is undoubtedly true but not very astounding, nor even, for that matter, very interesting. Second, it can be taken to refer to certain background characteristics of the violent person. Violence then 'indicates', or 'means' that the violent person is such and such a person. Another way to speak of a 'meaning' of violence is to say that a violent person makes a point by using violence. This is to say that he or she has a *reason* or a *motive* to use violence, and, as Robert Audi says, 'if we do not know for what reasons a person acts, we do not fully understand that person' (Audi, 1997: 75). This links up with a third way of speaking of the meaning of private violence, since knowing the reason a person has to perform an action is then not only to understand the action, but also to understand the person performing the action, since an action for a reason is 'sustained by a motivating want and a connecting belief' (Audi, 1997: 104). More generally still, one might say that the violent person attaches a certain subjective meaning to violence. Only one version of this third way to interpret the meaning of violence would then also emphasize that the violent person intentionally communicates (as a 'sender' in the well-known primitive model of communication) a certain message through violence. And the stronger one holds this with regard to a perpetrator of violence, the stronger the agency of that person one assumes to be with respect to violence.

These ways to speak of a meaning of violence all run into trouble at some point. The problem with the interpretation of the meaning of violence as being an indication of certain etiological factors, such as done in deterministic research of violence, is that the meaning of violence is made dependent upon statistical variance, and is thereby in the end made dependent on theoretical choices of the researchers – the problem is then, as Joseph Conrad said, that 'they can only see the mere show, and never can tell what it really means' (Conrad, 1995: 52). The problem with the various ways of presupposing a subjective meaning of violence is, first, that the meaning of violence is left to the rationalizations of perpetrators. Thereby the possibility of a second order observation of the meaning of violence that is privileged relative to such first order rationalizations disappears. Second, it is not obvious that *the* meaning of violence should be exclusively seen as the meaning a perpetrator allots to it. Third, the model of an ego experiencing a subjective meaning may well be flawed, since it assumes 'meanings in people's heads'. I will emphasize the problems of this model by emphasizing a deficiency in Weber's theory of action. Weber, who explicitly assumes the possibility of a not subjectively experienced subjective meaning of an action, assumes such a meaning to be instrumentally rational (*zweckrational*). Weber himself makes a distinction between an understanding (*Verstehen*) of something like $2 \times 2 = 4$, and a motivational understanding of the meaning the person saying or writing '$2 \times 2 = 4$' had when he or she said or wrote it in a specific incidence. We can then place this person's action within a larger network of relations. We then understand a man chopping wood because we know he gets paid to do this (Weber, 1988: 546–7). The *erklärendes Verstehen* Weber advocates reaches its highest degree of evidence in the explanation by means of instrumental rationality (Weber, 1988: 428). The sociology Weber advances is not exclusively concerned with (instrumentally) rational behaviour, and the category of instrumental rationality is an ideal-type. Nonetheless, as soon as action is instrumentally rationally comprehensible, it is tied to the means–end categories, as becomes clear when Weber speaks of the way events and objects devoid of meaning can be understood as tied to human action. Sociology constructs a strict, ideal-typical category of instrumental rationality, so as to consider any deviations from that type as instrumentally irrational action (Weber, 1988: 430, 544–5). For Weber, the categories of means and end are always primary in the analysis of (social) action. If, therefore, violence is to have a meaning in this sense, it is to be shown to be connected to the categories of means and ends. If it is not, then it is instrumentally irrational action. However, the will to violence that has been discussed earlier shows that the categories of means and end can become confluent. It is highly questionable whether Weber's theory of instrumental categories can accommodate this. As Audi (1997: 102) notes, 'it is not clear whether intrinsically motivated intentional actions – roughly, actions performed just for their own sake – are actions for a reason'. It is questionable whether, in the absence of such a reason in the regular sense, Weber could still speak of a *Sinn* of such action. Even if it were possible to speak of reasons of intrinsically motivated intentional actions, Weber's theory of action runs into difficulties precisely when the category of instrumental rationality is put forward. In emphasizing the need for sociology to put forward the category (the ideal type) of instrumental rationality, he explicitly says that action has reference to something *outside itself* (Weber, 1988: 430). The case of private autotelic violence therefore cannot be accommodated for by Weber's theory of action. A complementary problem of this theory of action is that the subjective meaning of action need not be subjectively experienced as such, since Weber does not go for the idea of 'inner' meanings of action as all there is to action. On the other hand, however, he deduces from this that the sociological understanding (*Deutung*) is therefore 'evident' irrespective of actual empirical validity. The reason for this is that the same action can take place under vastly differing motivations. Now, a motivation is defined elsewhere by Weber as a complex of meaning that appears as a meaningful 'basis' of action either for the actor or for an external observer (Weber, 1988: 550). By thus tying the real empirical validity to such inner motivations, and assigning to sociology only a degree of 'evidence' (*Evidenz*), these inner motivations are yet again given both ontological and epistemological priority while sociology cannot properly deal with them. This is another reason for the inadequacy of Weber's theory of action when the meaning of the meaning of such action is considered in the case of violence.

Now, as Anthony Giddens has said, reasons are the 'theoretical aspect of the reflexive monitoring of conduct' (Giddens, 1976: 91). However, other aspects of the meaning of a violent situation can be identified, and another aspect of the 'meaning' of violence can perhaps more systematically be taken as the *Sinn* of cases of private violence. It is therefore desirable to speak of the meaning of private violence in a way that is less Kantian with respect to subjective experience and instrumental rationality. Moreover, it is probable that it is more fruitful to refer to a situation of violence or a process of violence as a whole when the meaning of violence is concerned. A first reason to do this is that the meaning of violence does not consist of various individual meanings of various individual actions, but of a meaning, or of various meanings, of a conglomerate of actions that together form the situation, or, as has been explicated in Chapter 3, the *process* of violence. If individual actions within such a process were to be analysed as each having a subjective meaning or even as conveying a message, then there would be a very high level of redundancy in private violence, since the first punch delivered contains the information, whereas all consecutive punches would be redundant from this hermeneutic perspective. Only when each punch is seen as intrinsically motivated can one yet speak of the meaning of such individual actions, but there is no doubt that the social scientific advocates of 'subjective meaning' do not generally do this. Another way out of the problem of redundancy and therefore out of the problem of the meaninglessness of most actions, is to focus on the total practice, process or situation (these are all equivalent terms) of violence. An approach to the 'meaning' of private violence that is detached from the individual consciousnesses involved in such violence is one that sticks more closely to the definition of violence as reduction of being. What *happens* in a process of violence is that certain identities become actualized in practice. Especially in cases of 'physical personal private violence', the *body* is the surface of identity. Recall from Chapter 3 that one does not hit an arm or even a person's arm, but one hits a person as a whole. When one hits a person, one reduces that person's being and allots to him or her a situational identity. This process has been explained in terms of Husserlian phenomenology that are also deployed by Niklas Luhmann (1971). When Luhmann utilizes the concept of *Sinn*, it therefore takes on a completely different, and non-Kantian, form than its Weberian conceptualization allows for. Physical violence, like all violence, is an objectification of a person as a whole. That objectification entails a selection of certain aspects of the ontological horizon of a person, and a simultaneous non-selection of various alternative aspects of his or her being. Luhmann makes use of Husserl's concept of *Sinn* to denote a similar, albeit communicative selection and simultaneous non-selection. It now no longer refers to a 'meaning' that exists in someone's head, but it instead denotes a process that is (onto)logically prior to any meaningful experience, since in order to experience, a selection first has to be made effective. Moreover, what *Sinn* constitutes is a reduction of complexity that is, in social life, necessary to deal with contingency. To return to the case of physical violence between ego and alter, such a reduction of complexity is a way of dealing with the 'double contingency'. On the micro level of interaction, violence 'means' what it 'does': it reduces contingency for ego when interacting with an alter whose behaviour necessarily appears as contingent to ego. Private violence can thus be seen in light of its neutralization of the contingency of the other. Seen in light of this aspect, the 'meaning' of violence becomes de-individualized, detached from any individual consciousness 'experiencing' a 'subjective meaning'. Within this perspective, which is relevant as a systematic characterization of what a process of physical violence amounts to, a meaningful way to speak of the meaning of violence is to regard it as the neutralization of the contingency of the other in interaction that violence is as a reduction of the being of the other.

From the point of view of a violent ego, then, violence is indeed a neutralization of contingency. From the point of view of a victimized alter, violence is precisely the quintessence of his or her worst fears of the contingency of the other becoming reality. The double contingency that is characteristic of all interaction means that the freedom of the other is always expected to possibly appear. From the perspective of alter as the victim of violence, ego's freedom's worst realization is violence. From the perspective of ego as the perpetrator of violence, violence is a reasonably effective way of neutralizing the contingency of the other, since it is a reduction of the freedom of the other that might realize itself in a form that threatens ego. However, violence remains a risky neutralization of contingency. Alter's actions remain, after all, contingent upon ego's actions. And ego never can know for sure that alter, after being hit by ego, won't pull out a gun in self-defence. In such cases of violence, the double contingency is to a large extent removed, but what is left of it has narrowed down to the confines of the process of physical violence, which is inherently risky for anyone involved. Not without reason, many ways of neutralizing contingency exist as institutionalized forms in social life as alternatives to physical violence. These, however, are certainly characterized by their own specific forms of violence, since any reduction of contingency necessarily impeaches the freedom, and thereby the horizon of being, of the other.

Following the spirit of Wittgenstein's remark, mentioned above, that to understand a sentence, we first have to recognize it as a sentence, which means that we already understand it in one way or another, this way of speaking about the 'meaning of violence' highlights another aspect of that meaning than its subjective reflection or residue. It concerns the practical meaning that is immanent to the kinds of personal violence that have been discussed. Prior to a subjectively experienced meaning of violence, a meaningful aspect of violence, confluent with its recognition (in the practical sense of situationally eliciting actions based on a similar selection; not necessarily subjectively experienced) *as* violence, is the reduction of self and other to a certain identity. While that reduction is omnipresent in social life, it is only subjectively experienced in cases of relatively extreme violence, such as personal physical violence. Only then does the aspect of violence light up in consciousness as the dominant aspect of a situation in which a person knows him- or herself immersed. While social scientific researchers usually refer to this subjectively experienced meaning as the 'meaning of violence', it is clear that there is another way of speaking of such a meaning, one that is prior to the subject, since it concerns the meaning of the subject *qua* subject, the very way in which a subject is subjectified in a social process in which the aspect of violence is significantly highlighted.

I have given a more 'detached', second-order analysis of the meaning of private violence. The reason I have done this is that the conventional analysis of the semantics of violence is immersed in a semantic that functions within the social system as a whole and that conventional analyses are unable to observe as a consequence of a lack of detachment from the *status quo*.

The aetiology of violence

Very much a part of that status quo is research into the aetiology of private violence, which therefore needs to be briefly discussed here. Specifically the popularity of socio-biology or, as it is today often called, 'evolutionary psychology', combined with a biological criminology-cum-forensic science, has given rise to research connecting private violence with various biological factors. There is thus, abundant research showing the determination of private violence by all kinds of both social and biological factors. These are all relevant in their own rights. Some attempts have been made to integrate these factors into a single theory (Anderson and Bushman, 2002), which can be said to be based on a 'nature–nurture interplay' (Rutter, Giller and Hagell, 1998). It is by now clear that the 'biological' is subject to environmental and social factors and that such an interplay must necessarily be presupposed in complex forms of behaviour. But it is a challenge for social science to engage in such work. If there is one branch of research which is lacking in reflexivity with respect to the (mis)recognition of violence, it is the new bio-sociology of crime. It is well known that one cannot have an inborn motivation towards crime, as crime is a social construct and genes are, generally speaking, not well prepared for the next change in the law. Not quite the same goes for violence as I have described it here, but the point is that the bio-sociology of violence reduces violence to the behaviour of individuals amid a field of internal and external causal factors. And where socialization is involved in research of violence, the role of the violence of socialization is often forgotten. Pierre Bourdieu's concept of *habitus* compensates for this flaw. The habitus consists of 'durable, transposable *dispositions*, structured structures predisposed to function as structuring structures' (Bourdieu, 1977: 72). The habitus is an acquired structure of dispositions. As such, it does not differ much from common ideas of socialization (compare Habermas, 1968; Lazar, 2002: 117–34). However, Bourdieu stresses that the habitus, as an interiorization of the exteriority (a social space) is an incorporation of the play of power that such a space is characterized by. The space of positions is a continuous play of power, as indicated by the term 'field' (*champ*). It is structured on the basis of a logic that is, in the end, arbitrary because the 'highest' position within a field is only what it is in relation to all other positions. Since the habitus incorporates the logic of social positions, it becomes a source of reproduction of those positions, that is, of the distribution of power. Power is thus embedded in the habitus itself, and the struggle over the positions in a social field is in part a struggle over the legitimate classifications that are part of the habitus and that can (re)produce a space of relative positions. Bourdieu's concept of habitus thus gives more depth to the classical-sociological concept of socialization. It 'localizes' the effects of socialization and adds to it a quantum of (relational) power. What Bourdieu dubs 'practical reason' and 'strategic action' is produced by the habitus, which operates below consciousness: 'The schemes of the habitus, the primary forms of classification, owe their specific efficacy to the fact that they function below the level of consciousness and language, beyond the reach of introspective scrutiny or control by the will' (Bourdieu, 1996: 466).

However, as Bourdieu's is a theory of social reproduction, there is no space for biological predispositions in his theory (cf. Bourdieu, 1997: 169). In light of the evidence pointing at the relevance of various biological factors as perhaps not causes but surely conditionals and predispositions of private violence, this needs to be amended. To this end, the notion of a *diathesis* of violence is helpful. The concept of diathesis is much used by Aristotle to denote 'predisposition'. It is currently used in linguistics – which will be foregone here – and in psychology and medicine, where a diathesis is usually understood as an aptitude or a predisposition to develop a certain disease or disturbance. This disposition is said to be congenital, but it only leads to the related disturbance or disease when triggered by external, environmental stimuli (cf. Broadley, 2000). In psychology, diathesis-stress models have been used for over a century (cf. Maudsley, 1889; Dunham, 1947) and have become a widespread way of explaining, among other things, depression (Monroe and Simons, 1991; Rende and Plomin, 1992; Flett and Hewitt, 1995). Research into the causes of crime has been conducted making use of the concept of diathesis relatively early – Stanley Hall wrote in a 1913 paper in the *American Journal of Sociology*: 'The psychologist, on the other hand, is more interested in the heredity and the psychic diathesis of the criminal mind' (Stanley Hall, 1913: 618). However, the concept has only recently entered the outskirts of criminology (Markward et al., 2000; Burk and Burkhart, 2003). While other dispositional theories have tried to explain violent behaviour (cf. Walters, 2000), the concept of diathesis seems to be most encompassing. That is to say, the notion of a diathesis for violence offers the greatest possible integration of (scientific) experience. Given the available data on private violence, the existence of a diathesis for violence that consists of a set of biological predispositions, combined with certain psychic dispositions, which increases the likelihood of violent behaviour when certain social preconditions are met that trigger a relatively dormant disposition to violence to become 'active', is a most realistic hypothesis. This hypothesis cannot be tested here. In fact, it is nearly impossible to find a model that encompasses all possible causal factors leading to private violence. To speak of private violence in terms of a diathesis does however mean that a degree of conceptual clarity is gained. Like the habitus, a diathesis is a conceptual tool with the use of which actions can be 'localized'. It assumes that (1) predisposing biological factors exist which are themselves neither necessary nor sufficient to cause violent behaviour, (2) predisposing psychic factors exist which are themselves neither necessary nor sufficient to cause violent behaviour and (3) triggering social factors exist which are themselves neither necessary nor sufficient to cause violent behaviour. The various social factors make what can be called *diathetic connections* with existing biological and psychic predispositions, thereby increasing the likelihood of violent conduct.

A diathesis model therefore combines an *egological* with an *ecological analysis*. Mediators at the level of the individual are substances such as alcohol and drugs, which are unequivocally found to be related to private violence. These mediators themselves, however, are mediated at various social levels. The scholastic error of finding a relation between substance use and violent behaviour and claiming to find a cause at the level of the individual is to be avoided. Drug use is regarded as an influencing factor at the level of the individual, and while this is in a sense correct, it also blots out the fact that drug use and violent behaviour often stem from the same broader social origins. A theory of a diathesis of violence will, to conclude, seek to find the specific combination between predisposing factors and triggering factors at the various biological, psychic and social levels, as well as the various mediators that facilitate diathetic connections between such levels. From the perspective of aetiology, such a combination which integrates various aetiological aspects is without doubt the least one-sided analysis possible. However, as argued in Chapter 5, when seen from another profile, the aetiological analysis is itself still extremely one-sided.

8.3   Structural violence

Next to state violence and private violence, structural violence is a form of violence most often neglected. Reasons that have been given for its neglect have been discussed in Part I, and these generally amount to the idea that violence should be defined in a less broad sense. In the preceding chapters, I have stated my reasons for including structural violence in the taxonomy of ideal-typical forms of violence. In keeping with the critique of Galtung's concept of structural violence put forward in Chapter 2, structural violence may be alternatively defined as *the aspect of violence of the differentiation of the social system as a whole*. It therefore does not originate in the state, since the differentiation of state and such subsystems such as the economy, politics and law is not directly controlled by the state. Rather, it is because of this differentiation that it makes sense at all to speak of the state and its violence. The state may play its part in the shape that the execution of structural violence takes, but it does not control it, nor can it therefore be said that structural violence in any sense originates in the state. While I will treat structural violence mainly in its macro-social aspect, it naturally makes sense to speak of structural violence within smaller subsystems. Structural violence is one aspect of a (macro-)social process that no agency controls. It is the aspect of violence of the differentiation of the social system as a whole, which is always already prior to any kind of social agency. Loïc Wacquant has for instance said that 'if blacks have become the foremost "clients" of the penitentiary system of the United States, it is not on account of some special propensity that this community would have for crime and deviance. It is because it stands at the point of intersection of three systems or forces that, together, determine and feed the unprecedented regime of carceral hyperinflation' (Wacquant, 1999: 215). It is therefore not these systems that determine the effect, but what is *between* these systems, that is, their differentiation. Structural violence concerns both the differentiation between a system and its environment and the internal differentiation between forms of meaning, position and symbolically generalized media. With respect to the internal differentiation of a social system, structural violence thus exists in a situation in which relative social position is a main structuring factor, where an uneven division of knowledge exists, where access to information is scarce and unevenly divided, where money as a generalized communicative medium structures a social system. With respect to the differentiation between societal subsystems, it exists in the dividedness of the subject which has become fractured, decentred. It also exists in the structural coupling of certain function systems, for instance when the economic system causes resonance in interaction-systems. Such resonance can help explain forms of domestic violence, which are related to notions of masculinity and femininity (Messerschmidt, 1999). As Wykes and Welsh (2008: 5) state in a book on violence and gender:

'violence is both the area where gender roles are most clearly differentiated and where the most danger and damage occur'. However, highly gendered forms of violence are also heavily related to structurally differentiated factors such as age and socioeconomic status (cf. Anderson, 1997).

Where state violence is related to the self-reproduction of the state by means of a negation of the difference between two forms of state violence (active and reactive), and where private violence in itself, as a negation of the being of an other, serves the self-maintenance of the individual(s) whose agency it emanates from, structural violence contributes to the self-maintenance of the social system in which it occurs as a whole by means of a negation of its violent character. Structural violence exists, in Foucault's terms, as a normalized state of affairs. It is the way things are. The subsistence of relations of dominance and dependence that arises out of the particular differentiation of a social system is itself a form of violence, of reduction of being, which is unrecognized as such because of the very character of structural violence: no agency can be pointed out as its intentional source. Since the ideology of violence accords only to intentional agentic violence the label of 'violence', the status quo of any social system cannot be recognized as violent. The next chapter further develops the relationship between the social system as a whole and the ideology of violence. For now, it is relevant to consider some forms of structural violence.

Qua substance, structural violence is in many cases (though not necessarily) a *socially distributed* form of reduction of being, which, in its most severe forms, is *endemic to the social differentiation of means and ends of life*. That structural violence is socially distributed is to say that it affects some people more than others. That it is often related to the differentiation of means and ends of life is to say that (1) it is an aspect of social life emanating from the definition of legitimate means and ends of life, and (2) it is, in many of its most severe forms, an aspect of social life emanating from the allocation of means to achieve natural ends of life, such as food and shelter. Within Western societies, the latter form is relatively little present, whereas this form of structural violence is highly relevant on a global scale. Marx's idea of a proletarization might be said to have nowadays expanded in scale. Whereas western (or northern) states have managed to raise the mean standards of living, on a global scale proletarization has taken place. The economic dependence of many countries due to crippling debts and the policies of G7, GATT, IMF and World Bank (cf. Harvey, 2005) constitutes a form of globalized structural violence. Within the West, globalization can have the consequences of strain on welfare budgets and the disappearance of jobs to so-called 'low-wage countries', which has the effect of playing workers in different countries out against each other, thus breaking traditional socialist strongholds (Bourdieu, 1998a: 85).

That is to say that economic relations and policies enforcing them are accompanied by an aspect of violence that is highlighted more in some cases than in others. For those where it is relatively highlighted and those where it is less so, Bourdieu uses a terminology of 'exploited' and 'exploiters'. Bauman (1998) also speaks of 'tourists' and 'vagabonds'. Specific to structural violence is, however, the lack of agency that 'plans' it. While, in the bulk of his writings, Bourdieu recognizes the fact that those who occupy the dominant positions do not consciously plan their domination, his later public interventions increasingly did appear to assume such conscious agency. Yet structural violence has no agentic origin in a locatable subject. The reduction of being that is structural violence is, like in the other ideal-typical forms of violence, the endpoint of an *inter*subjectivity. Yet in the case of structural violence, the origin of violence is neither the state nor a private agency. Any social system is endowed with regulatory mechanisms that result, on the level of the individual undergoing its consequences, in a balance of enhancing or enabling factors and reductive or restraining factors. Structural violence thus lies in famine, unemployment, poverty, illness and other consequences of a specific kind of social organization. One might therefore describe any social system, in the words of Henri Lefebvre, as a 'terrorist society' (*société terroriste*). Any society, he says, will be dominated by a certain class, and this domination will be accompanied by both ideological persuasion and punitive mechanisms of repression (Lefebvre, 1968: 268). One need not, however, assume the existence of a dominant class to be able to highlight this aspect of a social system. Although at the time he wrote, Lefebvre could not see another society than one dominated by a certain class, this has become more difficult to state since a few decades. That only means that structural violence has become more diffuse. This is what Bourdieu's remarks concerning 'flexibility in work' highlight. It is for this reason that Bourdieu uses the concept of structural violence:

> The ultimate basis of this economic order placed under the banner of individual freedom is indeed the *structural violence* of unemployment, of insecure employment and of the *fear* provoked by the threat of losing employment
>
> Bourdieu (1998a: 98)

In a more interdependent economic system there is no telling where labour will be moved to, who will be competitors for work, who is hit by a global credit crunch and who, therefore, threatens to lose his or her job (compare Beck, 2000).

The mistake made by advocates of the concept of structural violence such as Galtung is that they equate job insecurity, famine, and so on, to structural violence. This is then not taken in by advocates of a 'restricted definition' of violence, because the concept of violence is inflated if it is used to denote such vastly different things. With the definition of violence as reduction of being, however, this is amended while at the same time the possibility is preserved of meaningfully speaking of structural violence in relation to such phenomena. What can be said on the basis of the definition as explicated in Chapter 3 is that phenomena such as famine and poverty *are not* violence, but that they nonetheless are characterized, to a relatively great extent, by the being-highlighted of the *aspect* of violence. And, furthermore, it can be added that the aspect of violence that is highlighted in these phenomena has the character of structural violence, not of private violence or of state violence. This is the only way of speaking of structural violence that does justice to the violence in such phenomena without wholly encapsulating them in a totalizing view of violence that leaves no room for other, non-violent aspects of these phenomena.

Structural violence is diffuse, hard to account for, and hard to protect from, since it runs through various social systems, none of which have control over it. Because structural violence pertains to the social distribution of means and ends of life, it follows precisely from the specific differentiation of societal function-systems, and can therefore be controlled by none of these systems. For the same reason, structural violence is hard to recognize. Because it is at the basis of the differentiation of societal subsystems and can be traced to none of them, it is, from the first-order point of view of every (sub)system, part of the system's environment. That environment is always many times more complex than the system itself, and, moreover, that environment is only seen from within each system by means of a system-specific distinction between system and environment. It is, in other words, highly unlikely for a first-order observer to see what actually enables a system to be operationally closed, since it is impossible for such an observer to observe both system and environment, *and* the distinction between system and environment that facilitates the observation. Because of the fundamental role played by structural violence in the organization of social life, it is clear that there exists a continuous reproduction of structural violence. This reproduction cannot be quantified, but it can be observed in the differentiating effect of whichever social organization one considers. Next to state violence and private violence, such organization is necessarily accompanied by a certain amount of structural violence that functions autonomously and of which the autopoiesis cannot be discerned from the autopoiesis of the social system that it simultaneously facilitates and works upon. As Nietzsche's Zarathustra (1979 II: 307) says, 'we are sorest bent and troubled by invisible hands'.

Symbolic violence

A form of violence closely related to structural violence has been aptly described by Bourdieu under the name of *symbolic violence*. Symbolic violence is defined by Bourdieu as a kind of violence that takes place with the (silent) consent of those to whom it befalls (compare Sartre, 1961: 14).

This is the main reason why symbolic violence is misrecognized as such. In *Raisons pratiques*, Bourdieu therefore describes symbolic violence as violence which entails submissions not recognized as such (Bourdieu, 1994: 188). The fact that this violence is not counteracted by those it works upon, can be regarded as a falsification of possibly the broadest definition of violence there is, namely that of Aristotle, to whom violence is that which is external to a body and with which the body undergoing it does not in any way cooperate. Symbolic violence, on the other hand, is wilfully undergone. The specific effectiveness of symbolic violence lies in its negation. Bourdieu's attempts to uncover symbolic violence and its negation are thereby based on the idea that knowledge is power, a theoretical acknowledgement but practical reversal of the Machiavellian idea that power works best when unnoticed. Symbolic violence, for Bourdieu, is indeed related to the schemes of perception, of knowing, that people are endowed with. The theory of symbolic violence must start with the processes of socialization that produce the durable dispositions Bourdieu terms *habitus*. Symbolic violence is the violence of the hierarchy of a social space, which is perpetuated by means of a naturalization of the legitimate schemes of perception by means of *doxa* and *illusio*. It manifests itself in the acceptation of domination by those dominated. The distinctions 'high–low', 'universal–particular', 'masculine–feminine' are sources of symbolic violence. Rites of bondage are sites of symbolic violence. For Bourdieu, symbolic violence comes with the very organization of the social field as a play of power between dominant and dominated positions. It is, so to speak, *an incorporated form of structural violence*, for it is embodied in agents. According to Bourdieu, it is out of his own choice that a lower class worker admits that the *Wohltemperiertes Klavier* is 'higher', 'better' music than the music he himself listens to, he 'knows' this. Bourdieu can trace this knowledge to a social production of knowledge, which, once effectuated, has all the characteristics of an 'inborn', 'natural knowledge'. Bourdieu's theory of symbolic violence therefore shows how structural violence can become incorporated, embodied even in a person's *hexis* (the arrogant distinction of the aristocrat, the self-indulged prudence of the bourgeois, the other-worldliness of the religious person, the contemplative detachment of the intellectual and the humbleness of the lower-class worker in the presence of any of these others). Symbolic violence is a violence one accepts while one suffers it.

While one can critique the exact application of the theory of symbolic violence to a three-class system the way Bourdieu has done in *La Distinction*, the value of this theory lies, on the one hand, in its conceptual refinement, which becomes especially apparent in the idea that people are themselves accomplices in the violence they undergo. This allows for a realistic theory in which violence is situated in a between-subjects, and in which it is not reserved for a few violent people encroaching upon the many non-violent. Secondly, the application of the theory of symbolic violence has proved fruitful in analyzing contemporary suffering in the research of *The Weight of the World* (*La misère du monde*), which Bourdieu directed. The analyses of the French countryside and of the American ghetto offer numerous examples of structural violence in general and symbolic violence in specific. In a chapter entitled 'site effects', Bourdieu lucidly states the embodied nature of symbolic violence in a passage I wish to quote extensively:

> the mute injunctions and silent calls to order from structures in appropriated physical space are one of the mediations by which social structures are gradually converted into mental structures and into systems of preferences. More precisely, the imperceptible incorporation of structures of the social order undoubtedly happens, in large part, through a prolonged and indefinitely repeated experience of the spatial distance that affirms social distance. More concretely, this incorporation takes place through the *displacements and body movements* organized by these social structures turned into spatial structures and thereby *naturalized*. They organize and designate as ascent or descent ('to go up to Paris'), entry (inclusion, cooptation, adoption), or exit (exclusion, expulsion, excommunication), what is in fact closeness to or distance from a central, valued site. Here I am thinking of the respectful demeanor called for by grandeur and height (of monuments, rostrums, or platforms) and the frontal placement of sculptures and paintings or, more subtly, of all the deferential and reverential conduct that is tacitly imposed by the simple social designation of space (the head of the table, the right side of the tracks, etc.) and all the practical hierarchizations of regions in space (uptown/downtown, East Side/West Side, foreground/wings, front of the store/backroom, right side/left side, etc.). Because social space is inscribed at once in spatial structures and in the mental structures that are partly produced by the incorporation of these structures, space is one of the sites where power is asserted and exercised, and, no doubt in its subtlest form, as symbolic violence that goes unperceived as violence
>
> Bourdieu (1999: 126)

What this passage clearly illustrates is the deep-rootedness of this type of violence. Violence may exist as a reduction of being that is effectively a self-reduction of the self-undergoing violence. This perhaps most inconspicuous form of violence is symbolic violence. Yet a conceptual refinement is still called for. Symbolic violence, as has been pointed out, is a subtype of structural violence. Yet structural violence can be a more severe form of violence, since its severe forms are directly related to means and ends of life. Marx's remark that he did not see people, only workers, civilians and intellectuals reflects a situation of symbolic violence insofar as people accepted their fate as natural and thereby reduced themselves to agents of their own reduction. But at the same time it reflects a situation of structural violence to the extent that workers, in Marx's time, did or did not want their misery but suffered it anyway. I will now regard symbolic violence as a form of *incorporated or embodied structural violence*, in which subjects are structurally violated but *accept the legitimacy* of the structure from which this violence emanates. This clarifies a confusion that is not adequately solved by Bourdieu's concept of symbolic violence, which pertains to the question whether the violence of symbolic violence lies in this self-reduction or whether it lies in the negative effects people undergo as a result of it. Bourdieu's concept does not allow for a clear distinction between these. This is probably a result of the lack of substance in his concept of violence. For what Bourdieu defines in 'symbolic violence' is the symbolic, not the violence. In fact, it is wholly unclear how Bourdieu conceives of 'violence' itself. The definition of violence as reduction of being is of aid here, since it can be said that structural violence is a form of reduction of being emanating from the macro-organization of social life as such, while symbolic violence is the *self-reduction through which people accept the legitimacy of structural violence*. Once violence is seen as a reduction of being, and once symbolic violence is defined as pertaining to a tacit agreement to undergo violence, the 'stuff' of symbolic violence is located in the self-reduction that is the result of a structural reduction and that tacitly condones this structural reduction of being.

8.4 The *trias violentiae*

In the above, I have elaborated upon the three general forms of violence. However, an analysis that isolates these forms of violence will never be quite adequate for an understanding of the production and reproduction of any of these forms of violence, since they are not unrelated to each other. The perspective I will unfold to conclude this chapter is necessarily hypothetical, but it is nonetheless useful in order to gain conceptual clarity. It is a proposal to see things in a certain light. When one does so, aspects are highlighted that would otherwise not be seen, and an understanding is gained that is of enough evocative power to replace the embarrassing silence that up to now reigns in the social science and philosophy of violence when the relations between general forms of violence – if properly discerned at all – are concerned. My claim is that there is a lot that can be said and understood with respect to each isolated form of violence, but each of these forms can be understood in yet another way, that is, in light of its connections with the other main forms of violence. I propose the notion of a *trias violentiae* to indicate that there always exists a balance of forms of violence. These forms influence each other in the sense that more of one form will lead to either more or less – this depends on the type of violence concerned – violence of the other two general forms. The conceptualization of violence that comes closest to that of the trias violentiae is Bourdieu's notion of the *law of the conservation of violence* (Bourdieu, 1997; 1998a). This 'law' implies that violence

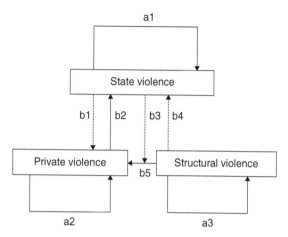

Figure 8.1   The Trias Violentiae

always translates in other forms of violence, although Bourdieu does not conceptually clarify which forms of violence produce which other forms of violence. As a visual aid illustrating the nature of the trias violentiae, the following schematic is helpful:

In Figure 8.1, the arrows denote the production of violence. First of all, the various ways in which the general forms of violence reproduce themselves are present in this figure as a1, a2 and a3. In the remainder of this chapter, the influences that exist between these three forms of violence that have as yet not been discussed (b2, b3, b4 and b5) will be given attention. It is to be clear at the outset, though, that 'influences' is here taken in a figurative sense, as 'forms' in themselves can never 'influence' anything. What is meant is that ontic violence participating – to make use of Scholastic language – in one of three ideal-typical forms of violence tends to elicit ontic violence participating in the same form and/or in other forms. In that sense, the trias violentiae gives a reformulation of the commonly held belief that 'violence leads to violence'. However, it differs from this perception in that it claims that translations between forms of violence may occur. Private violence does not always lead to private violence, state violence may lead to private violence, and structural violence is a third factor in the balance of violences that is usually left out of the picture. One cannot, however, fully understand the production of both private violence and state violence if their relations with structural violence are not acknowledged. First, the differences between this approach and more conventional (social) scientific approaches need to be briefly outlined, after which the conceptualization of the law of the conservation of violence has to be explicated further than has been done up to now.

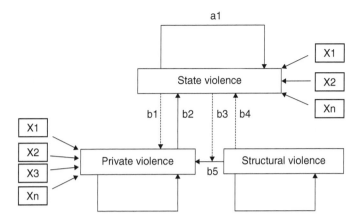

Figure 8.2 Conventional analyses of violence

The difference between the theory of the trias violentiae and more conventional scientific approaches to the various forms of violence can be summarized by means of Figure 8.2.

Conventional research focuses mainly on private violence, although not on its autopoiesis. Several factors are singled out that are said to be causally related to perpetrators of private violence. Such factors may, as has been reviewed above, be either endogenous or exogenous to such perpetrators. The list of such factors is seemingly endless, ranging from unemployment to the susceptibility to the pull of a gun, from childhood abuse to hearing disability (cf. Vernon and Greenberg, 1999). In addition to, and in isolation from this, state violence is researched first of all in its response to private violence, and secondly in its relation to the state of international relations (concerning questions of war) and to the characteristics of different systems of state (concerning questions of, for instance, totalitarianism versus democracy). Structural violence is usually not researched at all. The bulk of research on violence is focussed on private violence.

The law of the conservation of violence and the translation of violence

Without having a perspective on the connections between the three ideal-typical forms of violence as crystallized as that of the trias violentiae, Bourdieu has formulated the *law of the conservation of violence*. It is fitting to touch upon this at the end of Part II of this book, after having discussed various forms of violence in relative isolation. The law of the conservation says that violence of one specific form will translate into other forms:

> You cannot cheat with the *law of the conservation of violence*: all violence is paid for, and, for example, the structural violence exerted by the financial

markets, in the form of layoffs, loss of security, etc., is matched sooner
or later in the form of suicides, crime and delinquency, drug addiction,
alcoholism, a whole host of minor and major everyday acts of violence

Bourdieu (1998a: 40)

It can be assumed that Bourdieu here treats 'drug addiction' and 'alcoholism' as forms of self-inflicted violence, or at least as forms of violence
exerted by a self upon itself. If we assume that Bourdieu calls these things
violence because they are socially produced by means of structural violence,
then his argument would lose ground, since he would then no longer speak
of various violent consequences of structural violence, but of structural
violence itself. That Bourdieu does not do the latter becomes apparent in
a passage explicating the law of the conservation of violence in *Méditations
pascaliennes*:

there is a *law of the conservation of violence*, and all medical, sociological
and psychological research attests to the fact that being submitted to mal-
treatment during one's youth [...] is significantly linked to the changes of
subsequently exerting one's own violence upon others [...] and also upon
oneself, through alcoholism and drugs (*toxicomanie*)

Bourdieu (1997: 275)

Bourdieu invokes the general characteristic of theories of socialization and
of social learning theory to show how violence instigates the inclination to
violence. And he speaks of at least two of the general forms or ideal types of
violence. He is mainly concerned with the translation of structural and symbolic violence into private violence. In fact, he tends to *reduce* private violence to structural violence when he says that it is 'in the end the product of
an "inert violence" of economic structures and of social mechanisms relayed
by the active violence of men'. Private violence takes the place of structural
violence but is at the same time born from it (relation b5 in Figure 8.1).
That is why Sartre says in his introduction to Fanon's book that the violence
of the colonized is not theirs, but that it is the violence of the colonizers,
turned in opposite direction (Sartre, 1961: 13).

What is missing in Bourdieu's formulation of the law of the conservation
of violence is an explicit connection to the violence of the state. The concept
of the trias violentiae and the definition of violence as reduction of being
can be useful in broadening the scope of Bourdieu's analysis. According to
this definition, for instance, it becomes plausible that structural violence
can lead to private violence, since reduction of being generates a diathesis that prompts reductive behaviour towards others. Whoever has been
reduced to an extreme extent, that is, whoever has suffered violence to a
high degree, stands a greater chance of entertaining a highly reduced view
of man in general. The specific mediation between state violence, structural

violence and private violence is a diathetic mediation. The law of the conservation of violence, however, does not imply that violence balances out.
A significant increase in state violence might diminish many forms of
private violence, albeit at the cost of the execution of state violence in the
form of private violence. The law of the conservation of violence, thus
expanded, is the most comprehensive conceptualization of the autopoiesis
of violence. It is a radically anti-Hegelian concept that recognizes that violence is not dialectically sublimated, and that the very notion of such an
Aufhebung is itself fraught with violence.

What is gained by the combination of the definition of violence as reduction of being with the concept of the trias violentiae is thus the possibility
of balancing the scale on a conceptual level. By doing this, the problem of
the *generatio spontanea* of private violence and the problem of *translation* are
resolved. Most of the time, violence is not born out of an individual that
has experienced non-violence, but it is the re-action of violence. It is often
the re-action of previously experienced private violence (and then it is part
of an autopoiesis of private violence), but it can also be a re-action of experienced structural violence. Social science usually gets to work the moment an
individual exerts private violence, assuming that this private violence takes
place by means of private initiative, as a spontaneous occurrence which may
have various causes, but the violence of which is something spontaneously
produced. Where non-violent causes are usually presupposed to produce
violent effects, I assume that already violent causes lead to a translation of
violence into a violent effect. The problem of translation from non-violence
to violence is resolved by speaking of *translations between various forms of violence*. A translation between private violence and state violence, for instance,
means that private violence elicits state violence. Thereby, I mean to point
out a somewhat less inaccurate process than that designated by the 'law of
the conservation of violence'. For that law is not a natural law, nor does the
fact that various forms of violence translate into each other mean that there
is a Newtonian 'conservation' of violence, as if the sum total of the quantity
of reduction of being is a constant. Translations between forms of violence
exist at least in the ways pictured in Figure 8.1, but these translations may
depend on the levels of violence existing. For instance, when state violence
reaches extreme levels, the level of private violence might rise proportion-
ately, but it is equally possible that it drops significantly. To describe such
a process, the nomenclature of a 'law' sounds too positivistic, of the sort
Reichenbach deployed when figuring out for the RAND corporation the
exact chance that the USSR would start a nuclear war.

It is nonetheless possible to examine more closely the relations within the
trias violentiae as outlined in Figure 8.1. In this figure, the autopoietic cycles
of a1, a2 and a3 have already been discussed, as have one form of relation b1
(the production of private violence by state violence as private violence against
state violence), b2 (the production of state violence by private violence)

and b5 (the production of private violence by structural violence). These relations pertain to the commonly recognized translation between private violence and state violence. In order to expand the view of the triad of forms of violence, I have discussed other forms of violence. Other translations can therefore be seen to exist as well.

One translation between ideal-typical forms of violence concerns the production of private violence by state violence (b1). Private violence against state violence is not the only way of translation that exists between these forms. Another and less well-documented translation between state violence and private violence has to do with the violence of war. Not only is such state violence sometimes repaid to soldiers coming home and being discriminated, and not only does this in turn lead to private violence on their part; there also exists a relation between war and general post-war private violence. Archer and Gartner have performed research into the nature of this relation and have concluded that

> The major finding of the study was that most of the nation-wars in the study did experience substantial postwar increases in their rates of homicide. These increases were pervasive, and occurred after large wars and smaller wars, with several types of homicide rate indicators, in victorious as well as defeated nations, in nations with both improved and worsened postwar economies, among both men and women offenders and among offenders of several age groups. Homicide rate increases occurred with particular consistency among nations with large numbers of combat deaths
>
> Archer and Gartner (1976: 937)

There thus seems to be a relation between extreme forms of externally directed state violence and private violence. This may have to do with the destabilizing impact a war may have on a people, but whichever the cause, a translation of violence does appear to take place. Another way in which state violence translates in private violence concerns the attraction of violence in a bureaucratic system, as formulated by Hannah Arendt, which is relevant to repeat here, since it can be seen in a different light now: 'in a fully developed bureaucracy there is nobody left with whom one can argue, to whom one can present grievances, on whom the pressures of power can be exerted. Bureaucracy is the form of government in which everybody is deprived of political freedom, of the power to act; for the rule by Nobody is not no-rule, and where all are equally powerless we have a tyranny without a tyrant' (Arendt, 1970: 81). This situation, according to Arendt, can give rise to private violence. The mechanism she assumes to be working here is similar to that put forward by frustration–aggression theories and by theories of resentment.

Another translation takes place between structural violence and state violence. The state's monopoly of legitimate violence is based on a specific relation between the state and the subjects of the state. That relation is the object of a self-observation of the social system by means of which that social system de-tautologizes itself. The specific manner in which this is done in a modern society leads to a negation of the difference between active and reactive forms of state violence over against illegitimate forms of private violence. This negation is the basis of the state's legitimate use of violence. In the end, the modern theory of the state opposes the state's violence to private forms of violence and posits the state as the way out of the 'war of every man against every man' in which *homo homini lupus est.* But state violence is not only concerned with, or related to, private forms of violence. The state may both act against and with structural violence. In both cases this is done primarily by means of economic policy and by prevailing notions of justice. State violence against structural violence is a kind of reactive violence that is in this respect similar to state violence elicited by private violence. In Figure 8.1, it is shown as relation b4. In the figure of the trias violentiae, this line is dotted since it is not all that clear in what ways structural violence leads to state violence. Reason for this is that the state's monopoly of the use of legitimate violence is defined only in relation to private violence, not to structural violence. It is therefore doubtful whether structural violence will actually lead to state violence countering it, since the definition of the violence of the state entails a blind spot for structural violence to begin with.

Mixes of violence

An observation that needs to be made when the connections between the three ideal-typical forms of violence are concerned is that mixes between them exist. In such a mix, one ideal-typical form of violence assumes the *executive shape* of another form without being reducible to it, or without having its essential character and agentic (or, in the case of structural violence: non-agentic) origin. That is to say that each of the following possibilities may be realized:

1 *State violence takes the shape of private violence.* This happens, for instance, in the police or in the bureaucracy, which do in some degree rely on executive decisions by people. It is important to stress the limited level of agency in such cases in order not to place responsibility at the wrong level. However, it is equally important to note that there does, in the end, remain a private agentic responsibility, in order not to reduce all such violence to social systems and to thereby evaporate the moral substance of the execution of state violence. In the end, the policeman and the prison guard make use of legitimized forms of private violence in their execution of state violence. Their violence will usually only be recognized as private violence the moment it becomes excessive and exceeds the bounds of the legitimated. However, whenever those bounds

appear to be too contingent or are perceived of as allowing excessive violence themselves, executioners of state violence may be called to justify operating under such conditions. They will then not be able to hide behind the moral anaesthetic of institutionalized rules or of a command structure, but are held accountable for their actions themselves. It is significant to note in this respect that Rudolf Höss, commander of Auschwitz concentration and extermination camp for over three years, describes in his autobiography how he personally punished German soldiers displaying personal cruelty towards prisoners. He wanted all to be smoothly and efficiently run, and in such a bureaucratic organization there was no place for personal sadism (Höss, 1960). A similar case is provided by Machiavelli, who describes how Borgia had his all-too cruel lieutenant Ramiro d'Orco (governor of Romagna) killed (with the politically opportune effect of gaining both the love and fear of people). Reason for this was that 'having observed the past rigour of Ramiro had engendered some hatred, he wished to show to the people, for the purpose of removing that feeling from their minds, and to win their entire confidence, that if any cruelties had been practised, they had not originated with him, but had resulted altogether from the harsh nature of his minister' (Machiavelli, 1997: 28). Another example here are the charges against American soldiers in the Abu Ghraib prison in Baghdad that participated in practices of torture. While their superiors allowed for this to happen and even encouraged it, the executive soldiers are nonetheless held co-responsible. The thin balance between state violence and private violence is in such a case exposed for instance by the strategy of the American army to stress that these soldiers were not operating under orders but acted on their own initiative, thus making it appear wholly as a case of private violence of a few deranged individuals. An equally interesting case is that of a Dutch soldier in Iraq suspected of murder by the public prosecutor's office, much to the dismay of the Ministry of Defence. It turned out that he was part of a special operations unit, the existence of which was a Dutch state secret. The interesting point in case is that part of the state did not know of this secret (state secrets are usually 'head-of-state secrets'), and so the internal differentiation of the state causes the difficulty in deciding whether the soldiers' violence was private violence or state violence.

However, the mixes between state violence and private violence become apparent in the events of everyday, not just in relatively spectacular cases. The way a police officer handcuffs a person offers a daily mix between state violence and private violence. State violence takes the executive shape of private violence, but in fact private violence is always lurking. A policeman can't shut down his own will to violence. The decision to put on handcuffs in a normal manner or to use the more restraining manner by way of which any movement on the prisoner's

behalf tightens the cuffs belongs to the discretionary power of the policeman, and in the subtlest of movements he may add private violence to
the mere private executive shape of state violence. The trias violentiae is
a web of connections that can be found on the level of the micropolitics
of getting a detainee in a police car.

2   *Structural violence takes the shape of state violence.* While state violence
may be reactive against structural violence, as discussed above, it may
also become the shape of structural violence. State violence then does
not simply strengthen structural violence; it becomes the form through
which structural violence is executed. Debate exists over when this is
the case. While Bourdieu's writings on structural and symbolic violence
for instance denounce the dominance of neo-liberal economic policies for being structurally violent, neo-liberal thinkers themselves base
their ideas on a tradition that goes back to the early utilitarians who
are convinced – as Mandeville already was – that the economics of the
homo economicus is a model that will, in the end, be for the benefit of
all. The modern-day 'free markets' associated with this model are then
regarded as non-violent when it comes to structural violence, and they
are moreover regarded as promoting non-violence at the level of private
violence. However, any policy starting from a notion of the human being
as reductive as the *homo economicus*, might be said to be relatively violent
from the start. A less violent image of man would be that of Plessner, who
considered man to be the 'being not yet determined' (*das nicht festgestellte
Tier*) (cf. Plessner, 1975). Like Heidegger critiqued humanism's notion of
the *animal rationale*, the *homo economicus* can be seen as an *a priori* reduction of being, and any policy based on it as reductive. In that sense, such
policies contribute to structural violence when they legitimate economic
inequalities, for instance by means of such theories of justice as put forward by Robert Nozick (1974), who has pleaded for a 'minimal state' out
of concern over constraints of freedom. Nozick, however, fails to appreciate the fact that freedom is equally bound by an economic system that
is not so easily kept in check. With respect to the economic realm, he
does not speak of freedom and non-freedom at all, and his is therefore a
political theory that has the political effect of legitimating an economic
differentiation and therefore of reproducing structural violence.

There is another way in which the violence of the state becomes the
shape assumed by structural violence. It has been said above that the
very presence of the state's juridical apparatus implies a legitimization
of some actions versus a condemnation of others. And here always lies
a certain degree of historical contingency. At the same time, here lies a
facilitation and execution of structural violence. Of course, from Marx's
point of view, the state merely reproduces class-distinctions. And so, it
is forbidden for both the rich and the poor to sleep under bridges. The
meaning of this of course being that economic differences are juridically

legitimized by the state, and this, precisely because of the law's egalitarian principles. The law has a tendency to ignore differences, to flatten out, and turn a differentiated sociality into a uniformity. That is precisely what it is supposed to do. But it does disadvantage some while benefiting others in an unequal fashion. The equal treatment of unequal situations leads to inequality (Albrow, 1996). Anatole France's example is telling. But others can be given. To a person not inclined to be violent, the law that prohibits private violence is not an obstacle, it does not deprive him of preferred possible courses of action. On the other hand, the person that prefers to exert private violence is severely hampered by such a law. Again, that is precisely what the law is intended to do. But then, all comes down to the precise definitions of violence the law provides for. Which actions are regarded as illegitimate? And what people are prone to engage in such actions, for what reasons? The key point here is, that if there is an already violent reason for the violence of a person, to prohibit only the latter's violence in effect legitimates the former violence. It means an unjust treatment of the person actively engaged in private violence. This is how relation b5 comes into being. In accordance with the law of the conservation of violence, structural violence leads to private violence, but it does so *with the help of state violence, or, more precisely, in the shape of state violence*. The violence inherent for instance in the economy teams up with the state violence of the law. The early socialists had a keen eye for this. Gerrard Winstanley, for instance, commented on the 'particular propriety of mine and thine' that 'It tempts people to doe an evil action and then kils them for doing it: Let all judge if this be not a great devil' (Winstanley, 1965 [1649]: 276).

Structural violence is the aspect of violence of the differentiation of the social system, and the state is that subsystem of the social system that is actively involved in retaining the status quo of that differentiation, and thereby of its violence, in the name of concern over 'social cohesion' and 'integration'. The ensuing dialectic reads as follows: state violence accompanies structural violence and thereby generates private violence. That private violence legitimates the state because of the reactive violence it exercises against such private violence. The very notion of the state's 'monopoly of violence', which is merely a monopoly of state violence, serves as a violent construct to legitimate the fact that the state sanctions private violence that is the result of structural violence furthered, in part, by the state.

3   *Structural violence takes the shape of private violence.* Individuals may make use of structural or symbolic violence in order to further their interests. While their doing so is in fact part of what is contained in the concept of structural violence (since the 'dominant', in terms of Bourdieu, are also subjectified), it may take the shape of private violence each time they do so to their advantage. When an explicit reference is made in interaction

to what Weber has called the 'legitimate order' by a first-order observer, structural violence takes the shape of private violence. Moreover, in cases of symbolic violence, violence quite literally takes the shape of private violence, which is then, qua execution, self-inflicted. An extreme example of this might be the relatively high number of suicides in Japan (while for many years, the number of homicides has been relatively very low). These can be said to be a private execution of a structural violence of a highly competitive social system in which honour is a highly relevant communicative medium of interaction, while the sense of individuality and of the importance of the individual person is less developed. In the absence of an individualized morality, suicide is structural violence turned inward by means of the executive shape of private violence.

4 *Private violence takes the shape of structural violence.* Structural violence takes the shape of private violence in the case of a first-order observer, yet the opposite occurs when a second-order observer consciously uses structural violence to further his or her own interests. When an explicit reference is made in interaction to the 'legitimate order' by a second-order observer, that is, by an observer observing the differentiation of the social system and the aspect of violence that this entails, what happens is that private violence takes the shape of structural violence. An example of such a second-order observer would be a social scientist using his or her knowledge of the differentiation of the social system and the aspect of violence thereof in order to further his or her own interests. In such a case, Bourdieu speaks of a 'cynical use of sociology' (as opposed to a 'clinical use') (Bourdieu, 1998b: 70).

5 *Private violence takes the shape of state violence.* This happens when individuals or groups manage to further their interest with the help of the executive violence of the state. In political systems characterized to a large degree by corruption, the boundaries between state violence and private violence become blurred. In order to sustain the legitimacy of the state in such cases, a strong ideology needs to be in place. An example is Confucianism in feudal China, which legitimated the difference between farmers and elite, while members of the elite regarded their political activities as extensions of their means to further their self-interest (cf. Stover, 1974).

Concluding remarks on the trias violentiae

If violence is regarded as a reduction of being (with all the further qualifications that have been discussed in Chapter 3), it becomes possible to see how such at-first-sight different things as, for instance, poverty and violent crime are actually related. The correlation between violent crime and economic deprivation that is time and again reproduced in itself does not tell us anything. It is the specific light in which this correlation is seen that allows for a grasping of the *relation* that lies behind the correlation.

The perspective I have developed here starts from three ideal-typical forms of violence. I contend that private violence – the kind of violence social scientists usually focus exclusively on – cannot be wholly understood if it is cut loose from other forms of reduction of being that are in reality related to it. It has been my choice to search for a wholly different perspective and to conceive of people and their private violence as but one link in a triade, the *trias violentiae*. The trias violentiae is meant as a conceptual tool, devised for the sake of *seeing connections*, as Wittgenstein advocates. With the help of it, one sees that in the midst of state violence and structural violence is man, the executor of private violence. By means of diathetic connections, state violence and structural violence have the effect of instigating private violence. Violence, as reduction of being, is a way of subjectifying and objectifying, and of categorizing. Categories of perception and interpretation are acquired in a web of social relations to connect with biological systems and form what I have called a diathesis. Through such a diathesis, a person acts and perceives, or, in other words, reduces complexity. Private violence is one way of reducing complexity. The degree to which diathetic categories are acquired by means of violence determines the likelihood of the production of actions of private violence through that diathesis. That is to say that the degree to which the aspect of reduction of being is highlighted in a person's socialization, that person will be likely to exert a reduction of being (private violence) on others as a means of reducing complexity, that is, as a means of living. Structural violence is especially important here. The correlation between private violence and economic deprivation is nothing other than the expression of the translation of structural violence to private violence, a translation not of wholly different entities, but of one process of reduction of being to another. That is what the trias violentiae most of all is intended to bring into the light: the translation between different forms of reduction of being.

One might argue that this fractured realist perspective adds to the facts of violence certain presuppositions and relations that should not be added to them. One might argue that the facts of violence should be scientifically studied with a 'naked eye'. Contrary to such arguments, I wish to draw attention to a social science which imposes, as if it concerns a *sensus communis*, an intellectualistic stance towards violence that entails that violence can neither be senseless nor sensible, but only non-sense; a social science which imposes, furthermore, a view of violence that is imposed on social science; a social science that predominantly ignores structural violence, as well as the active side of state violence; a social science that is able to do all this under the guise of a 'science' that is based on either naïve realism or self-indulgent social constructivism, both excommunicating relevant aspects of its actual object of research in a violation of the complexity of social reality.

9

For a New Social Science of Violence

Speaking, writing, is not without violence – it is not without an *aspect* of violence. This is all the more true in the case of speaking or writing about violence. For not recognizing aspects of violence has a euphemizing and thereby legitimizing effect of such aspects, and even of forms of violence. That euphemization and legitimation are the complementary aspects of violence of a double violent movement. First, there is the misrecognition of a social phenomenon, which is as such characterized by an aspect of violence. This aspect is, however, hardly highlighted. Any science studying its research-object misses aspects of that object, if only by turning it into an 'object'; every science sees only partial truths, and there is no particular reason to lay emphasis on the aspect of violence that accompanies such science. That goes for all science, in almost every field of enquiry, *except for that of the study of violence*. Here, the scientific study and its necessary aspect-blindness, or one-sidedness, has the aforementioned second violent aspect, an aspect of violence much more highlighted, although hardly ever reflexively highlighted within the social sciences. When studying violence, therefore, the performative power of social science is likely to contribute to violence and to an ideology of violence. A special kind of social scientific reflexivity is required when violence is the object of study. The problem of the violence of speaking of violence is in fact a version of the problem of social science being a part of its general object of enquiry, which is usually labelled 'society', but which actually consists of all social life, not just the social life that coagulates into 'society'. Especially in the case of the study of violence, even when the social scientist opposes himself to his research-object, subject and object cannot be wholly discerned. All the attempts that have been made to overcome Cartesian and Kantian dualism, when seen in light of the aspect of violence, always already sprung from a confluence of subject and object. It is, so to speak, the nature of the social relation of the social scientist with his or her research-object that is, especially when that object is violence, always already violent. When we study violence, we are violent in a very particular way. The knowing subject cannot 'objectively' study the object of violence. Precisely because that object is always necessarily

203

seen in but one particular light, the effects of the knowledge claims concerning violence are violent in themselves, as they attribute cause, as they define, as they repudiate and ignore. In this chapter, I will try to complete a reflexive turn that focuses not only on violence from a social scientific point of view, and not only on the social science of violence, but that highlights the violence of the social science of violence. Social science has its place in the trias violentiae.

To gain a view of the violence of the social science of violence, one most of all should distance oneself from the dominant semantics of violence. I will narrow my discussion of the social science of violence down to two points. The first concerns what may be termed the 'demographic correction' that takes place in quantitative comparisons of violence ratios. From this discussion, a tacit assumption concerning social ontology will become visible, which in turn entails an *a priori* definition of violence that is highly problematic. The second point concerns what can be called the 'ethics of violence'. Linking up with the discussion of the dominant semantics of violence in Chapter 2, the concept of violence that is used in social science is value-laden and obscures the view from forms of violence that, remaining unrecognized as such, have all the more that quality which Bourdieu called 'symbolic'. The question is then legitimately raised to what extent the social science of violence contributes to the sustenance of the current *trias violentiae*.

The demographic correction (or how a social science negates itself)

One of the most problematic aspects of the social science of violence is related to the mathematics of the *demographic correction*; the 'correction' that is made in statistics of violence when the numbers are 'corrected' for demographic changes or proportions. As a certain 'flat' version of a nominalist social ontology is the consequence of the demographic correction, I will defend the realist position which accords to sociology an object of study with some relative degree of ontological independence from social levels aggregated to a lesser degree.

First of all, it is clear that the demographic correction is a feature of social science that is taken for granted. It has become such a common tool in social scientific analysis that it has been 'blackboxed' (Latour, 1987), thus making theoretical reflection on its presuppositions *prima facie* unnecessary. Social scientists have not wanted to simplify matters by dealing with police-statistics as they are, since that would lead to false conclusions regarding the questions concerning the quantitative fluctuation of violence. The 'correction' for demographic changes has been deemed a necessary first step in the discussion. This first step has furthermore been deemed so elementary, so scientifically basic, that it is usually taken without further explanation. It is, for instance, rare to find a researcher take the time to comment that the use of the yearly mean per 100,000 cases is 'a regular instrument of measurement'. After all, one does not elucidate every basic move, performed almost tacitly by any freshman student in criminology or sociology. So the gesture is a silent one: police statistics are 'corrected' for demographic changes, which means violent crime is expressed as a ratio of 100,000 people. Why? To make this explicit, the following reasoning might be offered to students:

> 'If violent crime statistics show an increase in crime, but, during that increase, the population to which these statistics apply grows, you would be mistakenly alarmed if you wouldn't correct the crime-figures for that population-increase. For when more people live together in a society, more violence is likely to occur. Therefore we express violence in terms of the number of cases per 100,000 people. In the Netherlands, for example, 90 cases of "violence against the person" per 100,000 people were registered by the police in 1965, whereas in 1985, 190 of such cases were registered for every 100,000 people (Kosec and Kapteyn, 1991). Or, one can display violent crime rates in percentages of the population experiencing cases of violent crime. In 1997, for instance, 5.2 per cent of the Dutch people above 12 years of age was a victim of violent crime; in 2001, 5.9 per cent was (CBS, 2003: 161). When the numbers are presented in this way, a link between demographic changes and changes in violent crime rates is established in research, and, as I explained, you will want to do that if you want to come to scientific conclusions. In the end, you will have to acknowledge the fact that a growth of the population will have an effect on the development of violent crime.'

The reason for this demographic correction must lie in its relevance of some sort. That relevance can only exist if the correction makes something visible about the relation between changes in population and changes in rates of violence. The very possibility of the demographic correction making something visible about that relation is what I contest. I do so on theoretical grounds, although empirical critiques of the demographic correction have been rendered as well (cf. Rudé, 1988: 262). In its weakest form, the use of the demographic correction assumes that it shows us something about the impact of the population on rates of violence. My main point here is that it cannot show us anything, since the use of this demographic correction is based on faulty assumptions and therefore leads to an altogether mistaken view on violence and its quantitative development.

Society and the gas law

Two things become apparent in the logic of the demographic correction: (1) a quantitative view of the social and (2) a respective and in some cases latent conception of social science as modelled by a conception of (natural) science. I will combine these in my discussion, since they are inextricably linked together. The demographic correction implies assumptions regarding the nature of the social that are not made explicit. Such basic assumptions usually aren't made explicit, which need not be a problem in research, except when they steer research in such a direction that the scientific discussion becomes encapsulated in theoretical constraints that lead to research results that are highly questionable, as I will show is the case in the basic assumptions of participants in the social scientific discussion of violence. For since these constraints are regarded as the parameters of reality, they cannot be broken free from. The result of this is that research results aren't questioned in that which makes them questionable. In the present case, we are dealing with a quantitative view of the social, which is at the same time a nominalist view of society. Here, the social is reduced to people, subjects, individuals. These then form the quantities of society in a linear, proportionate way: a society of four people is assumed to be twice as big as one of two people; ten million individuals on a plot of land make for twice the society of five million individuals on the same plot of land. And so, in the case of violence, the quantifying logic of criminological, historical and sociological discussions of the possible quantitative growth of violence is similar to the logic of Boyle and Gay-Lussac, expressed in the ideal gas law. The gas law states:

$$\frac{PV}{T} = nR,$$

where P is the absolute pressure, V the volume of the vat containing n moles of gas, T the temperature of the gas, n the number of gas moles and R is the universal gas law constant.

As readily becomes clear, the ideal gas law states that a *ceteris paribus* increase in the number of gas moles is linearly related to the pressure in the vat containing the gas. This is in line with Boyle's mechanicist view of reality. A similar assumption forms the bedrock of the demographic correction in social science. For the demographic correction in research of violence is based on the assumption that there exists, like in the case of the compression of gas, a linear relationship between the variables in question: violence between individuals (pressure of an ideal gas) increases with a percentage proportionate to an increase in the number of people in a society (the number of gas moles in Boyle's or Gay-Lussac's vat), when the same space is occupied by them (when volume of the gas – and temperature – stay the same). People are like gas moles: put more of them together in the same space, and their pressure, conflicts, their violence increases proportionally to the increase in their number. This is the logic underlying the demographic correction. And it is a logic that is indicative of a view of the social as nothing but a collection of people. The social, which is first objectified as 'society', becomes a collection of individuals, a whole that equals the sum of its parts. Only with the help of such an anti-sociological assumption can social scientists apply a demographic correction to rates of violent crime. What happens is that each individual is allotted a certain amount of violence. Thereby, the social is conceptualized in an a-social way, and violence is stripped of its social character. To whoever makes use of the demographic correction in research of violence, violence is no longer a social process that transcends the individual.

For a relational perspective

The demographic correction is part of a *Queteletismus*, which has already been critiqued by many nineteenth-century (German) neo-Kantian statisticians. Quetelet, who rewrote his book *Sur l'homme* under the title (reminiscent of Condorcet) *Physique sociale*, and who argued that society is formed out of atomistic individuals, which display statistical regularities that are to be thought of as statistical laws that are themselves representative of causal factors (Hacking, 1990: 126–32). The result is, as G. F. Knapp has aptly characterized it, an 'astronomical conception of society'. But this quantitative, or atomistic nominalist conception of society delivers a highly unsociological view of the social. This is not due to its nominalism per se, but rather to the combination of quantitative individualism and nominalism. Here, social science loses its ground. The autonomy of the social as a sphere of reality relatively independent from other spheres is done away with. If twice as many people are thought to cause twice as much violence, which is the inescapable assumption of the demographic correction, social science would be nothing but a psychology that counts violent individuals and that plots 'violence' and 'population' in such a way that a ratio of violence is allotted to each individual. This is actually what happens in the demographic correction. It is based on the assumption that such a calculation is possible and justifiable due to the nature of the social.

This social ontology is not only a denial of the social nature of violence, but of the social as such. Luckily, social thought has been more than mere 'footnotes with Plato'. The autonomy of the social sciences rests precisely on the reality *sui generis* of the social, that transcends individual beings and that cannot be 'traced back' or reduced to them without leaving a residue. Any decomposition of society is an attempt to reduce the social to another sphere of reality and/or to another aggregate level of reality. It is in fact an attempt to get rid of the social altogether that social scientists in the discussion of the quantitative amount of violence are, probably unknowingly, involved in. Any such attempt fails because the social is more than the sum of its parts. Decomposition and/or reconstruction of the social ends up with a residue that cannot be attributed to individuals. This is not a metaphysical belief; it is rather a (fractured) realism that forms the basis of all theoretically informed social science. In fact, it is rather the attempt to reduce the social to individuals that affiliates itself with an ancient tradition of a metaphysics of presence. What becomes apparent in the use of the demographic correction is an attempt at a *reduction of being of the social*. A certain violence is exerted upon reality in the social scientific discussion of the quantitative amount of violence. The demographic correction is informed by a tacit notion of the social as nothing but a collection of individuals that does not acknowledge the possibility of influences between those individuals or between aggregate levels of individuals that transcend the actions or the being of those individuals. That is the only way one can justify correcting rates of violence for a growth of population the way this is done, the way this is even *required* of 'good social science'. When one assumes that an increase in population leads to a proportionate increase in violence, one at the same time assumes that the social does not exist as a sphere of influence beyond individual people. The sociality, or the *relationality*, of the population is omitted from consideration.

I will give an argument against the use of the demographic correction that is, in itself, a refutation of the correctness of the use of the demographic correction, though it does not yet provide an alternative basis for dealing with the relationship between changes in violence and changes in population. The demographic correction is based on the silly idea that a growth of the population by 100 per cent, leads to a 100 per cent increase in violence within the society of that population. If it wasn't based on this idea, then there would be no point in assuming a linear relationship between population and violence. Now let's stop looking at individuals, but look instead at the social processes *between* those individuals. So let's look at something which can at least be regarded as referring to something *social*. It is then necessary to look at the growth of the number of possible *relations* between people when the number of people increases. After all, what you want to 'correct' for is not the number of people, but rather the number of times people may meet, which, in a certain amount of cases, is what leads to or even constitutes violence. In other words, *you don't want to know how many extra individuals exist in a society, but how many possible relations between those individuals exist in that society*, since violence may exist in some of these relations, and not 'in' some of the individuals.

Start with an easy example. An increase of a population of four people by two people leads to an increase of nine in the number of theoretically possible direct relations between any member of the population and some other member between these people, since six combinations of two exist between four people, whereas fifteen are possible for a population of six. When we add two more people, the result is an increase of thirteen in the number of possible combinations of two members of the population. So the increase in direct relations between people in case of an increase in population is *not* a linear one. The formula for the number of combinations of k individuals in a population of n is $n!/(k!(n-k)!)$. For combinations of two, this gives $n!/(2!(n-2)!)$, which can be rewritten as $\frac{1}{2}n^2 - \frac{1}{2}n$, which can of course not be linear, and which also excludes the possibility of asymptotic linearity. So the presupposition underlying the demographic correction that an increase in population leads to a proportionate increase in violence cannot be taken as self-evident. In case one would want to find a mathematical relationship between the growth of population and the growth of violence, one would surely need to be aware of the fact that what matters is the number of possible relations between people. And a growth in population means that the number of possible violent relations between people increases more than exponentially relative to the increase in population. The assumption of a linear relation between population and violence is based on nothing, as, therefore, is the demographic correction. To further substantiate this point, one might also look at the number of groups that are possible within a population. Since violence is a social process in which, very often, more than two persons are involved, it is also relevant to see how many more groups are possible with every increase in population. This relationship does not seem to be a linear one either: $A_{n+1} + 2A_n + (n+1)$, where A_n is the number of possible groups in a population of n members. This gives a more than exponential increase in the number of possible groups with every increase in population. Although groups of millions usually have to be counted out, smaller groups certainly would have to be counted in, which adds to the implausibility of the linear relation between violence and population presupposed in the demographic correction. What has not even been included here is the number of possible relations between groups as a function of changes in population. So, even when the idea of the demographic correction is adopted, namely that changes in population are accompanied by a change in the rate of violent crime that can be mathematically expressed, the assumption of linearity that is inherent in the demographic correction, the idea that a change in violence is proportionate to a change in population, cannot be taken at face value.

The tacitly performed decision to correct the numbers of violence for demographic changes by way of presupposing a linear correlation between these variables is (1) at odds with the bulk of social theory, and (2) extremely implausible.

The limits of quantification

Does this mean that we should conceptualize the relation between these variables as non-linear, perhaps exponential? No, it does not. The above argument was given, based on an assumption that also underlies the demographic correction as it is performed in social science: that the relation between changes in population and changes in rates of violent crime, *ceteris paribus*, can be mathematically expressed. If such an assumption is made, then the above way of pursuing the elaboration of that relationship should necessarily be made. For, once again, the social scientist does not want to know how many extra individuals are present in a society (or rather, he or she *should* not be primarily interested in this). In social science, one wants to know 'how many relations between those individuals are possible in a society, since violence may exist in some of these relations, and not 'in' some of the individuals. But the very assumption of the possibility of mathematical expression of the relationship between changes in population and changes in rates of violent crime can be disputed. For there is, quite simply, no way to tell in what way the transcendence of the social manifests itself empirically. The use of the demographic correction assumes that it shows us something about the impact of the population on rates of violence, but it cannot show us anything. There is, as yet, no way to interpret that relationship. There is no way to tell whether the 'actual' relationship between demographic changes and changes in rates of violence is in the end linear or non-linear, patterned or chaotic. Maybe we are in need of a demographic correction that makes use of fuzzy logic. Who knows? Social scientists have apparently always known. They have even known tacitly. But they have been wide of the mark. That the social transcends the individual is a basic premise of social science, but this premise is forgotten as soon as empirical research wanders off into quantitative debates without a solid theoretical foundation. Then, social science starts to undermine its own foundations and cuts off the branch on which it is sitting. Modesty with respect to the consequences of the grand premise of social science, that of the 'discovery of the social' and its transcendence over the individual, is in place. We simply don't know whether an increase in population necessarily leads to an increase in rates of violence. If 90 cases of 'violence against the person' per 100,000 people were registered by the police in 1965, and in 1985, 190 of such cases were registered per 100,000 people, these data still don't show anything about a possible growth of violence independent of a growth of the population. Since 'every 100,000 people' does not exist and only a total population exists, we should be able to know the exact influence of changes in population on social processes such as violence, but we don't. Maybe we are dealing purely with an effect of an increase of the population, which does not work in a linear fashion, since the social transcends the realm of the individual, where, all-too-human, each counts as one and the total is the sum of the parts. And if the 'change' in rates of violent crime is just such a non-linear effect of population changes, then maybe the level of violence is perfectly adjusted to the number of people – to the number of *these* people, not just any people. Maybe a combination of increase in population and other qualitative factors within that population, things like 'individualization', or 'functional differentiation' has been at work. Or maybe an increase in population leads to an increase in social control and thereby to less violence. Then again, maybe more social control of the 'wrong' people leads to more violence. Maybe an increase in population leads to a decrease in social control and thereby to an increase in violence. We simply don't know enough yet about the consequences of the basic premise of sociology – the premise that the social transcends the realm of the individual. We certainly don't know enough about it to make tacit decisions about them. But we do therefore know that the use of the demographic correction is unwarranted. It is the result of an implicit will to quantification, betraying a researchers' social-scientific socialization of little 'theory' and a lot of (normal) 'science' of quantification. The paradoxical result is a social scientific a-social view of the social, and an accompanying social scientific study of violence in which violence is no longer really seen as a specifically *social* phenomenon, since it is reduced to the existence of individuals and not to relations between individuals. The entire social scientific debate on the quantitative amount of violence can be liquidated, or even deconstructs itself, in the tacit assumption concerning the being of the social that underlies it.

The ethics of violence and the semantics of evil

Wir tun als die sunn, die scheint uber bose und uber gut: wir nemen gut unde bose in unser gewalt
                                                                                Der Ackermann aus Böhmen

The a-social way of analysing violence in a quantitative sense reduces violence to the level of the individual. This coincides with an *ethics of violence* – and of the social science of violence – that allots 'violence' to violent individuals. To analyse the allocation of responsibility for 'violence' means to take into consideration the functioning of that allocation in relation to the social system as a whole. First, let's consider this ethic of violence more closely, bringing back the distinction, explicated in Chapter 2, between *potestas* and *violentia*. The ethic of violence facilitates the most radical implementation of this distinction. In light of this, it has been beneficial that *potestas* is linguistically of a different root altogether, while *violentia* obviously retains the closest link to the root of 'violence'. The displacement of the legitimate violence by *potestas* and of illegitimate violence by *violentia* has led to a pre-dominant recognition of violence only in case of illegitimate violence. The normative semantics that accompanies this division is old, and can itself be seen as a result of the development of political theology. Distinctions in two have been recurring in thought concerning violence. Luther for instance makes a distinction between the worldly violence (*weltliche Gewalt*) of the sword and the spiritual violence or force (*geistliche Gewalt*) of the word. With the replacement of a transcendent order by a secularized state, the latter became *potestas*. It is relevant to note that the Greek concept to which *violentia* is related, *bia* ('life-force'; see Chapter 2), is opposed to *dike*, which translates as 'justice' since Plato, but which has more neutral connotations of lawful settlement as well in archaic Greek thought. Whether it was a moral concept at all has been subject to some debate among classicists in the 1970s (cf. Gagarin, 1973, 1974; Dickie, 1978). The main difference between the oppositions between *bia* and *dike* and between *violentia* and *potestas* is that the latter differentiation concerns two forms of violence, which are differentiated along the lines of a measure of legitimacy.

Any social system is characterized by a process of attribution of unwanted processes to its environment. Violence is one such unwanted process. While violence is constitutive of any social system, the modern differentiation between state and society is such that the violent origin of both needs to be denied. A paradox must be upheld: society is not what it is. This is done, as discussed in the last chapter, by means of turning the paradox into a tautology: society is *internally* differentiated into an 'inside' and an 'outside'. Individuals making use of private violence are said to be 'outside of society'. This symbolic exorcism is, to repeat what was said in Chapter 8, a functional a priori for the undisputed functioning of the differential unity that under-lies the self-definition of state and society. The paradox of one violence being legitimate because it acts upon something that is deemed not legiti-mate but which is violence as well is resolved by means of the tautology of a society which is non-violent, and 'outside' of which are certain violent individuals. The violence of the state is then legitimized because it no longer acts upon society, but rather upon those individuals 'outside of society' that form a threat to society, which defends itself against this threat by means of an autonomous state which acts on the basis of reasonable, contractual authority. The ethics of violence are such that 'violence' is regarded as a threat to society that emanates from individuals closed off from it, that is, operating in its environment. This way, society makes itself relatively immune to violence, since all violence comes from its environment and is indeed an external threat to society, but at least violence does not grow amid society itself. Violence has thereby become a modern-day secularized version of 'evil'. The attribution of unwanted processes to the environment of a social system has long since taken the normative form of evil. From the pre-Socratics on, the cosmos has been divided into good and evil forces. The Greeks thought of the powers of nature, externally determining them, as personified in Gods and demi-Gods who battled over supremacy. The Hebrew and Christian traditions mark the Fall – paradise lost – as the histori-cal root of all evil. The worldview of the Middle Ages stood in light of the divisions between Good and Evil, Light and Darkness. In modern times, this tradition has been secularized. Now, man himself becomes the source of all evil. The great Gnostic debates concerning the origin of evil were decided in allotting to man alone the roots of good and evil. The modern secularization of evil becomes apparent in Kant's notion of radical evil (*das radikale Böse*)

(Kant, 1974: Part I). Radical evil, in opposition to a Greek cosmological evil or a scholastic original sin and demonic counterpart of God, is evil emanating from man's individual freedom. After Kant, in Romanticism, God is replaced by nature, and evil by society. This echoes in Sartre's *Huis Clos*, with its famous 'l'enfer c'est les autres', as well as in Heidegger's supposedly non-normative yet privative notion of 'das Man'.

Today the so-called 'axis of evil' consists of states endorsing terrorist violence. Man has become the sole origin of evil. A further development that has led to the present situation is that this concerns especially the non-socialized and not fully 'integrated' man. If evil lies in man himself, this brings with it the problem that everyone is (potentially) evil, which leads to problems concerning the legitimation of punishment (one might say one was innately determined to do evil) as well as to problems concerning trust and solidarity (in times of 'organic solidarity' it is prudent to think of man as an egoistic animal – *homo economicus* – but not as innately bad, since that would destroy the trust needed for functional differentiation). These problems are overcome by the development of the idea that violence – which has become the main face of evil – exists outside of the truly social. As soon as the normative meaning of the social is pressed in this way, the violent individual can humbly be admitted to be a failure of society to produce, through moral education, a social individual, while in admitting such, a separation between society and the violent individual is nonetheless performed. Violence is the most prominent representation of evil, and violence therefore needs to be attributed to an environment of the social system. This attribution is facilitated by the differentiation between an inside of society – full of 'integrated' people – and an outside, which consists of non-integrated people: criminals, lunatics, immigrants. Evil is no longer a transcendent category, but an immanent possibility of the maladjusted who are in need of 'reintegration' and are excommunicated by means of the very emphasis on their lack of 'integration'. Evil has become, to speak with Arendt, 'banal'. Books on the topic of evil increasingly are about violence. Some examples are Hibbert's *The Roots of Evil*, Safranski's *Das Böse oder Das Drama der Freiheit*, Baumeister's *Evil. Inside human cruelty and violence*, and most recently Susan Neiman's *Evil in Modern Thought*. This equalization of 'evil' and 'violence' is possible on the basis of modern biaphobia. With the loss of a transcendent category that functioned as a 'black box' for the attribution of unwelcome social processes, a secularized alternative was ready at hand given the normativity that was embedded in violence as violentia with the development of the state's monopoly of legitimate violence. Weber once said that 'Many old gods ascend from their graves; they are disenchanted and hence take the form of impersonal forces. They strive to gain power over our lives and again they resume their eternal struggle with one another' (quoted in von Ferber, 1970: 8). Well today, the violent gods of before are people themselves, individuals, born out of what Durkheim called the 'cult of the individual'. Violence has become the inner-worldly equivalent of an outer-wordly Evil in the attribution of unde-sired processes by the social system. That way, *vis* and *fortuna* come together anew, in a strange way, and albeit that this time, *virtù* is completely separated from force in the sense of *vis*.

The modern obsession with violence

The expulsion of the violent person fulfils a necessary integrative function for the social system as a whole. This process is covered by the semantics according to which it is not the social system which is in need of integration, but the violent individual. Durkheim was already well under way in formu-lating this, although he in fact at the same time contributed to the concep-tual schism between criminal and society. Modern society, while said to be less violent than preceding ones, is obsessed with violence. This obsession is related to the function of 'violence' in the legal sense of *violentia* as a mod-ern-day equivalent of transcendent evil. Today, even evil is controllable. We use reason and science to root out the causes of evil in order to remove them. Hollway and Jefferson have said with respect to the 'risks' that are focused on in the 'fear of crime discourse', that they

> tend to have individual identifiable victims and individual identifiable offenders. This makes them *knowable*. [...] Second, offenders tend to be relatively powerless [...] This makes them *decisionable* (*actionable*). Third, offenders tend to be 'strangers', rather than known others [...] This blaming of the outsider builds loyalty and this assists social cohesion, as Douglas reminds us. It also renders the problem potentially *controllable* (even though the supply of 'criminals' is apparently endless)
>
> Hollway and Jefferson (1997: 260)

If we don't like what the social sciences have to say because it sometimes sounds apologetic, we turn to biology, neuroscience. As David Riches has remarked, ethologists' explanations of violence based on genetics tend to assume the shape of Anglo-Saxon 'folk ideas' concerning the innateness of evil (Riches, 1986: 2). Scientists studying violence have replaced preachers and their knowledge of evil. The semantic exclusion of private violence and its perpetrators has become a functional prerequisite of the contemporary social system. An obsession with violence needs to be upheld, with all the dangers of seduction by and succumbing to autotelic violence. It is this obsession with violence that becomes apparent in the rooting out of all kinds of violence where, in earlier times, nobody would have dreamed of speaking of *violentia*: domestic violence, sexual violence, racial violence, structural violence, symbolic violence, and with senseless violence and 'acoustic violence'[1] new forms of violence are discovered regularly. A Dutch philosopher speaks of 'a culture of violence', and he is speaking about private violence in the twentieth century (Verhoeven, 2000). Increasingly, types of crime are defined in terms of violence, which is of course always possible, since each crime has the aspect of violence – the question is to what extent that aspect is highlighted in practice. In the second half of the nineteenth century, this obsession with violence was less pronounced, as can be inferred from an analysis of media attention to street violence ('garotting', assault and 'ruffianism') in British cities between the 1850s and the 1880s. A moral panic was, so to speak, initiated by the media, yet the Victorian middle class saw through its arbitrariness and did not view street violence as a major problem (Sindall, 1990).

Today, the scientification of violence, parallel to the frictionalization of violence discussed in Chapter 5, has taken on tremendous size. Billions of dollars, pounds and euros are spent on the aetiology of private violence. This is the extension of nineteenth-century positivism. This positivism, both in law and in (social) science, is itself a consequence of an immanentization, as Voegelin (1968) says, of political theology. Individuals become the units of society; society can be analysed 'like an ordinary machine' (Sieyès). Lombroso's *L'uomo delinquente* marks the height of a positivism that cut man in two, as Mill voiced it: 'The only part of the conduct of anyone for which he is amenable to society is that which concerns others. In the part which merely concerns himself, his independence is, of right, absolute. Over himself, over his own body and mind, the individual is sovereign' (Mill, 1974: 68–9). The views of Beccaria, Mill and Lombroso are much closer to current research than to the views of old Europeans immersed in medieval political theology. Social scientific research of violence predominantly is deterministic research (in the sense deployed in Chapter 5), aetiological in kind. There is an obsession with the causes of private violence in 'individuals', while quite paradoxically, the causality of the causes is never thematized. Moreover, even the knowledge of causes would be rendered useless when *prediction* would be required. Perhaps Foucault's notion of a 'control society' is indeed a better term to observe the current situation with than that of the 'disciplinary society', its predecessor. There is an obsession with violence because there is an obsession with control. Violence is what escapes control, what threatens, what disturbs free and truthful communication. As one researcher has said: 'Violence has probably been the most researched topic in the vast literature on mass communications' (Cumbernatch, 1994: 492). The modern obsession with private violence is biaphobically motivated, and the social sciences seem to thrive on biaphobia.

The intellectualism of violence

Dem Volke habt ihr gedient und des Volkes Aberglauben, ihr berühmten Weisen alle! – und nicht der Wahrheit!

Also Sprach Zarathustra

The one-sided recognition of violence as private violence, *violentia*, might be called the *ideology of violence*. This ideology has violent effects, since it euphemizes and legitimizes those forms of violence which, according to it, are not violence at all. The ideology of violence is strengthened in various ways in different social systems. Dictionaries and encyclopaedia pin down violence on something destructive made of physical force. We find this for instance in the eighteenth century not only in Zedler's lexicon, but also in its French counterpart, in Diderot and d'Alembert (1967, 17: 315), whose *Encyclopédie* reads: 'a violent man is quick to lift his hand'. To the common-sensical observers immersed in everyday social life, the truth of the ideology of violence is self-evident, since the observer relies on his empirical observations and the practice he or she is foremost able to identify with the common-sensical notion of violence is the highly visible private physical violence. In everyday life, whoever receives a blow to the head, knows instantaneously he is being violated. Proponents of the 'restricted definition' of violence use this fact to argue that, therefore, one should not expand the concept of violence beyond such physical blows, since one would otherwise be dealing with wholly different phenomena. But this argumentation is flawed, because it mistakes a *form* which violence may assume for its *substance*. The point is to develop, as I have done in Part I, a metatheory of violence that specifies such a substance and can subsume different empirical *forms* under the generic name 'violence' without having to arbitrarily draw distinctions between forms on the basis of a contingent common sense.

In the system of law, the ideology of violence is strengthened by means of the specific programmes existing in this system. By definition (as its code, according to Luhmann, is *recht–unrecht*), the law only deals with violence as *violentia*. Thus, we find in Bouvier's well-known *Law Dictionary* the following: 'VIS (Lat. force). Any kind of force, violence, or disturbance relating to a man's person or his property. A person does anything by force (*vis*) when he does what he is forbidden to do by the owner' (Bouvier, 1914, II: 3403). And 'violence' is subsequently defined as 'the abuse of force. That force which is employed against common right, against the laws, and against public liberty. [...] Violence is synonymous with physical force, and the two are used interchangeably, in relation to assaults, by elementary writers on criminal law' (Bouvier, 1914, II: 3402). The law thus has its own ways to equate 'violence' to 'illegitimate physical violence'. Thus, 'violence' is ideally recognized if the following is present: 'a staunch complainant; a readily identifiable assailant; the absence of any prior personal relationship, particularly one of intimacy; serious, clearly visible injuries; and reliable witnesses' (Cretney and Davis, 1995: 98). In the systems of politics, science and philosophy, another way in which the ideology of violence is strengthened in its self-evidence is a biaphobia which entails a deontology of violence, and which is socially distributed in the form of an *intellectualism of violence*, a habitus or even diathesis of violence that washes the hands of the higher educated clean of violence. This is strengthened by the 'facts': the higher educated engage less in private physical violence than those with lesser education. The circularity in this reasoning is carefully avoided: the higher educated are less violent in general, since violence is only private physical violence and this occurs less among the higher educated. Any discussion of an 'extended definition' of violence meets with high resistance: from politicians, because they are unable to implement policy geared at an 'invisible violence'; from social scientists, because it is not 'empirically observable'; and from philosophy, because it goes against the laws of proper definition. Of course, all three arguments beg the question: only when alternative forms of violence are defined as invisible do problems arise in implementing policy with respect to such violence; only when the empirical observability of violence in general is related exclusively to the empirical observability of private physical violence do alternative forms of violence escape the categories of empirical perception; and only when violence is thus defined that the violence of definition is excluded from the definition of violence does it become possible to abide to rules of definition philosophically detached from social reality. The intellectualism of violence in these systems constitutes an enlightened rejection of supposedly all violence, which, since it only recognizes private violence – and at times especially in social science and philosophy, state violence, but hardly ever structural violence or the relations between these forms – offers a violent contribution to the sustenance of the trias violentiae.

Social science, by researching violence only in the restricted sense, very often appears to contribute to the reification of the intellectualist notion of violence. That is perhaps the reason why social scientists usually don't bother to define violence. Of the many characteristics of the intellectualism of violence, I will mention a few examples. (1) Violence is one-sidedly regarded as a negativity; its productive aspects are forgotten: 'We need to recognize that violence is a genus of behaviours, made up of a diverse class of injurious actions, invoking a variety of behaviours, injuries, motivations, agents, victims, and observers. The sole thread connecting them is the threat or outcome of injury' (Jackman, 2002: 404). Associated with this are the many paradoxes of 'non-violence' (cf. Sharp, 1973). Gandhi, for instance, is often quoted as having said: 'Victory, obtained by violence is tantamount to defeat, for it is momentary.' Or Martin Luther King: 'Nonviolence is the answer to the crucial political and moral questions of our time; the need for mankind to overcome oppression and violence without resorting to oppression and violence. Mankind must evolve for all human conflict a method which rejects revenge, aggression, and retaliation. The foundation of such a method is love.' Here, an opposition between violence and love becomes apparent, which remains paradoxical, since there is always still an *object* of love. Of course, Gandhi and MLK were speaking first of all of political violence. Social scientists usually restrict themselves to street violence or at most to physical violence in general. (2) Such violence is then predominantly seen as a *problem*, which has the consequence of not being able to identify as violence what does not pose an immediate problem. Furthermore, the semantics of violence as a problem is blind to the possibility that violence is a *solution* to a problem. A question of stance, of perspective, better yet: of aspect, seems to have been tacitly answered in the 'social problems' industry. (3) As the intellectualism of violence is a socially distributed diathesis of observing violence, it is accompanied by distinctive strategies on behalf of those who endorse it. The intellectualism of violence stresses the non-violence and in general the discipline and taste of the man who has devoted himself to a life of detachment, a *bios theoretikos* of contemplation, far removed from such vulgar behaviour as 'violence'. Accordingly, those who do engage in private physical violence are portrayed as defected in all kinds of ways. Isaac Asimov has thus remarked that 'violence is the last refuge of the incompetent'. Two well-known social scientists writing about post-industrialism stress that 'violence provides a kind of emotional high for some people whose emotional communication with others is blocked' (Hage and Powers, 1992: 100). This connects with the idea that violence and communication are somehow opposites. In psychology and psychiatry, defects are sure to be found in violent individuals – one nonetheless wonders what defects would be found in the population as a whole. A Dutch social scientist writing on violence speaks of private physical violence as 'impulsive behaviour' (Van den Brink, 2001: 342). The classification of behaviour as 'impulsive' declassifies it, and misses the obvious point that the existence of predispositions – habitus, diathesis – makes it problematic to speak of 'impulsive' behaviour at all – lest one would want to maintain that having a disposition to 'non-violent', 'normal' behaviour means one 'impulsively' behaves normally or non-violently. Even Machiavelli was not free of intellectualism, since he differentiates between two ways of contest: 'the one by law, and the other by force. The first is practised by men, and the other by animals; and as the first is often insufficient, it becomes necessary to resort to the second' (Machiavelli, 1997: 67). While recognizing the necessity and productivity of 'force', Machiavelli still relates it to 'the nature [...] of the beasts', thus intellectually ascribing truly human capacity to the law.

In the context of Dutch intellectual debate, two cases may serve as illustrations of the intellectualism of violence. The first is that of a philosopher of high reputation, who has written *Against violence* (*Tegen het geweld*), in which he opposes the irrationality of violence to the rationality of technology. First of all, he does not write *about* violence, but *against* it. According to him, reflection on violence 'does not so much have as its ultimate goal or ideal to know exactly what it is but rather to deliver a contribution to its liquidation' (Verhoeven, 1967: 7). Paradoxically, it is admitted that without seeking the best possible knowledge concerning violence, violence is to be countered. Yet even from the intellectualist point of view, this would in any case be a faulty way to proceed in the eradication of the evil of violence. Did not Spinoza say that the best way to transcend an evil is to know it in all its forms and if possible in its causes? What is more, it appears as a presupposition that violence is an evil, even without striving for full and accurate knowledge about it. The possibility, then, that violence may turn out to be positively productive in the end, is ruled out *a priori*. This philosopher's solution to the 'problem' of violence, then, is a remarkably violent one. Violence is opposed to technology, since in technology everything is controllable and predictable and in violence it isn't. What this philosopher preaches is a Foucauldian control society. Apart from the fact that such a 'society' is, in itself, not controllable by any one, but has developed relatively autonomously, the philosopher is apparently oblivious of the violence of technology. And apart from the fact that technology does not adequately counter private violence, there is the violence of technology, of its potential to reduce, of its reduction by means of Orwellian surveillance. A realistic answer to the utopian view of technology is Wim Wenders's movie *The End of Violence*, which incorporates all these ingredients and can be seen as a picture of the violence of technology.

Another case that highlights the intellectualist diathesis of biaphobia is that of a Dutch sociologist, who was in fact recently voted no. 1 Dutch intellectual by his colleague-intellectuals. I quote this sociologist and public intellectual (in my translation): 'That it is particularly intellectuals that are shocked by the violence of torture, may be related to the fact that they especially have sworn off rigorously all physical exercise of power, that they never hit wife or children, never fight with other men and also know no acceptable form of fight' (Swaan, 1982: 118). This sociologist first of all insinuates that intellectuals – who are, according to this quote, always male – make a wholly individual and autonomous choice to not engage in 'physical forms of exercise of power'. Again, to social science, determining factors – such as embodied in habitus or diathesis – are only at work in case of violence. The 'normal' case of supposed non-violence, such as the choices of the intellectual, are a form of social behaviour free of such factors. What shines through the intellectual's remarks is the well-known dictum that violence is 'primitive', where 'violence' is of course equated to private physical violence. This, however, does not mean that the intellectual has evolutionarily transcended violence in general, but at best that he makes use of further evolved forms of violence that are all the more effective since they are not recognized as such, and that very well may invoke an indirect physical violence, or threat thereof – for instance when intellectuals gain ground in advisory boards on crime, committees and 'expert' teams affiliated with the state. The intellectualist attitude of course also has a social origin and covers up the structural violence that is performed under the cloak of intellectualism. All the while, the supreme intellectual within the Dutch field of intellectualism proves the justness of his position, since his article starts by his being shocked, after which he explains that *intellectuals* are particularly shocked. Whoever can be at once intellectual, *explain* the behaviour of intellectuals, and then also dissociate the intellectual in general with all violence must indeed be a top intellectual himself.

These two cases are examples of a biaphobic attitude towards violence as secularized evil, an attitude that is expressed at different social levels, one of which is that of the enlightened intellectual, continuously thinking against evil. And as Voegelin says, 'enlightened intellectuals are not a harmless curiosity: they are dangerous maniacs. They take themselves seriously, they really believe they represent mankind, and if a recalcitrant *masse totale* insists on being formed in the image of God, they will use force to correct the mistake and remould man in their own image' (Voegelin, 1962: 182). Intellectuals continuously run the risk of euphemizing destructive forms of violence and of contributing to a status quo by becoming immersed in the ideology of violence. Nietzsche's Zarathustra has said the following of the relationship between what I will translate as 'the famous intellectual' (*von den berühmten Weisen*) and a political power: 'And many a powerful one who wanted to run well with the people, hath harnessed in front of his horses – a donkey, a famous wise man' (Nietzsche, 1979: 360). The true 'detached' intellectual, one would say, would rather keep his or her distance from dominant ideologies and would question his or her own biaphobia.

The social sciences; reflexivity and violence

I have set up many possible paradoxes throughout this book. By making the epistemological point that the social sciences always uncover aspects of social reality at the cost of blind spots, and by then defining violence in relation to the selection and negation of aspects of being, violence necessarily enters the social sciences in an unfamiliar familiar way. In a familiar way, because its operational process is where violence always already takes place, since the violence of social science is related to its necessarily one-sided observation of social phenomena – like violence. Yet this familiarity of social scientific violence is at the same time unfamiliar, since it is hardly ever observed. Once again, what is most familiar escapes observation. The story then continues, for if the social sciences are blind to their own violence, they do violence to themselves because they negate an aspect that is fundamental to its very being – remember that without violence, no social scientific observation of reality could exist! This violence that the social sciences perform unto themselves – a form of symbolic violence that incorporates the intellectualist notion of violence – is, however, a perfect illustration of the positivity and the productivity of violence. For it is by means of the violent negation of its violence that the social sciences are able to observe social reality the way they do.

What am I doing? The highlighting of the unfamiliar familiar violence of the social sciences leads to a level of reflexivity that is usually suppressed precisely because of the productivity of that suppression. The paradox of social scientifically violently observing violence is usually de-paradoxized by means of a further violence: the violence of negation of the paradox by means of the definition of violence as 'private physical violence', which automatically refers violence to something *outside* social science, but *studied by* it. To re-paradoxize the social sciences by pointing out the unfamiliar familiarity of their violence is to endanger their operational process. However, to reflexively highlight this means at least to do away with the violence of negation of the unfamiliar familiarity of violence. That means, though not without paradox, to be *less violent* in social science. I will now admit, for once, to paradoxically endorse the biaphobic position that a reflexive social science is a less violent social science. This entire book can be read as a critique of social theory. That is to say that one *aspect* of this book may be highlighted to show a text in social theory. I have argued that the nature of social scientific observation is violent, especially when that observation concerns violence. Of course this only holds true within the framework of my own text, since the commonsensical notion of violence does not allow for the violence of social science to be even thematized – unless if it were in the form of a World Congress of Sociology turning into a big physical fight, for instance on the occasion of a keynote speaker declaring sociology to be violent. But this is unlikely to happen, if only for the institutionalized de-paradoxization of sociology which would prevent it from having a keynote speaker that might turn the sociology of violence reflexively topsy-turvy. But my point is that the social sciences, if they truly are 'sciences', should do something more than unreflexively incorporate familiar, commonsensical notions of violence. They should, in Zygmunt Bauman's view that I have quoted earlier on, 'defamiliarize' what is familiar. As it stands, the social sciences have no theory, or better, no *metatheory* of violence. What is needed is the courage to observe, which is the courage to alternate perspective, to change the aspect. Find a consistent perspective that highlights aspects of social life in a way that has an evocative power, in a way that enables a consistent relating of these aspects to each other, and in the knowledge – grounded in the history of science – that a fracture-less realism will be impossible. The perspective I have thus developed, discards *arbitrary* boundaries between violence and non-violence, and replaces them by a *substance* of violence that allows violence to be seen as an *aspect* of social situations that is highlighted in different degrees, thus constituting a sliding scale. The social sciences are characterized by an aspect of violence somewhere along that scale. Especially where the concepts of social science are not fully metatheoretically developed, chances are that these concepts contribute to a status quo which necessarily involves a structural violence that is at times significantly highlighted. Contemporary social science incorporates a semantics of violence as if it were a *sensus communis*. This semantics separates a normal, non-violent social life from a pathological and violent social life. Moreover, it violently reduces people to fit one one-sided anthropology. The violent basis on which this semantics of violence claims moral superiority illustrates that violence is not that easily wholly attributed externally. From the scientific point of view, however, the unreflexive incorporation of the popular notion of what violence is, is itself a *pathos*.

What the social sciences need to do is therefore to learn to live with paradoxes. A level of reflexivity needs to be attained that uncovers biaphobia by means of the biaphobic contention that more reflexivity is less *violent* than less reflexivity. Reflexivity in social science means a being prepared to change the aspect of social science by changing the aspect of the object of social science. It is in this sense that the aspect of violence of a reflexive social science is less highlighted than it would be in case of lesser reflexivity.

The current social scientific research attitude towards violence is voiced – and propagated – well by Mary Midgley (who is herself a moral philosopher): 'It is fatalism – the superstitious acceptance of unnecessary evils as inevitable – not determinism, which can menace our freedom. Determinism is, or should be, only a pragmatic assumption of order, made for the sake of doing science' (Midgley, 1984: 113). This not only highlights the blindness to the 'non evil' aspects of violence; it also illustrates a problem I have dealt with in Chapter 5. Why is autotelic violence – violence for the sake of itself – hardly ever observed in social science, whereas art for art's sake is, as is love for the sake of love? If there is 'unmotivated, divine love', as the scholastics used to say, is there not 'unmotivated, divine violence'? Much of current social science does not allow for such observations to be made, or even for such hypotheses to be formulated, since it biaphobically presupposes violence to be diametrically opposed to all aspects of creation, such as art and love. Yet even contemporary art raises reflexivity to the level that its own violence is observed. Why couldn't social science do the same? Prior to the distinction between 'facts' and 'perceptions' of violence lies a semantics of violence that instigates a particular perception of the facts. Violence is only recognized as violence insofar as it is *recognized* as such. This sounds trivial and tautological, but it alerts to the fact that violence has to inscribe itself in a public order, and consequently in modes of perception. It has to leave a *trace* to be seen. Violence that does not leave a trace within biaphobic apparatuses of perception is, in the dominant semantics of violence, denied the entitlement of violence. Herein lies the inherent violence of that semantics.

Like biaphobia can be seen as a 'denial of life', its social scientific embrace is a denial of the social world, in which causes and consequences are only seen as tied to concrete empirical beings, immersed in concrete identifiable situations. Structural violence is much harder to pin down in concrete, individualized entities. State violence is hardly thematized in relation to private violence, and this may be a consequence of the semantics of the state as *pater familias*; domestic violence has long been a blind spot among the many forms of private violence. There is therefore a constant danger of the criminalization of violence, especially when violence is in social science left in the hands of criminology, which continuously runs the risk of acting as enforcer of a violent semantics of violence. The criminalization of violence makes it increasingly difficult to see the connections between various forms of violence. I have given these connections the conceptual designation of the trias violentiae. This entails the idea that no one form of violence can be adequately understood if it is not related to the other forms, that is, if it is not seen in light of the trias violentiae. A criminological isolated study of private (physical) violence cuts into its own hermeneutic potential. One of the problems preventing a reflexive truth in the social science of violence is that – as is the case in the social sciences in general – certain 'classics' form a basis that is too little problematized (Luhmann, 1984: 7). A sub-discipline like criminology has the disadvantage of being based on 'classical' middle-range theories – theories, therefore, that are even less sophisticatedly embedded in a general theory or a metatheory of social life in general and of violence in particular. Fundamental reflection within criminology is difficult, because it will be excommunicated as part of sociology of philosophy. Too little room therefore exists for genuine reflexivity, and the danger of a criminological monopolization of the social scientific study of violence is therefore a danger of losing fundamental reflection that is a necessary precondition for reflexivity. Current criminology is itself partly a result of the modern obsession with private violence. A dominant semantics herein is the semantics of 'risk'. By means of a simultaneous individualization and de-individualization of violence (individualization, because violence is predominantly treated as the private physical violence of isolated individuals – which is all too clear from the above discussion on the demographic correction, and de-individualization, because it is after all not the individual that is researched, but rather various endogenous and exogenous factors determining the individual), the individual becomes the unit of a research focused on 'risks' of the individual displaying violent behaviour. The obsession with violence is thereby carried to another level: the collective risk, at once a risk to the collective, that private violence is deemed to be, is now individualized and planted in the individual, not in the potential victim of risk, but in the person 'at risk of becoming violent'. Like a terrorism alert system, modern criminology finds its cause in the modern functional differentiation. An industry of 'violence risk assessments' has begun to emerge (compare Feeley and Simon, 1992; Ericson and Haggerty, 1997).

It is instructive to recall from Chapter 1 what Wittgenstein says about seeing aspects. We see something the way we do, he says, because we have a certain *relation* with it. Thus, in the social scientific observation of violence, what is and what is not seen is the expression of a relation between the social sciences and violence. That relation is not the relation of the knowing subject opposed to an object (lying, literally, before the subject). The relation in question is not an 'objective' scientific relation. What the history of the semantics of violence shows is that a historical development of a way of speaking about and of observing violence is tied up with structural changes in the social system and that moral overtones are part of the core of the modern concept of violence. At the near end of that historical process, the institutionalized social sciences enter the scene, and it is evident that they lacked, and still lack the objective distance it claims to have the legitimate monopoly on. Social science simply jumped on history's bandwagon, incorporating a semantics of violence that it should in fact take as an object of research. All the dismissiveness towards 'conceptual work' because it is not 'practical', 'empirical', 'implementable' and 'societally relevant' prevents the social science of violence from in fact becoming what its name suggests. For without a solid conceptual ground that utilizes concepts not arbitrarily defined, or borrowed from a semantics of violence that is the handmaiden of a status quo, whatever 'empirical' work is done will involve not only aspect blindness, but also its violence, doubled by the violence of the blindness to aspect blindness. One possible way to move towards a reflexive social science would be to provocatively turn the semantics of violence upside down, as Sorel has done in his *Réflections sur la violence*, where he calls the violence of the dominant class a *force*, which perpetuates power, while the violence of the proletariat is *violence*, a morally pure rebellion against 'the ideology of the state' (*l'idéologie de l'Etat*) (Sorel, 1919: 29). A liquidation of these reflections on violence – that means not a literal utilization but a putting to work of contemporarily relevant aspects – might prove instrumental towards a reflexive social science of violence.

In conclusion

Perhaps the most significant change in the relation between violence and the modern western state is the dramatic semantic driving back of violence. It is not unreasonable to assume that, during what Elias has called the 'process of civilization', private physical violence has decreased. Yet it is unlikely, as Cicero says, that anything has been done against violence without violence. 'Civilization' consists of a redistribution of violence, of improved and subtle forms of control, of biopolitics, and, most significantly, of a semantic change enabling a sovereign state to emerge by means of a monopoly of legitimate violence. It is crucial that, while private physical violence may have decreased, other forms of violence have been used in the generalization of expectations, for instance in maintaining the law. In history, the subtle illusion has been created of a decrease of violence *sec*, but only at the cost of the misunderstanding that 'violence' denotes private physical violence. The self-definition of the state as executor of re-active violence against private violence is enabled by means of a blind spot for the violence constitutive of sociality, for structural violence, and for the 'active' violence of the state. In fact, the state quite often facilitates structural violence. As discussed in Chapter 8, mixes of forms of violence may appear, and the state may become executor of structural violence. The dichotomy of state–society is in modern times accompanied by a replacement of religion by the economy as the main sphere of legitimation (see Luhmann, 1988: 30). 'Society' has become semantically equal to the working economy and the state has become an institution predominantly stimulating economic growth. Thereby, the violent nature of the economic order is obscured, just as the violent origin of the state is forgotten, as Pascal says it needs to be. The state's monopoly of legitimate violence rests upon the secularized cosmological authority of sovereignty (the 'point' of secularization may be analytically located in Hobbes). A rationalist layer was placed underneath the sole legitimate use of force, thus obscuring the fact that the sovereign power's very ability to do so rested on the use of force *before* a legitimation by means of an ideology of rationality could exist. It takes an initial state of exception, brought about by force, to decide upon the state of exception. Over time, the sovereign state absorbed many forms of private violence, sucking it up, so to speak, turning violent persons into disciplined police-men, soldiers, bureaucrats, and keeping an immense machine of violence ready at hand, dispersed through a system of procedures and rules, making use of education and all other available disciplinary tools of – as its discipli-nary name is – 'socialization'. Individuals resorting to private physical vio-lence are not recognized as having been socialized differently, but as having been 'defectively socialized', which stresses the *difference* but attributes it to only *one side* of that difference. All the while, the neglect of structural vio-lence in effect means a legitimation of it, which is a necessary consequence – as structural violence is the violence inherent to the differentiation of the social system – of the legitimation of the social system itself. What goes for other forms of relatively severe violence, goes for structural violence in a similar fashion: 'The key to justifying violence to others [...] is to make what was in fact rape appear ambivalent in terms of consent' (Maguire et al., 1997: 868).

If one were to take a look into the possible future of violence, it would seem that several developments are putting the state's monopoly of legiti-mate violence under pressure. As for private physical violence, increasing individualization may lead to an upsurge due to the aforementioned double effect of individualization facilitating techniques of neutralization and rationalization of private physical violence, as well as the weakening of social control. Moreover, private physical violence may become, more than it already is, a way of securing an identity that is hard to find in a function-ally differentiated social system differentiating itself ever more, creating insides and outsides, placing individuals on paradoxical borders, in multiple insides and outsides. The increasing privatization of state violence, moreover, seems to mix state violence and private violence. When private violence becomes the form assumed by state violence, the state is in danger of losing control of its own violence, which can then hardly be called 'legitimate' (Shearing, 1997). Probably the biggest threat to the state is the current globalization. Of all the dangers this process presents the state with (questions of autonomy, for one), from the perspective of this book the 'democratization of violence' is especially relevant. Worldwide terrorist movements have become a primary challenge to state authority in the West. Though terrorism has beneficial effects for states in a globalized world – it provides a chance to prove their autonomy and discernability, that is, their identity as political units anew – it remains a constant hassle for states, since it is almost impossible to control. Through terrorism, the smallest group can challenge the mightiest state, and this puts the state under pressure because it becomes painfully obvious that the state's monopoly of legitimate violence is really not a monopoly of all violence, and the question continually is: is this helpless state really what we need? One strategy to avoid such questions is to start one or two wars against nations and to classify these under the general heading of a 'war on terror', which, taken literally, is a contradiction in terms. Globalization has, on another plane, been hailed as the solution to problems of inequality, that is, of structural violence. For the moment, however, it seems to provide just as many possibilities for structural violence to occur. For structural violence is the violence that exists by virtue of the breaches between social systems and of their internal differentiations. Since world-society is increasingly complex, such breaches are only multiplying, for complexity in social systems is related to (functional) differentiation. The trias violentiae of the future may therefore be a trinity wholly different from the current one.

To return to the current situation, I wish to once more highlight the effects of the modern semantics of violence. Some things are as yet unresolved. The paradoxical character of this semantics means that anyone effectively deploying it needs to have some method of de-paradoxization. And since it has been clear from Chapter 1 onwards that the current study is not without paradoxes itself, it is likely to end in the paradoxical awareness of its aspect-blindness in the study of the paradoxes of the aspect-blindness that may be called violence.

To summarize what has been said above, 'violence' has become the innerwordly equivalent of evil. Psychiatrists have taken the place of exorcists; retribution has replaced repentance, death penalty and purgatory have been replaced by incarceration and prison. Absolution, for lack of transcendence, has been replaced 'reintegration'. Violence has thus become a theme on the basis of which the social system is able to deal with contingency and supposedly disruptive elements. This however, has a double paradoxical character. First, there is the paradox of one-sidedly attributing the difference between a 'society' of 'integrated' individuals and an 'outside society' of, among others, 'violent' individuals to only one side of that difference, whereas a difference necessarily takes two. Secondly, there is Cicero's paradox of fighting violence with itself. Because the productive side of violence is biaphobically repressed, 'violence' is to be countered. Paradoxically, violence itself seems best equipped to do this. The first paradox is resolved by means of an emphasis on the normality of non-violence and the pathological making-a-difference of the violent individual. The difference between society and the violent person can thus safely be attributed to one side of the difference (which is always the *other* side of the difference), since it is the violent individual who *makes* the difference through his violence. The second paradox has been bugging political theory for a long time. It touches upon the very basis of legitimation of the state. This paradox is apparent in Cicero's aforementioned dictum, and from the consolidation of the sovereign state onwards, it seems to have been resolved or in any case lived with. Thus, we find for instance in Zedler's *Universallexikon* immediately following the definition of violence and its semantic differentiation into *potestas* and *violentia*, and with respect to *violentia* the same process of attribution, enabled by the semantic differentiation of *potestas* and *violentia* (Zedler, 1732ff.: 1377).

Violence (*violentia*) first of all springs from maladjusted individual evildoers, after which the violence of the state (*potestas*) is merely a *reaction*, which in fact not really be called 'violence' at all. The problem that remains in this resolution of the paradox is that, apparently, a few individuals are able to threaten the existing order. This problem is resolved by the combined individualization and de-individualization of violence: *individuals* commit illegitimate violence, but all kinds of endogenous and exogenous determining factors, causes, are observed as being in fact responsible for their behaviour, thus dissolving the 'individual' to which violence is yet ascribed. It therefore once again comes down to 'society' versus 'nature'. This way, 'society' regains control over violence by means of the subsystem of science, coupled to policy. Society can now frankly and patiently admit that the 'integration' does not succeed in every individual case – since there are always abnormals – while at the same time it is only these individuals – not the social system itself – which are not well 'integrated'. The reasons for violence can now be scientifically known and controlled. As Charles Thorpe has noted, 'A central faith of modernity has been in science as a solution to the problem of violence' (Thorpe, 2004: 59). How harsh, therefore, are the judgements concerning both psychiatrists and politicians responsible in case of a 'psychologically' disturbed inmate repeating offence when on leave. The paradox of outlawing violence by means of lawful violence allows non-physical forms of violence to escape attention. Psychic violence (for instance in the form of bullying) is unregulated since unrecognized. When a victim of severe psychic violence then commits suicide, this latter action is outlawed once more, since it is physical and visible, and thereby threatening the state for the sole reason that the state should authorize any physical, visible violence. Private physical violence threatens the state already because the state's self-definition entails an opposition to physical violence, for instance in the case of the Hobbesian 'natural state' that is based on the opposition between non-violence and legitimate physical violence. All physical violence that after all occurs in the realm of supposed non-violence is necessarily illegitimate violence, *violentia*. It becomes apparent that the state's recognition and the negation of forms of violence are situated on the borders between the semantic oppositions by means of which the state forges its self-definition. In the violence it does and does not prosecute and exert, the state is always primarily concerned with its own survival as a social system.

As for the social sciences, their ability to observe violence is equally enabled by the distinction between *potestas* and *violentia*, and by the paradoxical observation of *violentia* as violence with the help of a negation of both *potestas* as violence, of structural violence, and of everyday forms of violence constitutive of the simplest forms of sociality. The de-paradoxization of this mode of observation is performed by means of an appeal to the commonsensical ontology and deontology of violence, that is, by unreflexively incorporating into social science the modes of first-order observation that it is actually supposed to observe from a second-order point of view. Incorporating the popular semantics of violence, it becomes apparent that the social science of violence is surely on the right track, since 'everybody knows' what violence is (the ontology) and 'everybody knows' that it is undesirable, even dangerous, a 'problem' (the deontology). Problems of legitimation of social science do not appear until the first-order commonsensical perspective is abandoned in favour of a genuinely social *scientific* second-order mode of observation. In fact, for social science, the degree to which it needs to justify itself towards other social systems, that is, the degree to which questions concerning its legitimation are asked in relation to its output, is almost a measure of its level of science, but in the sense that more *questioning* of its legitimation means a *higher* standard of social science. As it stands, the endless repetition of the same correlations with its negligible relevance in both attribution of causality and in prediction of private physical violence is not denounced by other social systems because it is in itself such a great help after all, but because it ratifies and keeps up the appearance of 'violence' first of all being a 'problem' that, secondly, is being scientifically kept in check. Such being the function of the social science of violence in the functional differentiation of the social system at large, it appears – who would have thought it? – that social science *is* the veil of ignorance. As such, it is even more 'societally relevant' than it would dream possible.

It is time to face the consequences of what has been said in Chapter 1. A first epistemological criterion of observations such as the ones expounded in this chapter is that they are paradoxical. To observe the blind spots of the social science of violence within social science itself is to bring into social science the blind spots that are the conditions of possibility of its ability to observe. Such a 're-entry' is not without paradoxical consequences. One of these is the observation that the observation that the social scientific observation of violence is not without violence; it is characterized by its own violence. Such paradoxes are, however, what needs to be endured if aspects of violence are to be observed scientifically at all.

Notes

2 The Definition of Violence – Part I

1. This is a simplification, since *Gewalt* saw a historical widening of denotation, not so much in the (Latin) concepts it referred to, but rather in the generalization in its practical use. As Grimm and Grimm cite from a text from the 'mittelhochdeutsche Periode': 'gewalt ist aber sô manicfalt' ['yet violence is so multifarious']. See (Grimm and Grimm, 1911: 4920).

3 The Definition of Violence – Part II

1. I will henceforth drop the term 'empirical', as it is now clear what I meant when I used this imprecise term in the preceding chapter.
2. Robert de Niro in the movie *Jackie Brown*.
3. This becomes particularly clear in the documentary entitled *First Kill* (2001), by Coco Schrijber.

4 From Critique of Violence to Autotelic Violence: Rereading Walter Benjamin

1. In Benjamin's philosophy of history, most explicitly formulated in his *Geschichtsphilosophische Thesen*, the historian's (which is, the historical materialist) task is not to follow the line of history towards its progressive goal, but rather to gather the fragments of the past and to come to a 'now', a *Jetztzeit* in which past and present are captured in a messianic relation. The 'idea of the end' of violence will as such have to be 'saved' from the past.
2. Ibid., p. 42: 'die rechserhaltende Gewalt ist eine drohende'.
3. This point has been mentioned to me by Kees Schinkel, a Dutch theologian and philosopher.
4. The concept of the autotelic has been used by Benjamin as well, although not in relation to violence, but in his philosophy of language, where he speaks of the *unmittelbarkeit* of an original (non-mythical) language. Benjamin took the concept from an earlier use by Novalis and Todorov.

5 The Will to Violence

Part of this chapter has been published in an earlier version in *Theoretical Criminology* 8(1), pp. 5–31.
1. http://www.esrc.ac.uk/esrccontent/ourresearch/violence.asp.

6 The Continuation of Violence by Other Means: Terrorism

1. http://www.whitehouse.gov/infocus/nationalsecurity/faq-what.html (accessed 26 July 2006).

2. http://www.whitehouse.gov/infocus/nationalsecurity/faq-what.html (accessed 1 August 2006).

7 A Note on Causes of High School Violence

1. For additional information, see *Jefferson County Police Report*, for instance at http://www.portalofdallas.com/columbine/TOC.htm.
2. http://www.cnn.com/US/9904/21/school.shooting.01/.
3. Quoted at http://denver.rockymountainnews.com/shooting/0516bguy2.shtml.
4. http://www.cnn.com/US/9904/21/harris.profile.02/.
5. http://www.cnn.com/US/9904/21/school.shooting.01/.
6. Quoted at http://www.cnn.com/US/9904/20/school.shooting.08/index.html.
7. http://www.disastercenter.com/killers.html.
8. Quoted at http://www.cnn.com/US/9904/20/school.shooting.08/index.html.
9. Quoted at http://www.westword.com/issues/2001-12-06/news.html/1/index.html.
10. Ibid.
11. http://www.cnn.com/US/9904/21/harris.profile.02/

9 For a New Social Science of Violence

1. See for instance the proceedings of the 'Fourth International Multidisciplinary Conference on Acoustic Violence', Rosario, Argentina, 22–24 October 2001: http://www.eie.fceia.unr.edu.ar/~acustica/violac4e.htm.

References

Agnew, R. (1997): 'The Nature and Determinants of Strain: Another Look at Durkheim and Merton', in Passas, N. & R. Agnew (eds): *The Future of Anomie Theory*. Boston: Notheastern University Press, pp. 27–51.

Akers, R. L. (1985): *Deviant Behavior: A Social Learning Approach*. Belmont: Wadsworth.

Albrow, M. (1996): *The Global Age: State and Society Beyond Modernity*. Stanford: Stanford University Press.

Alexander, J. C. (2004): 'From the Depths of Despair: Performance, Counterperformance, and "September 11"'. *Sociological Theory* 22(1): 88–105.

Allison, H. E. (2002): 'On the Very Idea of a Propensity to Evil'. *The Journal of Value Inquiry* 36: 337–48.

Amussen, S. D. (1995): 'Punishment, Discipline, and Power: The Social Meanings of Violence in Early Modern England'. *Journal of British Studies* 34: 1–34.

Anderson, K. L. (1997): 'Gender, Status, and Domestic Violence: An Integration of Feminist and Family Violence Approaches'. *Journal of Marriage and the Family* 59(3): 655–69.

Anderson, C. A. & B. J. Bushman (2002): 'Human Aggression'. *Annual Review of Psychology* 53: 27–51.

Archer, D. & R. Gartner (1976): 'Violent Acts and Violent Times: A Comparative Approach to Postwar Homicide Rates'. *American Sociological Review* 41(6): 937–63.

Arendt, H. (1968): *The Origins of Totalitarianism*. New York: Harcourt, Brace & World.

—— (1970): *On Violence*. San Diego: Harvest.

Aron, R. (2003): *Peace & War. A Theory of International Relations*. New Brunswick/London: Transaction Publishers.

Audi, R. (1997): 'Acting for Reasons', in Mele, A. R. (ed.): *The Philosophy of Action*. Oxford: Oxford University Press, pp. 75–105.

Badiou, A. (2002): *Ethics. An Essay on the Understanding of Evil*. London/New York: Verso.

Barak, G. (2003): *Violence and Nonviolence. Pathways to Understanding*. London: Sage.

Barry, B. (1965): *Political Argument*. London: Routledge & Kegan Paul.

Barry, K. (1979): *Female Sexual Slavery*. New York: Avon Books.

Bateson, G. (1972): *Steps to an Ecology of Mind*. Chicago: Chicago University Press.

Bauman, Z. (1990): *Thinking Sociologically*. Oxford: Blackwell.

—— (1995): *Life in Fragments. Essays in Postmodern Morality*. Oxford: Blackwell.

—— (1998a): *De moderne tijd en de holocaust* (Dutch translation of *Modernity and the Holocaust*). Amsterdam: Boom.

—— (1998b): *Globalization: The Human Consequences*. Cambridge: Polity.

Beck, U. (2000): *The Brave New World of Work*. Cambridge: Polity Press.

Beiner, R. (1984): 'Walter Benjamin's Philosophy of History'. *Political Theory* 12(3): 423–34.

Benjamin, W. (1965a): *Zur Kritik der Gewalt*. Frankfurt/M.: Suhrkamp.

—— (1965b): 'Geschichtsphilosophische Thesen', in (1965): o.c., pp. 78–94.

—— (1965c): 'Schicksal und Charakter', in Benjamin, W. (1965): o.c., pp.66–77.

—— (1965d): 'Theologisch-politisches Fragment', in (1965): o.c., pp. 95–6.

—— (1977): *Das Kunstwerk im Zeitalter seiner technischen Reproduzierbarkeit*. Frankfurt/ M.: Suhrkamp.

—— (1996): *Maar een storm waait uit het paradijs. Filosofische essays over taal en geschiedenis*. Nijmegen: SUN.

Berents, D. A. (1976): *Misdaad in de middeleeuwen. Een onderzoek naar de criminaliteit in het laat-middeleeuwse Utrecht*. Utrecht: De Walburg Pers.

Berg, M. van den & W. Schinkel (2009): '"Women from the Catacombs of the City". Gender Notions in Dutch Culturalist Discourse'. *Innovation: European Journal of Social Science Research*. Forthcoming.

Berger, P. (1977): *Facing up to Modernity: Excursions in Society, Politics, and Religion*. New York: Basic Books.

Bergesen, A. J. & O. Lizardo (2004): 'International Terrorism and the World-System'. *Sociological Theory* 22(1): 38–52.

Bergesen, A. J. & Han, Y. (2005): 'New Directions for Terrorism Research.' *International Journal of Comparative Sociology* 46(1–2): 133–151.

Best, J. (1999): *Random Violence. How we talk about New Crimes and New Victims*. Berkeley: University of California Press.

Black, D. (2004): 'The Geometry of Terrorism'. *Sociological Theory* 22(1): 14–25.

Blok, A. (1991): 'Zinloos en zinvol geweld', in Franke, H., N. Wilterdink & C. Brinkgreve (eds): *Alledaags en ongewoon geweld*. Groningen: Wolters-Noordhoff, pp. 189–207.

—— (2001): *Honour and Violence*. Cambridge: Polity Press.

Blomberg, T. G. & Cohen, S. (1995): *Punishment and Social Control. Essays in Honor of Sheldon L. Messinger*. New York: Aldine de Gruyter.

Bobrow, D. B. (2004): 'Losing to terrorism: An American work in progress'. *Metaphilosophy* 35(3): 345–64.

Bohman, J. (1996): *Public Deliberation. Pluralism, Complexity and Democracy*. Cambridge, MA: MIT Press.

Bonger, W. A. (1936): *An Introduction to Criminology*. London: Methuen.

Bourdieu, P. (1977): *Outline of a Theory of Practice*. Cambridge: Cambridge University Press.

—— (1993): *The Field of Cultural Production*. Cambridge: Polity Press.

—— (1994): *Raisons pratiques. Sur la théorie de l'action*. Paris: Seuil.

—— (1996): *Distinction. A Social Critique of the Judgement of Taste*. Cambridge, MA: Harvard University Press.

—— (1997): *Méditations pascaliennes*. Paris: Seuil.

—— (1998a): *Acts of Resistance. Against the Tyranny of the Market*. New York: The New Press.

—— (1998b): *Over Televisie* (Dutch translation of *Sur la télévision*). Meppel: Boom.

—— (1999): *The Weight of the World. Social Suffering in Contemporary Society*. Cambridge: Polity Press.

—— (2000): *Les structures sociales de l'économie*. Paris: Seuil.

Bouvier, J. (1914): *Bouvier's Law Dictionary and Concise Encyclopedia* (Third revision by Rawle, F.), Vol. II, St. Paul: West Publishing Company.

Braukmann, C. J. & M. M. Wolf (1987): 'Behaviorally based group homes for juvenile offenders', in: Morros, E. K. & C. J. Braukmann (eds): *Behavioral Approaches to Crime and Delinquency. A Handbook of Application, Research and Concepts*. New York: Plenum, pp. 135–59.

Brewer, J. & J. Styles (eds) (1980): *An Ungovernable People. The English and their Law in the Seventeenth and Eighteenth Centuries*. London: Hutchinson.

Brezina, T. et al. (2001): 'Student anger and aggressive behaviour in school: an initial test of Agnew's macro-level strain theory'. *Journal of Research in Crime and Delinquency* 38(4): 362–86.

Brink, van den G. (2001): *Geweld als Uitdaging. De betekenis van agressief gedrag bij jongeren*. Utrecht: NIZW.

Broadley, S. A. (2000): 'Autoimmune disease in first-degree relatives of patients with multiple sclerosis'. *Brain* 123: 1102–11.

Bunge, M. (1959): *Causality. The Place of the Causal Principle in Modern Science*. Cambridge: Harvard University Press.

Burk, L. R. & B. R. Burkhart (2003): 'Disorganized attachment as a diathesis for sexual deviance. Developmental experience and the motivation for sexual offending'. *Aggression and Violent Behavior* 8: 487–511.

Butler, J. (2007): *Opgefokte taal. Een politiek van de performatief* [Dutch translation of *Excitable Speech: The Politics of the Performative*, with new preface]. Amsterdam: Parrèsia.

Camus, A. (1951): *L'homme révolté*. Paris: Gallimard.

—— (1962): 'Les Justes', in: *Théâtre Récit Nouvelle*. Paris: Gallimard.

Caputo, J. D. (ed.) (1997): *Deconstruction in a Nutshell. A Conversation with Jacques Derrida*. New York: Fordham University Press.

CBS (2003): *Statistisch Jaarboek 2003*. Voorburg/Heerlen: Centraal Bureau voor de Statistiek.

Chauncy, C. (1754): *The Horrid Nature and Enormous Guilt of Murder*. (A sermon preached at the Thursday-lecture in Boston, November 19, 1754, the day of the execution of William Wieer, for the murder of William Chism). Boston: T. Fleet.

Chomsky, N. (2001): 'U.S.: A Leading Terrorist State'. *Monthly Review* 53: 10–19.

Coady, C. A. J. (2004): 'Defining Terrorism,' in: Primoratz, I. (ed): *Terrorism: The Philosophical Issues*. New York: Palgrave Macmillan: 3–14.

Collingwood, R. G. (1958): *The Principles of Art*. Oxford: Oxford University Press.

Collins, R. (1974): 'Three Faces of Cruelty: Towards a Comparative Sociology of Violence'. *Theory and Society* 1(4): 415–40.

—— (1993): 'What Does Conflict Theory Predict about America's Future?'. *Sociological Perspectives* 36: 289–313.

—— (2004): 'Rituals of Solidarity and Security in the Wake of Terrorist Attack'. *Sociological Theory* 22(1): 53–87.

—— (2008): *Violence: A Micro-Sociological Theory*. Princeton: Princeton University Press.

Conrad, J. (1995): *Heart of Darkness*. London: Penguin.

Copleston, F. C. (1972): *A History of Medieval Philosophy*. London: Methuen & Co.

Coser, L. (1956): *The Functions of Social Conflict*. New York: The Free Press.

Craig, E. (ed.) (1998): *Routledge Encyclopedia of Philosophy*, Vol. 9, London: Routledge.

Crenshaw Hutchinson, M. (1972): 'The concept of revolutionary terrorism'. *The Journal of Conflict Resolution* 16(3): 383–96.

Crenshaw, M. (1981): 'The Causes of Terrorism'. *Comparative Politics* 13(4): 379–99.

—— (2001): 'Terrorism', in: *International Encyclopedia of the Social & Behavioral Sciences*. Amsterdam: Elsevier: 15604–6.

Cretney, A. & G. Davis (1995): *Punishing Violence*. London: Routledge.

Crettiez, X. (2008): *Les formes de la violence*. Paris: La Découverte.

Cumbernatch, G. (1994): 'Legislating mythology: Video violence and children'. *Journal of Mental Health* 3: 485–94.

Dahrendorf, R. (1990): *The Modern Social Conflict: An Essay on the Politics of Liberty*. Berkeley: University of California Press.

Dante (1996): *Inferno* (Translated by Durling, R.M.). Oxford: Oxford University Press.

Davis Graham, H. & T. R. Gurr (eds) (1969): *Violence in America, Volume I. Historical and Comparative Perspectives. A Report to the National Commission on the Causes and Prevention of Violence.* Washington, DC: National Commission on the Causes and Prevention of Violence.

De Cauter, L. (1999): *De dwerg in de schaakautomaat. Benjamins verborgen leer.* Nijmegen: SUN.

De Sade (1992): *De 120 Dagen van Sodom of De school der losbandigheid* (Translated by Hans Warren). Amsterdam: Bakker.

Denzin, N. K. (1984): 'Toward a Phenomenology of Domestic, Family Violence'. *American Journal of Sociology* 90(3): 483–513.

Derrida, J. (1974): *Of Grammatology.* Baltimore: The Johns Hopkins University Press.

—— (1978): 'Violence and Metaphysics: An Essay on the Thought of Emmanuel Levinas', in *Writing and Difference.* London: Routledge, pp. 97–192.

—— (1994): *Force de loi. Le 'Fondement mystique de l'autorité'.* Paris: Galilée.

—— (1995): *The Gift of Death.* Chicago: The University of Chicago Press.

Dickie, M. W. (1978): '*Dike* as a moral term in Homer and Hesiod'. *Classical Philosophy* 73(2): 91–101.

Diderot, D. & J. d'Alembert (eds) (1967): *Encyclopédie ou Dictionnaire Raisonné des Sciences des Arts et des Métiers.* Nouvelle impression en facsimile de la première edition de 1751–1780. Stuttgart: Friedrich Fromann Verlag.

Drake, C. J. M. (1998): 'The Role of Ideology in Terrorists' Target Selection'. *Terrorism and Political Violence* 10(2): 53–85.

Dugard, J. (1974): 'International Terrorism: Problems of Definition'. *International Affairs* 50(1): 67–81.

Dunham, W. H. (1947): 'Current status of ecological research in mental disorder'. *Social Forces* 25(3): 321–6.

Durkheim, E. (1915): *The Elementary Forms of the Religious Life.* London: George Allen & Unwin.

—— (1937): *Les règles de la méthode sociologique.* Paris: PUF.

Durkheim, E. & M. Mauss (1963): *Primitive Classification.* Chicago: University of Chicago Press.

Elias, N. (1970): *Wat is sociologie?* Utrecht: Het Spectrum.

—— (1975): *Die höfische Gesellschaft.* Darmstadt & Neuwied: Luchterhand.

—— (1980): *Über den Prozeß der Zivilisation. Soziogenetische und psychogenetische Untersuchungen* (1 & 2). Frankfurt/M.: Suhrkamp.

—— (1986): 'An Essay on Sport and Violence', in Elias, N. & E. Dunning (eds): *Quest for Excitement. Sport and Leisure in the Civilizing Process.* Oxford: Basil Blackwell, pp. 150–74.

Enders, W. & T. Sandler (2002): 'Patterns of Transnational Terrorism, 1970–1999: Alternative Time-Series Estimates'. *International Studies Quarterly* 46: 145–65.

Erasmus, D. (1969): *Oorlog (Dulce bellum inexpertis).* Amsterdam/Antwerpen: Wereldbibliotheek-Vereniging.

Ericson, R. V. & K. D. Haggerty (1997): *Policing the Risk Society.* Toronto: University of Toronto Press.

FBI (2006): http://www.fbi.gov, accessed at July 27, 2006.

Feeley, M. M & J. Simon (1992): 'The New Penology: Notes on the Emerging Strategy of Corrections and its Implications'. *Criminology* 30(4): 449–74.

Ferber, C. von (1970): *Die Gewalt in der Politik. Auseinandersetzung mit Max Weber.* Stuttgart: Kohlhammer.

Ferell, J., K. Hayward, W. Morrison & M. Presdee (eds) (2004): *Cultural Criminology Unleashed*. London: Glasshouse Press.

Ferell, J., K. Hayward & J. Young (2008): *Cultural Criminology: An Invitation*. London: Sage.

Flett, G. L. & P. L. Hewitt (1995): 'Perfectionism, life events, and depressive symptoms. A test of a diathesis-stress model'. *Current Psychology* 14(2): 112–38.

Foucault, M. (1966): *Les Mots et les Choses. Archéologie des sciences humaines*. Paris: Gallimard.

—— (1975): *Surveiller et punir. Naissance de la prison*. Paris: Gallimard.

—— (1976): *L'Histoire de la Sexualité I: La volonté de savoir*. Paris: Gallimard.

—— (1982): 'Afterword", in: Dreyfus, H. L. & P. Rabinow: *Michel Foucault: Beyond Structuralism and Hermeneutics*. Brighton: The Harvester Press.

—— (1994): *Power*. London: Penguin.

Fromm (1973): *The Anatomy of Human Destructiveness*. Greenwich: Fawcett Crest.

Gadd, D. (2000): 'Masculinities, violence and defended psychosocial subjects'. *Theoretical Criminology* 4(2): 429–49.

Gagarin, M. (1973): '*Dike* in the *Works and Days*'. *Classical Philosophy* 68(2): 81–94.

—— (1974): '*Dike* in Archaic Greek Thought'. *Classical Philosophy* 69(3): 186–97.

Galtung, J. (1968): 'Violence, Peace, and Peace Research'. *Journal of Peace Research*, 6(4): 167–91.

Garland, D. (2001): *The Culture of Control: Crime and Social Order in Contemporary Society*. Chicago: Chicago University Press.

Garver, N. (1998): 'What Violence Is'. *Nation*, June 24, pp. 817–22.

Gasché, R. (1994): 'Über Kritik, Hyperkritik und Dekonstruktion: Der Fall Benjamin', in: Haverkamp, A. (ed.): *Gewalt und Gerechtigkeit. Derrida – Benjamin*. Frankfurt/ M.: Suhrkamp, pp. 196–216.

Gay, P. (1993): *The Cultivation of Hatred. The Bourgeois Experience: Victoria to Freud, Volume III*. London: Harper Collins.

Geuss, R. (2001): *History and Illusion in Politics*. Cambridge: Cambridge University Press.

Gibbs, J. P. (1989): 'Conceptualization of Terrorism'. *American Sociological Review* 54: 329–40.

Giddens, A. (1976): *New Rules of Sociological Method. A Positive Critique of Interpretative Sociology*. London: Hutchinson.

—— (1984): *The Constitution of Society. Outline of the Theory of Structuration*. Berkeley: University of California Press.

Girard, R. (1982): *Le bouc émissaire*. Paris: Grasset.

—— (1985): *La Route des Hommes Pervers*. Paris: Grasset.

Gorman, L. & D. McLean (2003): *Media and Society in the Twentieth Century*. Oxford: Blackwell.

Gottfredson, M. R. & T. Hirschi (1990): *A General Theory of Crime*. Stanford: Stanford University Press.

Greer, C. (2004): 'Crime, Media and Community: Grief and Virtual Engagement in Late Modernity', in: Ferell, J., K. Hayward, W. Morrison & M. Presdee (eds): *Cultural Criminology Unleashed*. London: Glasshouse Press, pp. 109–118.

Grimm, J. & W. Grimm (1911): *Deutsches Wörterbuch*. 4e Bandes, 1e Abtheilung, 3e Theil. Leipzig: S. Hirzel.

Grossman, D. (2003): 'Schoolgeweld in de Verenigde Staten. Hoe kinderen geweld aanleren', in: Schuyt, C. & G. van den Brink (eds): *Publiek Geweld*. Amsterdam: Amsterdam University Press, pp. 75–82.

Gurr, T. R. (1979): 'Some Characteristics of Political Terrorism in the 1960s', in: Stohl, M.: *The Politics of Terrorism*. New York: M. Dekker.

Habermas, J. (1968): *Theorien der Sozialisation. Stichworte und Literatur zur Vorlesung im Sommer-Semester 1968*. Frankfurt.

Hacking, I. (1990): *The Taming of Chance*. Cambridge: Cambridge University Press.

Haddad, S. & Khashan, H. (2002): 'Islam and Terrorism. Lebanese Muslim Views on September 11'. *Journal of Conflict Resolution* 46(6): 812–28.

Hage, J. & C. H. Powers (1992): *Post-Industrial Lives. Roles and Relationships in the 21st Century*. London: Sage.

Halbmayer, E. (2001): 'Socio-cosmological contexts and forms of violence. War, vendetta, duels and suicide among the Yukpa of north-western Venezuela', in: Schmidt, B. E. & I. W. Schröder (eds): *Anthropology of Violence and Conflict*. London: Routledge, pp. 49–75.

Hardman, J. B. S. (1948): 'Terrorism', in: Seligman, E. R. A. (ed.): *Encyclopaedia of the Social Sciences*, 14: 575–80.

Harvey, D. (2005): *A Brief History of Neoliberalism*. New York: Oxford University Press.

Hassemer, W. (1973): *Theorie und Soziologie des Verbrechens*. Frankfurt/M.: Fischer.

Hegel, G. W. F. (1969): *Werke*, in: Glockner (ed.), Bd. 4.

—— (1970): *Phänomenologie des Geistes*. Frankfurt/M.: Suhrkamp.

Heidegger, M. (1949): *Über den Humanismus*. Frankfurt/M.: Vittorio Klostermann.

—— (1953): *Einführung in die Metaphysik*. Tübingen: Max Niemeyer.

—— (1993): *Sein und Zeit*. Tübingen: Max Niemeyer.

Heineke, J. M. (ed.) (1978): *Economic Models of Criminal Behavior*. New York: North-Holland.

Henry, S. (2000): 'What is School Violence? An Integrated Definition'. *Annals of the American Academy of Political and Social Science* 567: 16–29.

Henry, S. & D. Milovanovic (1996): *Constitutive Criminology. Beyond Postmodernism*. London: Sage.

Hess, H. (2003): 'Like Zealots and Romans: Terrorism and Empire in the 21st Century,' *Crime, Law & Social Change* 39: 339–57.

Hirschi, T. (1969): *Causes of Delinquency*. Berkeley: University of California Press.

Hobbes, T. (1969): *Leviathan*. London: Collins.

Hoffman, B. (1998): *Inside Terrorism*. New York: Columbia University Press.

Hollway, W. & T. Jefferson (1997): 'The risk society in an age of anxiety: situating fear of crime'. *British Journal of Sociology* 48(2): 255–66.

Horkheimer, M. & T. W. Adorno (1944): *Dialektik der Aufklärung. Philosophische Fragmente*. Frankfurt/M.: Fischer.

Höss, R. (1960): *Commandant of Auschwitz: The Autobiography of Rudolf Hoess*. Cleveland/New York: World Publishing Company.

Hoyle, C. (1998): *Negotiating Domestic Violence: Police, Criminal Justice, and Victims*. Oxford: Oxford University Press.

Hume, D. (1984 [1739]): *A Treatise of Human Nature*. Harmondsworth: Penguin.

Husserl, E. (1976a): *Ideen zu einer reinen Phänomenologie und Phänomenologische Philosophie*. Bd. III Husserliana. Den Haag: Martinus Nijhoff, Bd. I.

—— (1976b): *Die Krisis der Europäischen Wissenschaften und die Transzendentale Phänomenologie*. Den Haag: Nijhoff.

Jackman, M. R. (2002): 'Violence in Social Life'. *Annual Review of Sociology* 28: 387–415.

James, W. (1953): *The Philosophy of William James James* (with an introduction by H. M. Kallen), New York: The Modern Library.

Jaspers, K. (1953): *Die Geistige Situation der Zeit*. Berlin: De Gruyter.

Jefferson, T. (1994): 'Theorizing Masculine Subjectivity', in: Newburn, T. & E. Stanko (eds): *Just Boys doing Business*. London: Routledge.

Jenkins, B. M. (1982): 'Statements About Terrorism'. *Annals of the American Academy of Political and Social Science* 463: 11–23.

Junger-Tas, J. & N. W. Slot (2001): 'Preventie van ernstig delinquent en gewelddadig gedrag', in: Loeber, R, N. W. Slot & J. A. Sergeant (eds): *Ernstige en gewelddadige jeugddelinquentie. Omvang, oorzaken en interventies.* Houten/Diegem: Bohn Stafleu Van Loghum, pp. 265–89.

Kant, I. (1957): *Kritik der Urteilskraft.* Frankfurt/M.: Suhrkamp.

—— (1961): *Kritik der praktischen Vernunft.* Stuttgart: Reclam.

—— (1974): *Die Religion innerhalb der Grenzen der blossen Vernunft.* Stuttgart: Reclam.

Katz, J. (1988): *Seductions of Crime. Moral and Sensual Attractions in Doing Evil.* New York: Basic Books.

Kelly, J. M. (1992): *A Short History of Western Legal Theory.* Oxford: Clarendon Press.

King, A. (2001): 'Violent pasts: collective memory and football hooliganism'. *The Sociological Review* 49(4): 568–85.

Kosec, H. & P. Kapteyn (1991): 'Geweld en eerste hulp. Een oriënterend onderzoek in een aantal Europese steden'. *Amsterdams Sociologisch Tijdschrift* 18(3): 117–37.

Laclau, E. & C. Mouffe (1985): *Hegemony and Socialist Strategy. Towards a Radical Democratic Politics.* London: Verso.

Landmann, M. (1982): *Philosophische Anthropologie. Menschliche Selbstdarstellung in Geschichte und Gegenwart.* Berlin/New York: de Gruyter.

Latour, B. (1987): *Science in Action. How to follow Scientists and Engineers through Society.* Cambridge: Harvard University Press.

Latour, B. (1996a): *Aramis or the Love of Technology.* Cambridge: Harvard University press.

—— (1996b): 'On Interobjectivity'. *Media, Culture & Activity* Symposium The lessons of simian societies.

Laqueur, W. (1987): *The Age of Terrorism.* Boston: Little Brown.

—— (1996): 'Postmodern Terrorism'. *Foreign Affairs* 75: 24–36.

—— (1999): *The New Terrorism. Fanaticism and the Arms of Mass Destruction.* New York: Oxford University Press.

Lazar, J. (2002): *La violence des jeunes. Comment fabrique-t-on des délinquants?.* Paris: Flammarion.

Lefebvre, H. (1968): *La vie quotidienne dans le monde moderne.* Paris: Gallimard.

Lefort, C. (2000): *Writing: The Political Test.* Durham: Duke University Press.

Lerner, M. J. & C. H. Simmons (1966): 'Observer's reaction to the "innocent victim": Compassion or rejection?'. *Journal of Personality and Social Psychology* 4(2): 203–10.

Levi, P. (1965): *If This Is A Man/The Truce.* London: Abacus.

Levinas, E. (1974): *Totalité et Infini. Essai sur l'extériorité.* The Hague: Martinus Nijhoff.

Lindenberger, T. & A. Lüdtke (1995): *Physische Gewalt. Studien zur Geschichte der Neuzeit.* Frankfurt/M.: Suhrkamp.

Lindqvist, S. (1996): *Exterminate All the Brutes.* New York: New Press.

Lorenz, K. (1963): *Das Sogenannte Böse. Zur Naturgeschichte der Aggression.* Wien: Borotha-Schoeler Verlag.

Luhmann, N, (1971): 'Sinn als Grundbegriff der Soziologie', in Luhmann, N. & J. Habermas: *Theorie der Gesellschaft oder Sozialtechnologie. Was leistet die Systemforschung?.* Frankfurt/M.: Suhrkamp.

—— (1984): *Soziale Systeme. Grundriß einer allgemeinen Theorie.* Frankfurt/M.: Suhrkamp.

—— (1988): 'Tautology and Paradox in the Self-Descriptions of Modern Society'. *Sociological Theory* 6(1): 21–37.

—— (1991): *Soziologie des Risikos*. Berlin: de Gruyter.

—— (1993): *Das Recht der Gesellschaft*. Frankfurt/M.: Suhrkamp.

—— (1995): *Gesellschaftsstruktur und Semantik*, Bd. 4. Frankfurt/M.: Suhrkamp.

—— (1997): *Die Gesellschaft der Gesellschaft*. Frankfurt/M.: Suhrkamp.

—— (2000): *The Reality of the Mass Media*. Stanford: Stanford University Press.

Lukes, S. (1967): 'Alienation and anomie', in: Laslett, P. & W. G. Runciman (eds): *Philosophy, Politics and Society*. Oxford: Blackwell.

Machiavelli, N. (1997): *The Prince*. Ware: Wordsworth.

Maguire, M. et al. (1997): *Oxford Handbook of Criminology*. Oxford: Oxford University Press.

Marcuse, H. (1965): 'Nachwort', in: Benjamin, W.: *Zur Kritik der Gewalt*. Frankfurt/M.: Suhrkamp, pp. 99–107.

Markward, M. et al. (2000): 'Culture and the Intergenerational Transmission of Substance Abuse, Woman Abuse, and Child Abuse: A Diathesis-Stress Perspective'. *Children and Youth Services Review* 22(3/4): 237–50.

Marquis de Sade (1992): *De 120 Dagen van Sodom of De school der losbandigheid* (Translated by Hans Warren). Amsterdam: Bakker.

Marsh, P., E. Rosser & R. Harre (1978): *The Rules of Disorder*. London: Routledge & Kegan Paul.

Martin, A. von (1932): *Sociologie van de renaissance*. (Dutch translation of *Sociologie der Renaissance*). Utrecht/Antwerpen: Aula.

Maudsley, H. (1889): 'The Double Brain'. *Mind. A Quarterly Review of Psychology and Philosophy* 54: 161–87.

Mead, G. H. (1962): *Mind, Self & Society from the Standpoint of a Social Behaviorist*. Chicago: Chicago University Press.

Merleau-Ponty, M. (1962): *Phenomenology of Perception*. London: Routledge.

Merton, R. K. (1968): *Social Theory and Social Structure*. New York: The Free Press.

Messerschmidt, J. W. (1999): 'Making bodies matter: Adolescent masculinities, the body, and varieties of violence'. *Theoretical Criminology* 3(2): 197–220.

Michaud, Y. (1986): *La Violence*. Presses Universitaires de France.

Midgley, M. (1984): *Wickedness. A Philosophical Essay*. London/New York: Routledge.

Mill, J. S. (1974): *On Liberty*. Harmondsworth: Penguin.

Mills, D. (1976): 'Kataki-uchi: The Practice of Blood Revenge in Pre-modern Japan'. *Modern Asian Studies* 10: 525–42.

Monroe, S. M. & A. D. Simons (1991): 'Diathesis-stress theories in the context of life stress research. Implications for the depressive disorders'. *Psychological Bulletin* 110: 406–25.

Muchembled, R. (1991): *De uitvinding van de moderne mens. Collectief gedrag, zeden, gewoonten en gevoelswereld van de middeleeuwen tot de Franse Revolutie*. (Dutch translation of *L'invention de l'homme moderne*). Amsterdam: Contact.

Mulhall, S. (1996): *Heidegger and Being and Time*. London: Routledge.

Muncie, J. & E. McLaughlin (eds) (1996): *The Problem of Crime*. London: Sage.

Nieburg, H. L. (1963): 'Uses of violence'. *The Journal of Conflict Resolution* 7(1): 43–54.

Nietzsche, F. (1964): *Der Wille zur Macht. Versuch einer Umwertung aller Werte*. Stuttgart: Alfred Kröner Verlag.

—— (1979): *Werke*. Frankfurt/M.: Ullstein.

Nozick, R. (1974): *Anarchy, State, and Utopia*. Oxford: Blackwell.

Nussbaum, M. (1993): 'Equity and Mercy'. *Philosophy and Public Affairs* 22(2): 83–125.

Nuzzo, A. (2004): 'Reasons for Conflict: Political Implications of a Definition of Terrorism'. *Metaphilosophy* 35(3): 330–44.

Pascal, B. (1976): *Pensées*. Mercure de France.

Plessner, H. (1975): *Die Stufen des Organischen und der Mensch. Einleitung in die philosophische Anthropologie*. Berlin/New York: Walter de Gruyter.

Portes, A. (2000): 'The Hidden Abode. Sociology as Analysis of the Unexpected'. *American Sociological Review* 65(1): 1–18.

Presdee, M. (2000): *Cultural Criminology and the Carnival of Crime*. London: Routledge.

Presser, L. (2003): 'Remorse and Neutralization Among Violent Male Offenders'. *Justice Quarterly* 20(4): 801–25.

Price, H. E. jr. (1977): 'The Strategy and Tactics of Revolutionary Terrorism'. *Comparative Studies in Society and History* 19(1): 52–66.

Primoratz, I. (2004): 'What Is Terrorism?', in: Primoratz, I. (ed.): *Terrorism: The Philosophical Issues*. New York: Palgrave Macmillan, pp. 15–30.

Pye, L. (1956): *Guerilla Communism in Malaya*. Princeton: Princeton University Press.

Rende, R. & R. Plomin (1992): 'Diathesis-stress models of psychopathology. A quantitative genetic perspective'. *Applied & Preventive Psychology* 1: 177–82.

Riches, D. (1986): 'The Phenomenon of Violence', in: Riches, D. (ed.): *The Anthropology of Violence*. Oxford: Basil Blackwell, pp. 1–27.

Ricoeur, P. (1967): 'Violence et langage'. *Rechreches et Débats: La Violence* 16(9): 86–94.

Ritter, J. (ed.) (1974): *Historisches Wörterbuch der Philosophie*. Darmstadt: Wissenschaftliche Buchgesellschaft.

Rodin, D. (2004): 'Terrorism without Intention'. *Ethics* 114: 752–71.

Rudé, G. (1988): *The Face of the Crowd. Studies in Revolution, Ideology, and Popular Protest*. (ed. Kaye, H. J.). New York: Harvester Wheatsheaf.

Runkle, G. (1976): 'Is Violence Always Wrong?' *The Journal of Politics* 38(2): 367–89.

Rutter, M., H. Giller & A. Hagell (1998): *Antisocial Behavior by Young People*. Cambridge: Cambridge University Press.

Safranski, R. (1998): *Het kwaad. Het drama van de vrijheid*. Amsterdam: Atlas.

Sandkühler, H. J. et al. (1990): *Europäische Enzyklopädie zu Philosophie und Wissenschaften*. Hamburg: Felix Meiner.

Sankey, M. & G. F. Huon (1999): 'Investigating the role of alienation in a multicomponent model of juvenile delinquency'. *Journal of Adolescence* 22: 95–107.

Sartre, J. P. (1961): 'Introduction', in: Fanon, F.: *De verworpenen der aarde* (Dutch translation of *Les damnés de la terre*). Utrecht: Bruna.

—— (1969): *Being and Nothingness. An Essay on Phenomenological Ontology*. New York: Philosophical Library.

Scheffler, S. (2006): 'Is Terrorism Morally Distinctive?' *The Journal of Political Philosophy* 14(1): 1–17.

Scheffler, T. (1997): 'Vom Königsmord zum Attentat. Zur Kulturmorphologie des politischen Mordes', in: Trotha, T. von (ed.): *Soziologie der Gewalt. Sonderheft Kölner Zeitschrift für Soziologie und Sozialpsychologie*. Opladen: Westdeutscher Verlag, pp. 183–99.

Scheler, M. (1992): 'Negative Feelings and the Destruction of Values: *Ressentiment*', in: Scheler, M.: *On Feeling, Knowing and Valuing* (edited by H. J. Bershady). Chicago: The University of Chicago Press, pp. 116–43.

Scheper-Hughes, N. & P. Bourgois (eds) (2004): *Violence in War and Peace: An Anthology*. Oxford: Blackwell.

Schiff, T. (2003): 'Developing Men's Leadership to Challenge Sexism and Violence. Working in University Settings to Develop "Pro-Feminist, Gay-Affirmative, and Male-Positive" Men', in: Wallace, B. C. & R. T. Carter: *Understanding and Dealing With Violence. A Multicultural Approach*. Thousand Oaks: Sage, pp. 161–82.

Schinkel, W. (2002): 'The modernist myth in criminology'. *Theoretical Criminology* 6(2): 123–44.

—— (2003a): 'Pierre Bourdieu's Political Turn?' *Theory, Culture & Society* 20(6): 69–93.

—— (2003b): 'Discipline or Punishment? The Case of the Dutch Prison'. *Innovation. European Journal of Social Sciences*, 16(3): 211–26.

—— (2007): *Denken in een tijd van sociale hypochondrie. Aanzet tot een theorie voorbij de maatschappij*. Kampen: Klement.

—— (2008): 'Contexts of Anxiety. The Moral Panic over "Senseless Violence" in the Netherlands'. *Current Sociology* 56(5): 735–56.

—— (2009a): '*Dignitas non moritur?* The State of the State in an Age of Social Hypochondria', in: Schinkel, W. (ed.): *Globalization and the State. Sociological Perspectives on the State of the State*. Basingstoke: Palgrave Macmillan, pp. 1–22.

—— (2009b): 'Illegal aliens and the state, or: bare bodies versus the zombie'. *International Sociology*. Forthcoming.

—— (2009c): 'On the Concept of Terrorism'. *Contemporary Political Theory* 8(2): 176–98.

Schmid, A. P. & Jongman, A. J. (1988): Political terrorism: A New Guide to Actors, Authors, Concepts, Data Bases, Theories and Literature (revised from 1983 ed.). New Brunswick: Transaction.

Schmidt, B. E. & I. W. Schröder (eds): *Anthropology of Violence and Conflict*. London: Routledge, pp. 1–24.

Schmitt, C. (1996): 'Politische Theologie', in *Politische Theologie. Vier Kapitel zur Lehre von der Souveränität*. Berlin: Duncker & Humblot, pp. 41–55.

—— (2002): *Der Begriff des Politischen*. Berlin: Duncker & Humblot.

Schröder, I. W. & B. E. Schmidt (2001): 'Introduction: Violent imaginaries and violent practices', in Schmidt, B. E. & I. W. Schröder (eds): *Anthropology of Violence and Conflict*. London: Routledge, pp. 1- 24.

Scholem, G. (1960): *Zur Kabbala und ihrer Symbolik*. Frankfurt/M.: Suhrkamp.

Schwartz, J. M. (2004): 'Misreading Islamist terrorism: The "war against terrorism" and just-war theory'. *Metaphilosophy* 35(3): 273–302.

Scott, J. C. (1985): *Weapons of the Weak: Everyday Forms of Peasant Resistance*. New Haven/London: Yale University Press.

Senechal de la Roche, R. (2001): 'Why is Collective Violence Collective?'. *Sociological Theory* 19(2), pp. 126–44.

Sharp, G. (1973): *The Politics of Nonviolent Action*. Boston: Porter Sargent Publishers.

Shearing, C. (1997): 'Gewalt und die neue Kunst des Regierens und Herrschens. Privatisierung und ihre Implikationen', in: Trotha, T. von (ed.): o.c., pp. 263–78.

Sherman Grant, D. & Wallace, M. (1991): 'Why Do Strikes Turn Violent?'. *American Journal of Sociology* 96(5): 1117–50.

Shiva, V. (1988): 'Reductionist Science as Epistemological Violence', in: Nandy, A. (ed.): *Science, Hegemony and Violence. A Requiem for Modernity*. Delhi: Oxford University Press/The United Nations University, pp. 232–56.

Simmel, G. (1993): 'Der Mensch als Feind. Zwei Fragmente aus einer Soziologie', in: *Gesamtausgabe*. Frankfurt/M.: Suhrkamp, pp. 335–43.

Sindall, R. (1990): *Street Violence in the Nineteenth Century: Media Panic or Real Danger?*. Leicester: Leicester University Press.

Sironi, F. & R. Branche (2002): 'Torture and the borders of humanity'. *International Social Science Journal* 54(174): 539–748.

Sloterdijk, P. (1998): *Sphären I: Blasen*. Frankfurt/M.: Suhrkamp.

Smith, A. (1978): *Lectures on Jurisprudence* (edited by Meek et al.). Oxford: Clarendon Press.

Smith, P. K. & P. Brain (2000): 'Bullying in Schools: Lessons From Two Decades of Research'. *Aggressive Behavior* 26: 1–9.

Sofsky, W. (1996): *Traktat über die Gewalt*. Frankfurt/M.: Fischer.

Sokolowski, R. (2000): *Introduction to Phenomenology*. Cambridge: Cambridge University Press.

Sorel, G. (1919): *Réflections sur la violence*. Paris: Rivière.

Sosa, E. (1975): *Causation and Conditionals*. Oxford: Oxford University Press.

Southern, R. W. (1970): *Western Society and the Church in the Middle Ages*. Harmondsworth: Penguin.

Sprandel, R. (1975): *Verfassung und Gesellschaft im Mittelalter*. Paderborn: Schöningh (UTB).

Stanko, E. A. (2003): *The Meanings of Violence*. London: Routledge.

Stanley Hall, G. (1913): 'Social Phases of Psychology'. *American Journal of Sociology* 18(5): 613–21.

Staples, J. S. (2000): 'Violence in Schools. Rage Against a Broken World'. *Annals of the American Academy of Political and Social Science* 567: 30–41.

Stern, J. (1999): *The Ultimate Terrorists*. Cambridge: Harvard University Press.

—— (2003): *Terror in the Name of God: Why Religious Militants Kill*. New York: Harper Collins.

Stover, L. (1974): *The Cultural Ecology of Chinese Civilization*. New York: The New American Library Inc.

Sugarman, D. (1992): 'Writing "Law and Society" Histories'. *The Modern Law Review* 55(2): 292–308.

Sullivan, R. F. (1973): 'The economics of crime: an introduction to the literature'. *Crime and Delinquency* 19(2): 138–49.

Sutherland, E. H. & D. R. Cressey (1978): *Criminology*. Philadelphia: J. B. Lippincott.

Swaan, A. de (1982): *De mens is de mens een zorg. Opstellen 1971–1981*. Amsterdam: Meulenhoff.

Thornton, T. P. (1964): 'Terror as a weapon of political agitation', in Eckstein, H. (ed.): *Internal War*. New York: The Free Press, pp. 71–99.

Thorpe, C. (2004): 'Violence and the Scientific Vocation'. *Theory, Culture & Society* 21(3): 59–84.

Tillich, P. (1959): *Theology of Culture*. Oxford: Oxford University Press.

Tilly, C. (2004): 'Terror, Terrorism, Terrorists'. *Sociological Theory* 22(1): 5–13.

—— (2005): 'Terror as Strategy and Relational Process'. *International Journal of Comparative Sociology* 46(1–2): 11–32.

Tolnay, S. E. & E. M. Beck (1992): *A Festival of Violence. An Analysis of Southern Lynchings, 1882–1930*. Urbana/Chicago: University of Illinois Press.

UN (2005): *Delivering Counter-Terrorism Assistance*. UN Office on Drugs and Crime Terrorism Prevention Branch.

U.S. Department of Justice, Federal Bureau of Prisons (1995): *Definition of Term – Crimes of Violence*, p. 2.

Vale, J. (2000): 'Violence and the tournament', in: Kaeuper, R. W. (ed.): *Violence in Medieval Society*. Woodbridge: The Boydell Press, pp. 143–58.

Vale, M. (2000): 'Aristocratic Violence: Trial by Battle in the Later Middle Ages', in Kaeuper, R. W. (ed.): *Violence in Medieval Society*. Woodbridge: The Boydell Press, pp. 159–82.

Verhoeven, C. (1967): *Tegen het geweld*. Utrecht: Ambo.

—— (2000): *Een Cultuur van het Geweld. Kritische Essays*. Leende: Damon.

Vernon, M. & S. Greenberg (1999): 'Violence in deaf and hard-of-hearing people: a review of the literature'. *Aggression and Violent Behavior* 4(3): 259–72.

Voegelin, E. (1951): *The New Science of Politics*. Chicago: The University of Chicago Press.

—— (1962): 'World-Empire and the Unity of Mankind'. *International Affairs* 38(2): 170–88.

—— (1968): *Science, Politics, and Gnosticism. Two Essays.* Washington: Regnery Publishing.

Volkskrant (2004): 'Opgefokte Murat regelt even een "pipa"; Verdachte van moord op Haagse Terra College zou volgens vrienden al jaren vete hebben met docent'. *De Volkskrant*, 15–01–2004, p. 1.

Vries, H. de (2002): *Religion and Violence. Philosophical Perspectives from Kant to Derrida.* Baltimore: Johns Hopkins University Press.

Wacquant, L. (1999): '"Suitable enemies". Foreigners and immigrants in the prisons of Europe'. *Punishment & Society* 1(2): 215–22.

Wade, F. C., (1971): 'On Violence: Comments and Criticism'. *The Journal of Philosophy* 68(12): 369–77.

Waddington, P. A. J., D. Badger & R. Bull (2005): 'Appraising the Inclusive Definition of Workplace Violence'. *British Journal of Criminology* 45: 141–64.

Walter, E. V. (1964): 'Violence and the Process of Terror'. *American Sociological Review* 29(2): 248–57.

Walters, G. D. (2000): 'Disposed to aggress? In search of the violence-prone personality'. *Aggression and Violent Behavior* 5(2): 177–90.

Walzer, M. (1977): *Just and Unjust Wars: A Moral Argument With Historical Illustrations.* New York: Basic Books.

Wardlaw, G. (1982): *Political Terrorism: Theory, Tactics and Counter-Measures.* Cambridge: Cambridge University Press.

Weber, M. (1972): *Wirtschaft und Gesellschaft. Grundriss der verstehenden Soziologie.* Tübingen: Mohr.

—— (1988): *Gesammelte Aufsätze zur Wissenschaftslehre.* Tübingen: J. C. B. Mohr.

Weerman, F. (1998): *Het belang van bindingen. De bindingstheorie als verklaring van verschillen en veranderingen in delinquent gedrag.* Groningen: Wolters-Noordhoff.

Weil, E. (1967): 'La violence'. *Recherches et Débats* 16(9).

Wellman, C. (1979): 'On Terrorism Itself'. *The Journal of Value Inquiry* 13(4): 250–58.

White, H. C. (2008): *Identity & Control. How Social Formations Emerge.* Second Edition. Princeton: Princeton University Press.

Wiener, P. P. (ed.) (1973): '*Virtù* in and since the Renaissance', in: *Dictionary of the History of Ideas. Studies of Selected Pivotal Ideas,* Volume IV. New York: Charles Scribner's Sons, pp. 476–86.

Wilkinson, P. (1997): 'The Media and Terrorism: A Reassessment'. *Terrorism and Political Violence* 9(2): 51–64.

Winch, P. (1958): *The Idea of a Social Science and its Relation to Philosophy.* London: Routledge & Kegan Paul, p. 102.

Winstanley, G. (1965 [1649]): *A Declaration from the Poor Oppressed People of England.* London, rptd. in: Sabine, G. H. (ed.): *Works.* New York: Russell & Russell.

Wittgenstein, L. (1969): *Philosophische Grammatik.* Frankfurt/M.: Suhrkamp.

—— (1984): *Philosophische Untersuchungen.* Frankfurt/M.: Suhrkamp.

—— (1989): *Vortrag über Ethik und andere kleine Schriften.* Frankfurt/M.: Suhrkamp.

WODC (1999): *Geweld: Gemeld en Geteld.* The Hague: WODC.

Wolfgang, M. E. & F. Ferracuti (1967): *The Subculture of Violence. Towards an Integrated Theory in Criminology*. London: Tavistock.

Wolin, S. S. (2004): *Politics and Vision. Continuity and Innovation in Western Political Thought*. Princeton: Princeton University Press.

Wykes, M. & K. Welsh (2008): *Violence, Gender and Justice*. London: Sage.

Zedler, J. H. (1732ff.): *Grossen Vollständigen Universallexikon*. Leipzig, X Theil.

Žižek, S. (1999): *The Ticklish Subject. The Absent Centre of Political Ontology*. London: Verso.

Index

Page numbers in **bold** refer to figures